BVR's Guide to Valuing Wholesalers

Warren D. Miller
CFA, ASA, CPA

First Edition

BVR
What It's Worth

Business Valuation Resources, LLC
1000 SW Broadway, Suite 1200
Portland, OR 97205
(503) 291-7963 • Fax (503) 291-7955 • www.BVResources.com

BVR
What It's Worth

Executive Editor: Colin Murcray
Chair and CEO: David Foster
President: Lucretia Lyons
VP of Sales: Lexie Gross
Managing Editor: Janice Prescott
Customer Service Manager: Stephanie Crader

ISBN: 978-1-935081-72-2
Library of Congress Control Number: 2011928043

To my beloved bride, Dorothy,

How I lived without you for 46 years, five months, and two days is beyond me. Your love, wisdom, presence, and encouragement have transformed my life. You have brought me joy and happiness that I never would have believed until I experienced it first-hand, all day, every day. I'm the luckiest guy on the planet, and I never forget that.

Note from the Author

Thank you for buying this book. As its writer, I am committed to helping you use it profitably. Toward that end, Business Valuation Resources, LLC, and I are working together to have some additional online tools for you. Here is the link:

http://www.bvresources.com/wholesaledownloads

This page has the Delaware Open MRI case referred to on page 173 for you to download. There is also a very cool Excel tool that will calculate risk premiums for the macroenvironment, domain, and company. The tool has a series of statements with "scaled" (1-5) radio-button responses. You must click on the radio button in each statement that best describes your client's situation, or else the template will not compute any of the risk premiums for you. Third, there is a set of graphics in a Word document that you are welcome to copy and paste. The images are in .JPG format, so you can size them just by dragging a corner; don't drag a midpoint, though, because it'll make the graphic look goofy. I respectfully ask that you insert the following in a footnote: © 2011 – Beckmill Research, LLC – Used with permission. You should check back to the website from time to time to see if there are new graphics, an updated Excel template, or other goodies. If there is something that you would like to see on this special page, please email me directly: SPARC@beckmill.com. I will respond to all suggestions.

I welcome your comments, questions, and constructive criticisms any time, of course. We're all in this thing together, you know. Again, email me at SPARC@beckmill.com.

Table of Contents

Preface

About This *Guide*

This volume is about valuing wholesalers. The perspective I take is multidisciplinary, with the primary discipline being strategic management. Don't worry if you don't know what that phrase means. It is friendly turf, and I will pass along simple and relevant ideas that you can use *today*. There is a plethora of wonderful and practical tools in the strategy arsenal, and I will drop them into the conversation whenever I think it can be helpful.

My writing style is conversational. Though some of the material will likely be new to you, I want it to be accessible and useful. The best way I know to do that is to write as if you and I were having a conversation. I welcome e-mails about this *Guide*, especially as your comments pertain to constructive criticisms, errors you've found, or ideas that don't make sense. Please don't hesitate to drop me a line any time at SPARC@beckmill.com.

Here is what lies ahead:

- ***Chapter 1*** sets out what makes valuing small and medium-sized distribution companies (SMDCs) different from appraising other enterprises. There are some key notions in this chapter that will pop up often in the rest of this *Guide*.

- ***Chapter 2*** is about engagement issues—scoping, due diligence, defining the domain (crucial at this early stage), eyeballing the warehouse before you price the work, pricing, and whether or not to include a value-map provision in the Engagement Letter.

- ***Chapter 3*** provides an overview of what, in my view, is the single most important aspect of valuing SMDCs: unsystematic risk. We spend at least 65% of our time in every SMDC engagement thinking about, researching, talking about, and writing about unsystematic risk. It doesn't help that our colleagues in financial economics assumed away its existence.

- ***Chapter 4*** draws from five non-traditional disciplines to offer three tools from each. These tools will come in handy in valuing SMDCs. You will find this perspective both unusual and, I'll wager, valuable.

- **Chapter 5** focuses on assessing risk in the *macroenvironment*—the six remote forces that affect every domain. In most engagements, this analysis is straightforward and uncomplicated.

- ***Chapter 6*** is about market structures with a special focus on one that is seldom seen nationally, but is often present at the regional and local levels: oligopoly.

- *Chapter 7* covers risk assessment in the *domain* itself. Six domain-level factors must be analyzed. The chapter includes an Appendix on competitive analysis.

- *Chapter 8* profiles SPARC archetypes in the SMDC context. We do so in the context of a wonderful paper by Stanford scholar Jim March on exploitation and exploration. If that sounds like "cost leadership" and "differentiation" to you, you're on the right track. We place special emphasis on the **Experimenter** because that is the appropriate competitive strategy for the vast majority of SMDCs.

- *Chapter 9* focuses on the company itself and the elements of the SPARC framework. This is a crucial chapter because it lays the foundation for Chapters 11 and 12.

- *Chapter 10* zeroes in on preparing a preliminary financial analysis of the client company. This includes key metrics, constructing an industry composite, and sources of potential normalizing adjustments.

- *Chapter 11* is devoted to a single SPARC element: Routines. That component accounts for the most causes of aberrant performance, good or bad. I believe that your understanding of routines is essential, and that is why I commit an entire chapter to the subject.

- *Chapter 12* tells you about how to prepare for the on-site visit and conduct the interviews that are the heart of it. I have said and written in many venues that this visit is the most underappreciated, underutilized aspect of the valuation process. Readers should find it extremely helpful.

- *Chapter 13* is called "Writing the Analysis of the SMDC's Outlier Metrics." That section of the report is *the* hardest task in writing. I give examples of how to make critical statements and how not to. I also provide you with details for how to compute your "Fog Index," a measure of writing clarity (we hope) or turgidity. This is arguably the most important chapter in the *Guide*: using our SPARC framework to gauge unsystematic risk at the company level. SPARC helps you identify underlying causes of certain effects that present themselves in the form of what we call "outlier performance metrics." SPARC also gives you a 38-percentage-point range within which the company level of unsystematic risk lies. I also address the crucial topics of "sustainable revenue" and "share of wallet" and offer some pointers about writing up this analysis.

- *Chapter 14* is all about writing the document we call "Incomplete Work Product—For Discussion Purposes Only"; in the bad old days, it was just the "Draft." Most of us can use some pointers about writing, and this chapter does that. We include a section on calculating your "Fog Index" and another on "Do's and Don'ts of Report-Writing."

- The last chapter in the book, ***Chapter 15***, highlights the value-map concept, how to recognize an add-on consulting opportunity, and how to price and sell the engagement. In non-adversarial contexts, especially with an owner looking to exit, a value map can do wonderful things for the client company.

The book nears its end with a bibliography of sources cited, plus others you'll find helpful. The last section is the Index, which, as a fierce critic of the indexes in most other valuation reference books, I did myself. If you have ideas about how I could have made it better, please drop me a line.

***

One last item: In the original manuscript for this *Guide*, I intentionally did not define the size of an SMDC because, like so much in business valuation, "It depends." However, a prospective customer asked one of the sales reps at Business Valuation Resources, LLC, to define the size range. That question, of course, came to me.

What we mean by "small and medium-sized distribution companies (SMDCs)" is not what we usually mean when we talk about size. We tend to mean "revenues" in those conversations, but revenues are a clinker in the distribution space because gross margins vary, and COGS has no labor. The smaller the gross margin, the higher the revenues must be for the company to be viable. In computer wholesaling, for instance, Ingram Micro is one of the big dogs. Even though its gross profit is $1.89B, its gross *margin* is barely 5%. To be sure, it's a huge business (revenues = $35.8B), not an SMDC at all. According to Yahoo! Finance, it employs 15,650 people. Let's assume they all work full time. Dividing $35.8B by 15,650 results in annual revenues per employee of almost $2.3 million. That sounds like a lot, and it is, but let's put a microscope on that $2.3MM. Start by multiplying it by the gross margin, 5.28%; the product is $121,440. That is gross profit per FTE (full-time-equivalent employee). The employee and fringes have to be paid out of that number. That won't leave much for all the other indirect expenses of Ingram Micro. That's why scale matters in a hypercompetitive low-margin business like Ingram Micro's. In its sector, the minimum efficient scale, as industrial economists call it, is huge because that's what it takes to survive.

Therefore, rather than revenues, we define an SMDC in terms of its number of FTEs. That's because, for instance, a hypothetical nano-Ingram Micro could generate, say, $25 million/yr., yet have only 10 or 11 employees. On the one hand, $25 million is a lot of money. But 10 or 11 employees don't pose much of a management challenge, and the business itself is pretty simple because it has to be highly automated (the substitution of capital for labor). In fact, this book first talks about technology in the SMDC context on page 3 in a section called "The Deployment of Technology in Wholesaling."

So, if we look at it in terms of head count—one of the eight size measures in the Duff & Phelps dataset—I think an SMDC is about where any other too-small-to-be-big/too-big-to-be-small company is: in the 15-100 FTE range. Some might start at a dozen, but I think 15 is a better number because the benefits of division of labor start to be clear there. If the company is smaller, many employees are apt to be wearing several hats. Of course, this could also be true in the 15-20 FTE range if the firm were poorly managed, so it's all pretty arbitrary. But I think 15 FTEs is a minimum, simply because the investment in technology has to have a return, and it takes a certain scale—measured in head count, not revenues—to produce that in low-margin businesses, which include most wholesalers, thanks to the price discovery afforded by the Internet.

If you doubt the impact of the Internet on pricing, ask someone who owned a travel agency 15 years ago how technology affected her business. But duck as soon as you raise the question!

Acknowledgements

As anyone who has written a book can attest, it is a tough journey. This is my second one, and the debt I owe to colleagues, mentors, friends, and family is enormous. At the top of my list of payables is my beloved bride, Dorothy Beckert. I don't know why good fortune put her and me at the same place on May 11, 1991, but it did. My life has changed permanently and for the better as a direct result. She is my muse, my editor, and my partner for life. Nothing good happens to me without her. Ever. Thank you, my love.

I have also received encouragement from David Foster, Gary Karlitz, Al King, Lucretia Lyons, Mike Mattson, and Bill Rister. Thanks to all of you. Please forgive any omissions; they are inadvertent and unintended.

As those who have worked with David's troops at Business Valuation Resources, LLC, can attest, they are first-rate. My primary contact there, Colin Murcray, Executive Editor, Guides & Books, is a man of endless patience, ceaseless good humor, and positive encouragement. This book wouldn't be in your hands today without him. I was fortunate to have the meticulous and exacting assistance of a woman I've never met or even spoken with: Janice Prescott. She has a pleasant habit of asking questions, rather than plunging ahead and making changes . . . at least most of the time. More important, her eyes spot things an eagle's can't see. I also appreciate the talents of Paul Erdman, who provided a crisp and accessible layout.

A key member of my family is no longer with us: Grandmother Miller. She was a third-generation college graduate, Cal/Berkeley, Class of 1912. She worked until she was 99 and lived to be 106. She was an upbeat, positive, forward-looking woman. I know that she would be busting her buttons with the publication of her only grandson's second book.

I cannot overstate the contribution to this *Guide* of Terry J. Allen, CPA, ASA, and former chair of the Business Valuation Committee of the American Society of Appraisers. She provided a wonderful technical review. She somehow found the time as a wife, mom, and sole practitioner with her own busy practice to read the manuscript and offer a slew of suggestions and comments that improved it by magnitudes. A million thank-yous, Terry.

Susan M. Saidens, ASA, CPA·ABV, and a fellow attendee at meetings of the Appraisal Issues Task Force, engaged me in a protracted e-mail exchange, and then a phone conversation, about how she uses the asset accumulation method; see the last two pages of the Appendix after Chapter 9. She offered insights and comments that stimulated my thinking in many ways. She also endured my interminable questions with patience and bemused good humor. Thank you, Susan.

To all of you—those I have named and those about whose names my memory has failed me—I thank you for your comments, error-spotting, and constructive criticisms. In most cases, I took your advice. In some cases, I didn't. In those instances, I know I erred. You tried to steer me right, but I was too stubborn to agree. Therefore, the errors that remain are mine alone.

Chapter 1

What's Different About Valuing SMDCs?

Introduction

The major challenge in valuing small and medium-sized distribution companies (SMDCs)—a.k.a. wholesalers—is that technological innovation has put them under extreme margin pressure. Think of Amazon.com's effect, not just on booksellers, but also on book publishers (think Kindle *and* the push for authors to self-publish under the Amazon banner), electronics outlets (we bought two HD television sets through Amazon), tool retailers, H&G (home and garden) outlets, haberdashers, and sporting goods retailers, among others. Technology allows consumers to price-shop and compare as never before. We pay $79/yr. to Amazon to ship all our books second-day delivery at no additional charge. We don't have to meet the $25 minimum, either. My beloved bride says that the day I die, "There'll be a layoff at Amazon."

This first chapter of the *BVR Guide to Valuing Wholesalers* will explore the technology issue in some detail. We will discuss its huge impact on the selling process, on purchasing, on logistics, and on CRM (customer relationship management). Next come short profiles of three distribution sectors upended by innovation in technology. We will then discuss what we believe is a key valuation multiple that many appraisers overlook in valuation distribution companies generally. We will talk briefly about what we believe are the keys to wealth creation in distribution. And then we'll lay out a brief roadmap for the rest of this *Guide*. First, however, we want to introduce you to two broad types of distributors and, within each, two subgroups.

A Brief Overview of Wholesaling

Standard Industrial Classification (SIC) and North American Industry Classification System (NAICS) codes define wholesalers by whether they sell durable or non-durable goods. Durables are long-lived bigger-ticket items—think appliances and automobiles. Non-durables are everything else—think goods that must be replenished in less than a year (e.g., office supplies, groceries, soft drinks, soap, and so on). The economics of these two types of goods have different demand cycles and different price elasticities of demand.

Even in recessions, for instance, people have to buy food. They might move down the food chain, as it were, in terms of what they buy, but they have to eat. They might buy cheaper wine, too, or beer that's not branded by billion-dollar ad campaigns. Even with high interest rates and high unemployment, grocery stores will still be in business.

The flip side of the food menu can be tough to swallow: institutional food sales. When a local economy is in the dumper, restaurants feel it big-time. And the closer to high end they are, they more they feel it. This, of course, helps grocery stores because those who might eat out eat in instead.

It's a similar economic story with, say, new-car dealers. Not only are they under pressure to realize economies of scale and of scope (which is why we see multiple brands under a single roof and even U.S. and non-U.S. cars being sold new by the same dealership), but they are also sensitive to the economic cycle, especially higher interest rates and the unemployment that inevitably follows. Unlike computers, whose prices tend to fall in the near term, the price of cars continues to increase. Part of that is the psychology of the business—consumers expect it, so auto manufacturers oblige them. Another part, though, is a productivity issue.

That came home to me in 1992. I talked my way into a two-week seminar at the Goldratt Institute near Yale University in New Haven, Conn. Eliyahu Goldratt, an Israeli physicist by training, wrote *The Goal: A Tale of Ongoing Improvement*. I'ts become a cult book among manufacturing experts, and I've never known a top-flight manufacturing professional who hasn't read it at least twice. Most re-read it at least annually. *The Goal* is all about something called "the theory of constraints." The shop floor in manufacturing, after all, is simply a sequence of mini-systems of supply and demand. Goods move through a plant from process to process. The no-no in a plant, however, is a bottleneck where everything comes to a halt or at least slows down. That leaves downstream processes idle and twiddling their thumbs, which is, of course, expensive. *The Goal* is all about how to finesse the bottlenecks issue. That seems like an obscure topic for a book that has sold over 3 million—that's right, three *million*—copies. Not too shabby. With royalties from *The Goal* and at least four follow-on books, Goldratt set up his institute, which he named in honor of his dad.

That Institute conducts training and education seminars and is not bashful about charging for its services. The seminar I attended in 1992 cost each of the other nine attendees 10 grand, not including travel, food, and lodging expenses. Yours Truly, who was then a newbie to self-employment, managed to wrangle a modest 95% discount. Yep, I paid 500 bucks, and the Institute even subsidized my hotel room. Bless 'em.

The first morning of the seminar, the discussion leader asked each of us to introduce ourselves and give a little background about what we did for a living and why we were attending. I had managed to seat myself between two shift managers from manufacturing. The introductions got to the guy on my right. He introduced himself and said he ran Intel's graveyard shift in Albuquerque. He leaned forward, pointed to his colleague on my left, and said, "And Bob here runs the swing shift. We're here because our CEO, Andy Grove, told us we had to improve plant productivity by 15%."

Pause.

"Per month."

At that moment I understood falling computer prices in a way that I never had before. Even today, whenever I think our business is a little soft, I remember that guy's "per month" comment and know that things in my little economic world are never as tough as they could be.

Productivity is a big deal in most economic sectors (except government and healthcare). It is crucial in distribution because of technology. Therefore, one of the first numbers you should look at is annual revenues per full-time-equivalent employee (FTE). Be sure to compare the client company's productivity with that of a public-company composite. If the gross margin is thin—anything less than about 40%—you will also want to calculate gross profit per FTE. Anytime basic compensation expense (gross salary only) divided by gross profit is more than 40%, you can safely assume that there are too many people on the payroll. And, in our experience, that is usually because the client has not deployed technology to the extent that it should. Companies under extreme margin pressure have no choice but to substitute capital for labor if they want to survive.

But before divvying up wholesalers between "establishments" (in SIC code parlance) that sell durables vs. those that traffic in non-durables, you will want to make a broader delineation. That is the one between B2B and B2C—"business to business" and "business to consumer," respectively. B2B means that the *end user* of what's being sold is a business, not a person; B2C is just the opposite.

You won't be surprised to hear that B2B and B2C are about as different as heartburn and a heart attack. B2C gets all of the ink because slick advertising mostly targets consumers, and that is what most of us see and hear; little of B2B advertising and marketing hits the mass market. In fact, I estimate that at least 90% of a typical college marketing course is dedicated to the consumer side. In marketing, B2B is the stepchild to B2C, just as management accounting plays second fiddle to public accounting in the accounting trade.

Whether B2B or B2C, however, many of the same rules about what to do to be successful apply. Sam Walton said it best when he defined his business: to have the right amount of the right item in the right place at the right time at the right price. That's five "rights" in 17 words. Mr. Walton liked to say that he was from Arkansas, but that even he knew that those five required one heckuva computer system. Walmart is arguably the pre-eminent performer in all of distribution, wholesale or retail. Ask P&G—Walmart accounts for over 20% of its annual revenue. In fact, a large cadre of P&G employees lives in, you guessed it, Bentonville, Arkansas. And Walton's early insistence on and embrace of leading-edge technology made it possible.

The Deployment of Technology in Wholesaling

It is not only computers, but also electronic innovation more broadly, that have made life a whole lot more exciting—and perilous—in wholesaling than it used to be. Think about EDI, bar-coding, RFID, pick-ticket software, CRM, automated ordering, and, well, the list goes on. Let's talk briefly about various aspects of wholesaling that show the effects of innovation.

Purchasing: The area ripest for improvements—and the one that often accounts for a disproportionate amount of unsystematic risk—is purchasing and its kissing cousin, inventory control. Today's software systems have built-in algorithms that take account of EOQ, safety stock, lead time, and recent SKU-level shipping trends to produce automatic purchase orders. They can also be manually adjusted on the fly if those who use the system have knowledge that hasn't reached the system yet. This software can also analyze trade-offs in incurring freight charges for a particular order vs. delaying or missing sales by being out of stock as a result of "saving up" for an order that will get the freight paid by the vendor.

Selling: Technology enables companies to have a SKU-level tracking system for what their customers have bought and when. Just as the purchasing side of the house uses similar algorithms that incorporate EOQ, safety stock, and recent sales trends into automated orders, the selling side can then encourage its own customers to replenish inventory when the latter's systems lack that kind of capability. With smaller retailers and those in the specialty segment, these kinds of systems are often conspicuous by their absence.

Outbound logistics: This process begins when the sales order hits the system. The software should batch orders to be delivered by the company's vehicles on a given day. The batch is then disaggregated in reverse sequence from that in which it will be delivered. In other words, the order that will be delivered last is picked first because it goes in the truck first. The within-order sequence in which SKUs are pulled tracks the layout of the company's warehouse and the location of various SKUs within it.

Customer relationship management (CRM): The phrase "CRM" gets a lot of press these days. Software vendors boast that their systems "can handle CRM." The problem with that, of course, is that CRM is only as good as the information that goes into it for each customer.

Sure, what customers buy will be a part of the CRM record. But what about those sales calls—by phone, teleconference, e-mail, or chance meetings in grocery stores or at sporting events after hours? Such encounters can produce "actionable intelligence" for sellers. But if the people on the ground don't get it into the system, then it's lost. Don't misunderstand: CRM *is* great stuff. How great is a function of what it comprises.

Even though this *Guide* is dedicated to wholesaling, it is worth mentioning that the use of technology on the retail side of the world is expanding in ways that manufacturers of innovative products did not anticipate. A 2010 article in *BusinessWeek* drew attention to the deployment of v1.0 of Apple's iPad in large corporations. The new gizmo is being used by peddlers of Mercedes Benzes to request on-the-spot financing, by CFOs to approve wire transfers through Wells Fargo, and by Tellabs to improve inventory control. In our own practice, a client in a construction niche is considering using iPads across its far-flung operations in 12 states with 1,400 employees.

More than operations in most other sectors, the operating side in distribution is information-driven. How else can an SMDC achieve Walton's right-thing/right-amount/right-place/right-time/right-price imperative?

Technology in Non-Distribution Sectors

Anyone reading this *Guide* knows businesses on the receiving end of the adverse effects of technology. I will discuss briefly just three of them here now.

Publishing: Except for software publishing, the publishing segment is at its greatest level of peril since its genesis with the Gutenberg Bible. The 24-hour news cycle that Ted Turner's Cable News Network began in the summer of 1980 has accelerated into the Internet, blogging, Twitter, and more. The impact on newspapers and news magazines has been huge and negative. *U.S. News & World Report* now publishes monthly. And not very well. *Newsweek* was sold for $1. The *Chicago Tribune* is in bankruptcy. The *Seattle Post-Intelligencer* is no longer in business. Neither is the *Los Angeles Herald-Examiner* or the *Philadelphia Evening News*. *Gourmet* magazine is gone. So is *Editor & Publisher* and a host of smaller magazines. They couldn't compete with either the price or the immediacy of the Internet.

Regardless of one's politics, the Fox News Channel is arguably the most successful media innovation of the last 50 years. It has taken up where CNN left off and hacked away at the market share of other networks—the "big three" of the mid-twentieth century (ABC, CBS, NBC) and spin-offs (MSNBC, CNBC, and CNN itself). Ironically, News Corporation, which is controlled by "Mr. Fox" himself, Rupert Murdoch, made a $5 billion cash tender offer for *The Wall Street Journal* in 2008; after much dithering and dysfunction, the Bancroft family that controlled it threw in the towel.[1] In 2009 the *New York Times* borrowed $250 million from Mexican magnate Carlos Slim Helú . . . at 14% interest.

Travel Agencies: Traditional travel agencies are under assault from all quarters. Starting in 1997, the airline industry gradually weaned them from commissions. Then came the online agencies—Travelocity, Expedia, Orbitz, Hotwire.com, and Hotels.com, among others. Priceline.com piled on by accessing excess inventory from hotels and offering it for bids, subject to the acceptance of each hotel. Even they understand that the revenue lost from an unoccupied room can never be recouped—unlike housing, for instance, there are no gains from pent-up demand in the hospitality sector.

Some segments within the travel-agency space have withstood the onslaught and done well. Agencies specializing in packaged travel and in cruise vacations still retain market share north of 70%. Buyers of those services know that the transactions are far more complicated than booking an airline ticket or hotel room online, and they have neither the time nor the expertise to do it themselves.

Telephone Companies: Then there's POTS (Plain Old Telephone Service), as it's called in the declining landline industry. As valuation professionals know, cellular service, the invasion of cable into POTs, and VoIP have combined to reduce demand for services from the old POTS companies. There is no reason that the decline should not continue. AT&T, Verizon, and, to a

1. For a fun read, try Ellison's *War at the Wall Street Journal*.

lesser extent, Sprint, have many billions of dollars invested in their landline infrastructure. They are now in the unenviable position of seeing steeply falling rates of return on that investment. Monopolists, of course, have no incentive to innovate, and the dinosaur telecoms are no exception.

A Key Valuation Multiple in Appraising Wholesalers

Any company that has a "gross profit" line on its P&L can be valued using MVIC/Gross Profit. In our experience with SMDCs, MVIC/GP often has a low coefficient of variation. If that multiple is not already in your guideline public company template, it should be.

Two Keys to Wealth Creation in Wholesaling

Productivity: The margin pressure under which most wholesalers find themselves elevates the importance of productivity among the concerns that owners and senior managers of SMDCs should be monitoring closely. As we noted earlier in this chapter, the easiest way to measure that is (Annual Revenues ÷ Full-time-equivalent Employees). The adroit substitution of capital for labor in the form of IT investment is essential to increasing productivity. But all the IT investment in the world won't do much for a company whose top dogs fail to lead the way—"walk the talk"—in cementing a company's commitment to IT. In the distribution space, luddites tend to become footnotes in history.

Without the gains that adroit investment in IT can provide, a struggling SMDC might be tempted to build share with lower prices. Good luck. Price-based competition is lethal for all but the market leader in a segment. Those who think they can out-low-ball the lead low-baller are deluding themselves. It might work for a while, but the returns are so low that the company is in a slow state of *economic* liquidation because the firm is not earning its cost of capital. Unfortunately, GAAP deludes some owners into thinking that, because their company is profitable, everything is just ducky. Try deducting from Net Income a capital charge equal to the equity cost of capital times net worth. If the adjusted bottom line is still positive, then the company is at least creating wealth.

Experimenter Strategy: The pre-eminent competitive strategy for most wholesalers is narrow-scope differentiation. I say "narrow" because few distributors compete industrywide. Most compete in what the strategy literature calls a "strategic group." Such a group is merely a segment of an industry. It is defined by two parameters, one of which is often geography; the other might be target market, or product line, or distribution channel, or price point. In his classic book, *Competitive Strategy: Techniques for Evaluating Industries and Competitors*, Porter put forth certain "generic competitive strategies." In my recent book,[2] I labeled Porter's 2x2 matrix with four alliterative names[3] beginning with the letter "E." Here is an updated graphic:

2. Miller, *Value Maps.*
3. I chose "E" because it is the first letter in Entrepreneur, too.

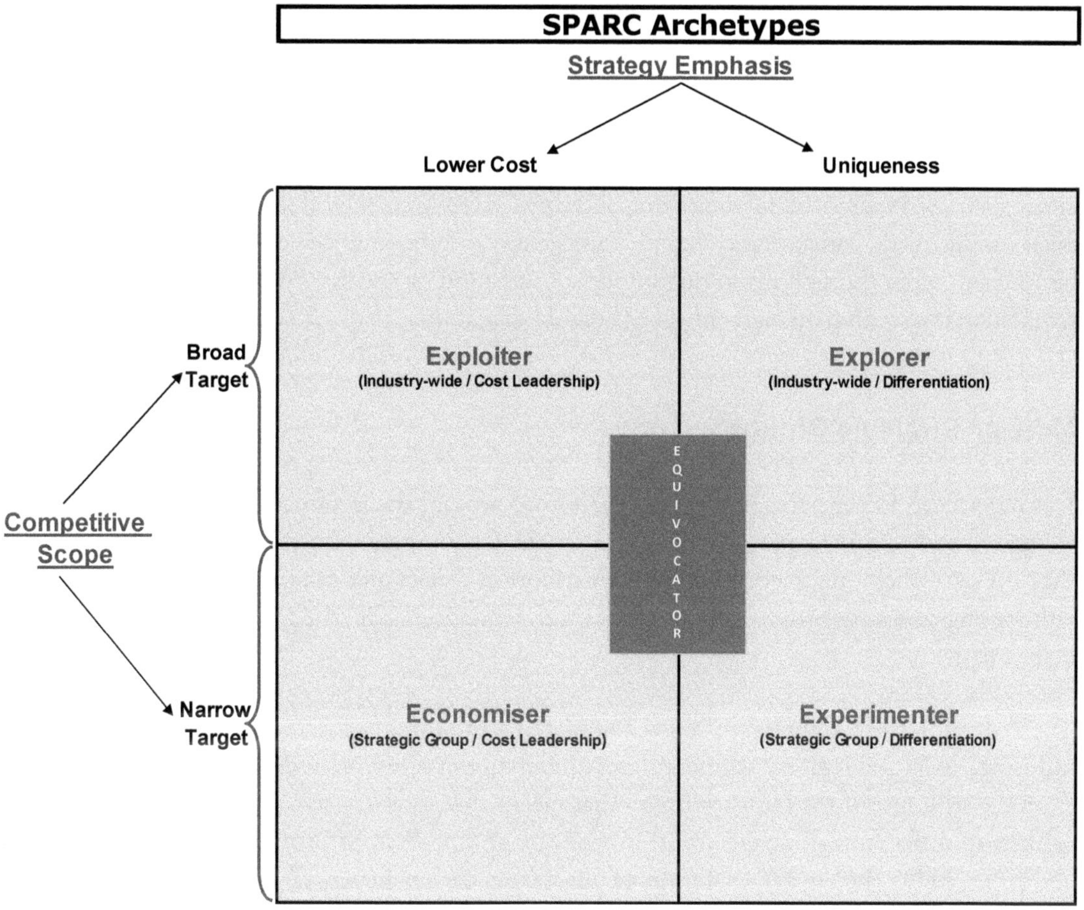

Porter called what I have labeled "Narrow Target" a "Focus" strategy. Such a strategy is *not* industrywide—think strategic group—and it can be either "cost leadership" (compete on price) or "differentiation." For virtually all wholesalers competing in any strategic group, the **Experimenter** strategy is the first one to consider. That is because the sources of differentiation are limited only by the imaginations of a company's people *and* their ability to convince customers to pay more for perceived greater value. As every person is unique, every company is also unique because of the combination of people and resources it comprises. Contrary to the neoclassical paradigm of microeconomics, a company is *not* an inanimate production function. It is a living, breathing entity.

That, in turn, places responsibility on the owner or top managers to (a) analyze the unique resource endowment of their company; (b) look for ways to derive new services from those resources; and (c) find a way to configure some of them into value for which customers are willing to pay more. It is a not-small order, but the Experimenter is the best strategy for the typical SMDC.

To be sure, even a successful Experimenter cannot willy-nilly ignore the price charged by the market leader. At some point, if the gap between the prices charged by the Economiser[4] and the Experimenter becomes too large, the Experimenter's customers will migrate to the Economiser. But differentiation works in small business. I know it does because we've done it since 1991 in our own consulting practice, and we have watched countless other small and medium-sized businesses (SMBs) create their own sources of differentiation and thrive, even in markets dominated by behemoths. It takes commitment, patience, investment, consistency, and stamina. The differentiation plant must be watered, often through marketing outlays of one kind or another. When times are tight, the temptation is to scrimp on marketing. SMDCs do that at their peril. *At their peril.*

More on Strategic Groups

It is important, I think, that readers get their arms around the importance of *strategic groups* to valuation. As I said a few paragraphs ago, few SMDCs compete industrywide. That alone means that the overwhelming majority of your distribution clients and ours are Porter-type focusers, either using cost leadership (Economiser) or differentiation (Experimenter). But there's more to it than that.

The Federal Trade Commission has accumulated a mountain of data that show that, in most industries, local and regional segments have underlying structures that differ, often in major ways, from the structure of the industry itself. That means that industry risk within the same industry is likely to differ from strategic group to strategic group. That, in turn, means that those copy-and-paste "industry analyses" that some of our colleagues buy from well-meaning vendors such as Integra and First Research are neither useful nor relevant to the domain of their client SMDC. The quality of your work will increase if you do your own such analyses. A key part of what I'm going to do in this *Guide* is show you how to do that. With luck, we'll save you some money *and* help enhance the quality of your valuation practice.

I want to allay any remaining doubt about the power and utility of strategic groups. If you practice in a metropolitan area, as the vast majority of valuation professionals do, look at the different segments of CPA practices in your area. At a minimum, there will be at least five strategic groups of such practices in a big city, and probably more. First, there are the four global CPA firms. Next come the large-but-not-global firms—Grant Thornton, BDO Seidman, McGladrey & Pullen, Crowe Horwath, Meyer Hoffman McCann, BKD, Plante & Moran, and Moss Adams. At least a couple of them have offices in large cities. Next are the regional CPA firms, then the large local firms, and finally the small locals. Right there are five (5) strategic groups of CPA firms present in most metroplexes. Some firms might specialize by industry, others by service (IT, software consulting, personal financial planning, etc.), and still others by type of client (i.e., no 1040 work without an 1120 or 1065 alongside it).

4. My use of 's' rather than 'c' in Economiser is not an attempt to be British. I use the 's' to emphasize the frugality of the narrow-scope cost leader.

The strategic groups construct also lends itself to lodging facilities, restaurants, models of automobiles, haberdashers, and, well, the list can go on and on. It is a crucial tool at the start of any valuation in defining your client company's "competitive domain." I'll have a whole lot more to say about that later in this *Guide*, but I wanted to get it on your radar screen now. Strategic groups are a vital concept in valuing SMDCs.

The Wrap

This chapter hit certain issues hard:

- the impact of technology on the distribution sector
- the importance of the MVIC/Gross Profit valuation multiple
- two keys to wealth creation in wholesaling
- strategic groups
- our "E wrinkle" addition to Porter's generic competitive strategies

Before we get to the real fun—valuing wholesalers—we have to cover the business side of business valuation: engagement issues. That is what Chapter 2 is about.

Engagement Considerations in Valuing SMDCs

Introduction

The business and administrative side of a craft can challenge crafts-women and -men like you and me. But that is the price we pay for the privilege of doing craft and being well-paid for it. As I'm fond of saying, "I don't mind working *pro bono*. I just want to able to choose at the *beginning* that it's *pro bono*."

In this chapter of our *Guide*, we will take on the practice-management side of valuation: scoping the engagement, preliminary documents, what I call the *sine qua non* of valuation, the "shake 'n' howdy" visit, how to get better pricing of calculations engagements, fees in general, and other issues. We will also explain how you can eliminate collection problems—not just reduce them, but get them out of your life.

Scoping the Engagement

Let's start with a question: What *does* "scoping the engagement" mean? Answer: Know enough to know what you're getting yourself into. I can remember early in my valuation career when I was hungry, both for work and for food (despite my silhouette today). A prospective client would call, and I would be all over myself to get the engagement letter done, get a retainer, and get going on the work. That's called Ready, Fire, Aim! I learned the hard way to slow down and learn about the client and the engagement before I gave the prospect the bum's rush.

That is because—and I have said this loudly and publicly—there are some clients we cannot afford to have. I'll wager that most readers can't afford them, either. We use a higher price to send them elsewhere, preferably to our closest competitors. You know the kind of client I'm talking about: the kind who, when you shake their hand, you're looking for the Lysol. You just *know* at a gut level that it's going to be not-fun, a hassle, and a "learning experience." That means it is going to cost money. The only question is how much.

You can avoid that with judicious scoping before you ask someone to sign on the dotted line. It is a lesson that we should have to learn only one time. It took me twice . . . but I'm a slow learner. What else can you say about a guy who crammed four years of undergraduate education into 14?

The *Sine Qua Non*

That's Latin for "without which, nothing." In other words, it's a gotta-do. You ignore this at your peril: ***Define the domain.***

What does that mean? We noted in Chapter 1 that few SMDCs compete industrywide. If they did, they probably wouldn't be "SM." So, instead of calling it "the industry" or "the strategic group," we use the word "domain" to encompass both. To determine the scope of the client's competitive arena, we ask two questions:

1. "*Where* do your company's competitors do what they do?" and

2. "*What else* makes them your competitors besides what they do?"

The answer to (1) defines the group geographically. The response to (2) further refines and defines the field of battle in another dimension; it is often the target market. But it could be just the high end of a product line, particular expertise in certain products, or technical knowledge that customers find indispensable to their own livelihoods—or something else.

Defining the domain matters because, as you will see in Chapters 4 and 5, the domain is *the unit of analysis* in assessing external risk. That has an obvious implication: all players in a domain *have the* same *external* risk premiums. They have to: they're all facing the same set of external forces, however friendly or hostile those forces might be.

Think about the elements of SWOT analysis: **S**trengths, **W**eaknesses, **O**pportunities, **T**hreats. A bright line separates the first two of these from the last two: strengths and weaknesses are *internal* to the company; opportunities and threats are *external.* Little in valuation is as clear-cut and simple as this is. Therefore, every competitor within a domain confronts the same external set of opportunities and threats as its rivals. Therefore, the magnitude of those "O's and T's" is the same for each domain player. It is *how an SMDC responds to them*—its strengths and weaknesses ("S and W"), if you will—that really tells the story.

Here are two examples of domain definition:

> In this engagement, the competitive domain is the cohort of building-materials distributors serving a portion of the "Tidewater" area of Virginia defined by the cities of Portsmouth, Norfolk, Virginia Beach, and Chesapeake. Here's a map:

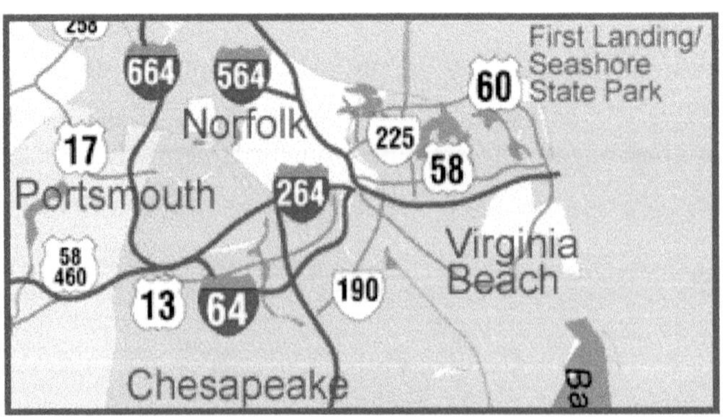

> The competitive domain in this engagement is the cadre of janitorial-supplies wholesalers in the Richmond metropolitan statistical area.

Defining the domain early, before you even land the engagement, will add efficiency to your valuation effort. You won't find yourself retracing your steps because you didn't understand domain issues. In our shop, we go so far as to include the domain definition in our engagement letters. It makes them seem less boilerplate, and it also shows the client that we've done our homework.

As I noted near the end of Chapter 1, domain definition reduces costs, too, by lowering, if not eliminating, the cost of canned industry analyses from third-party vendors. As we also noted in Chapter 1, data from the Federal Trade Commission show that the underlying structures of local and regional segments of industries differ in major respects from that of the industry as a whole. You can and should prepare your own domain analyses. Eliminating boilerplate so you can tell the *client's story* enhances your credibility better and faster than almost anything you can do.

Preliminary Information You Need About an SMDC

After getting a nondisclosure agreement in place with your prospective client—we won't spend much time talking to a prospective client without the execution of an NDA—we ask for the following for our due-diligence phase of the engagement:

1. financial statements for the last two years
2. federal tax returns for the most recent two years
3. Form W-3 for the last three years
4. number of SKUs
5. organization chart, including total number of employees in each function
6. list of locations in addition to the current one
7. name of engagement partner at CPA firm
8. name of attorney at primary law firm

That short list allows us to get a quick reading of productivity, tax compliance, attest/not-attest financials, organization structure, and the likely complexity of the engagement (from the number of SKUs, number of locations, and org chart). Each of these affects pricing.

We also calculate the following metrics:

- Bang for the Buck (BftB) %: [gross profit ÷ Box 1 of Form W-3] (s/b ≥ 2.5)
- Annual revenue per full-time equivalent employee
- Inventory turnover
- Employee turnover (compare # of W-2s with heads on the org chart)
- DSO

If the BftB is < 2.5, either the SMDC is overpaying or it has too many people on the payroll . . . or both. Typically it's too many folks because of too little IT deployment. Annual revenue per FTE should exceed $150K (more if gross margin is below 40%. Inventory turn will vary across SMDC sectors, depending on price and demand cycle, but 4x is minimal. DSO should not exceed 45 days.

As soon as we have computed the five simple metrics for two years and reviewed the other information we asked for, we then schedule a short meet-and-greet at the client company during regular business hours. We prefer doing it then in order to get a feel for the company's tempo and workaday atmosphere. If there's a business reason to do it off-hours, that's O.K., too.

Do Your Due Diligence: The Shake 'n' Howdy (S&H)

In the American south and southwest, the phrase "shake 'n' howdy" is common. It refers to an initial introduction between people with common interests. Even in an age of technology that enables us to work worldwide, we still like to look an owner in the eye. Sooner is better than later. It gives us a quick sense about the organization, its people, and its business. We believe it is essential to have that before we can price the engagement and invest the time to draft an Engagement Letter (ours runs to 13 single-spaced pages, including the Document Request List). An experience in 1999 affirmed our prudence.

We moved from Tulsa to Lexington, Va., in 1997. Lexington is a university town (VMI and Washington & Lee) of 7,000 in the beautiful Shenandoah valley of Virginia. We had bought acreage a couple of miles outside town in 1995. We wanted to build our dream house. Neither my bride nor I had ever lived in a small town before. A week after we arrived, an insurance peddler came to see us. At the end of his unsuccessful attempt to sell us some more life insurance, he gave us his definition of small-town living: "It's a place where you know whose check is good and whose spouse isn't." "Works for me," I said.

A couple of years later, a pillar of the local community to whom the insurance guy later introduced me referred a business-owner in another town in the Shenandoah Valley to us. The man owned some convenience stores. Like you, we would never knowingly embarrass a referral source.

Besides, the fellow who made the referral is a truly outstanding (and upstanding) member of the Lexington community. We thought that if the referred owner sang our praises later, more referrals would come along.

We got the NDA done and then asked for my attenuated list of documents. The C-store guy said he'd rather not fax or PDF anything to me. He said that if I'd come see him, he would show me whatever I asked for. He wasn't too far away, so I agreed to do it that way. I was wary, however.

Usually Dorothy and I make these visits together. She has sense and sensibility about people that I can only dream of. Unfortunately for me, she had other plans at the time the client wanted me to come out, so I made the trip by myself.

Sure enough, as soon as I shook the man's hand, my wariness went into overdrive. It is one of those gut-level things, I guess, but I knew I did not want any part of this engagement. Still, the man was taking his time to see me, so I owed him the courtesy of sticking around. And I didn't want to embarrass our referral source.

Unaware that I knew a lot about C-stores, the owner showed me his P&L. Gross margin was about 10 percentage points lower than it should be, even with a high component of gasoline sales (which his stores didn't have—there were just three pumps between the two stores). The guy then started talking about all the real estate he owned and the fact that he'd "paid hard cash" for it. I was born at night, but not last night, so the connection between cash real estate deals and lower gross margin was clear. Then the man started griping about the federal deficit.

"A foolish consistency," Waldo Emerson once said, "is the hobgoblin of small minds." Maybe. But an inconsistency like the one I was hearing was too much, even for me, a lifelong admirer of Emerson. (Dorothy and I tour his home every time we return to the scene of the crime where we got married in 1994.) I knew that there was no way that this guy's stores would become our client, but I also had to keep the referral source in mind. I drove back to the office, eager to discuss it with Dorothy.

By the time I got there, she was waiting for me. I explained the situation. We agreed that we didn't want any part of dealing with an industrial-strength tax crook. The next day I called the guy back because he wanted the appraisal report on a short timeline, shorter than we'd be comfortable with even if we were working with repeat clients. I walked a delicate tightrope between the referral source and the business owner. Here's about how the conversation went:

WM: *Well, sir, we can appraise your two C-stores.*

Owner: *That's great news.*

Me: *Ummm, I have some not-great news for you.*

Owner: *Oh? And what would that be?*

Me: *Well, sir, we have a lot of work in the house right now. You want this on a short timeline. To meet your needs, I have to call repeat clients and tell them that I must push back their delivery dates. That is going to put stress and strain on those relationships. They might even stop being our clients. That means I have to charge you more. In fact, this is probably going to cost a bunch more than you had in mind.*

Owner: *How much?*

Me: *Forty-five thousand dollars.* (This was in 1999.)

The phone line fell silent. I waited. I mean, it was his turn to talk. After what seemed like an eternity, he almost yelled through the phone.

Owner: *Forty-five thousand dollars??????*

WM: *Yes, sir. We'll understand if that's a little rich for your blood.*

Owner: *I can't afford that!*

I thought, "Sell some real estate, dude." Instead:

Me: *I understand.*

Owner: *Do you know anyone else who does this kind of work?*

I did, and I gave him the name of a gentleman in the Valley who likes to think he's a competitor of ours because he had low-balled an engagement a few years ago, which he got and which, I heard later, he screwed up badly enough that his client spent more in fees fighting the IRS on the appraisal than he would have spent with us in the first place.

I quickly called the referral source to thank him. I also said that, due to an unexpected expansion on one of the projects in process at that time, we were unable to accommodate the timeline that the business owner needed, so we had referred him elsewhere. The source was happy, and we were relieved. I figured that was the end of it.

Six months later, I attended an AICPA valuation conference in Atlanta. Sure enough, I ran into the guy to whom I'd referred the C-store owner. He shook my hand and began pouring out a tale of woe about a company he called "the client from hell."

Me: *Really?*

BV guy: *Yeah. You know anything about convenience stores?*

Bingo.

Lucrative Pricing for Calculations Engagements

You won't be surprised to read that calculations engagements are easier to sell than appraisals. However, there are times when they should not be done under any conditions, including the following:

- Gift- or estate-tax appraisals
- Litigation support

The problem with the typical calculations engagement is pricing: we have to do three of them to realize the revenue we get for a typical appraisal. In 2007, I figured out a way to try to get that calculations price up. It was to deliver something of real value: a mini-version of a "Value Map." (Heads-up, reader: shameless plug coming.) I called it a "Value Enhancement Memorandum" (VEM) back then; now it's a "Value Map." It didn't have the graphical zip that it has now, nor did it have a book standing behind it.[1]

When the valuation of a typical SMDC is done the way it should be, the analyst comes away knowing about risk exposures that the client company has. In our experience, the SMDC might not even know about some of the biggest risks it faces. The analyst identifies those later during the on-site interview when she uncovers causes of those "outlier metrics" I wrote about in Chapter 1. A short add-on deliverable describing major risk factors and what to do about them *in the context of the company's **current** resources and capabilities* can easily send what would be a $7K-$8K price tag north of $20K. And we guarantee our work.

In order to do that, though, we have to invest the front-end time in scoping the client and seeing that its risk profile is going to offer fruitful opportunities around which to construct a value map. Early on, we even went so far as to guarantee satisfaction or we would cut the price back to the calculations level. However, we would *not* give the client company the value map's predecessor until it had given us a check for the balance at the higher amount.

How did we accomplish this? It was easy. We would go to the client's office with the VEM in hand, nicely bound in a navy blue cover with maroon spine in it. We would open the VEM and say to the client company's owner or CEO something like the following:

> *We came across a lot of risk factors in this engagement. As you've heard us say more than once during our time together, reducing risk increases value. This document* (and I hold it up so the person can see it) *has detailed solutions for the following major risk factors: A, B, C, D, E, and F. However, as we have discussed, we need you to agree to pay us for the work we've done before we can discuss details of our findings. Are you up for that?*

1. www.amazon.com/value-maps-valuation-unlock-business/dp/0470437561.

A conniving owner or CEO could, I suppose, agree to pay and later claim not to be satisfied, in which case we would have to issue a refund. Maybe we were lucky back then, but it never happened. I think it was because we always found at least two big areas of risk that the owner had no idea his company was exposed to. Then and since, we have always gotten paid—in full.

Value maps come into play, first, in *non-adversarial engagements*. We would never try to do a value map if there were any such player as "opposing counsel." The value-map add-on is especially attractive when the engagement is compliance-related—"C" corporations making the "S" election, for instance, offer a great opportunity for the value map because a full-blown appraisal report is superfluous for such a conversion. However, the absence of the report also cuts the price way down. To compensate, we do a "letter appraisal" that has the figures that the client company and its CPA need. We have the supporting information in our files so that, if we later have to produce a valuation report, it will be easy. We've never had to, but there's always a first time.

Buy-sell agreements also present an opportunity for a value-map add-on. In this case, we deliver only a range estimate because it leaves the opposing parties with room to negotiate. As SMDC-savvy readers know, such clients are apt to have considerable difficulty producing a five-year DCF forecast that is up to the standards that readers of this *Guide* need. Because we do not use capitalization of free cash flow (or any other capitalization method) for any but a world-class SMDC (which we met for the first time last year, incidentally), we are left with the market approach and the asset-based approach. Guideline public company (GPC) analysis is a primary valuation method in our shop. Our GPC template has switches for size-adjusted valuation multiples[2] based on Morningstar/Ibbotson and on Duff & Phelps built into it, so we are not stuck relying on the old "4 to 7 companies" that Pratt's early editions cited. Instead, our typical GPC analysis has more than a dozen companies, often more than 20, and sometimes more than 30. The additional "degrees of freedom" (a.k.a. "large number of companies") makes any substantial error statistically improbable. In the absence of viable GPCs—which happens, but only rarely—we do a rough-cut estimate using the asset accumulation method to pick up intangible value. We consider adjusted book value to be useless except for a young SMDC with little intangible value.

Walk the Warehouse

I can't say it straighter than that. The warehouse is to the SMDC what the shop floor is to the small manufacturer. It's where what matters happens. The warehouse walk during your shake 'n' howdy visit will tell you whether or not a value map is likely to be plausible.

Here are some things to look for or ask about during this stroll:

- Are employees wearing hard hats and safety glasses? (OSHA requires it.) Are they wearing protective gloves (if necessary)?

2. Mattson, et al., "Adjusting Multiples."

- Is the warehouse floor marked to keep people away from hazardous activities? (Look out for that forklift!)
- Are the warehouse bins labeled?
- Are the bins labels bar-coded?
- Is there a map of the warehouse showing what's in every bin?
- How is a bin assigned for a new SKU? Is the map updated automatically?
- Can merchandise fall out of a bin, either into an adjacent one or to the floor?
- Does software generate the pick ticket?
- Has the company heard of using iPads to show pick tickets electronically, rather than hard copies which can be lost or torn?
- Does the company use cycle counting as a way of keeping its inventory levels accurate?
- Does the company make deliveries or does it use LTL trucking, FedEx, or UPS?
- If FedEx/UPS, does the firm use FedEx/UPS software or its own?
- If pick tickets are computer-generated, how is the sequence of an individual ticket determined?
- If the company makes deliveries, are the pick tickets arrayed in reverse delivery sequence when they arrive in the warehouse? (In other words, does the delivery to be made last get picked first, so that it can be put right into the truck?)
- Find out what the five SKUs in highest demand are, and then ask where "excess inventory" for each of those SKUs is kept? (Perfect answer: "We never have excess inventory of those SKUs because our software system and the vendors won't let that happen.")
- Look for dust on merchandise. Fast-moving SKUs won't have any.
- Ask what the five most expensive SKUs are, and be sure you observe the location of each in the warehouse. Are they fungible? Are they situated close to an exit? Are they light enough to be carried out? What kind of inventory adjustments has the company had to make for those five SKUs in the past, either during a formal inventory or through cycle counting?

- What is the company's incidence rate?[3] This is a crucial driver of the cost of workers' comp insurance. At this writing, 2009 data are available for download. The incidence rate for "wholesale trade—all sizes [measured by headcount]" in 2009 was 3.3, notably below rates in construction (4.6), manufacturing (4.3), agriculture (5.3), warehousing and storage (5.0), and even retailing (4.2), but higher than mining (2.4), information (1.9) financial activities (1.5), and professional and business services (1.8).[4]

- How many warehouses does the company have? If > 1, how are intra-company inventory transfers accounted for? Do all warehouses have the same layouts, the same pick-ticket technology, the same policies about safety and excess inventory, etc.?

- What routines does the warehouse function use to process incoming shipments, from either vendors or its own warehouses?

- Do any SKUs include HazMats (hazardous materials)? If so, how rigorous are company policies regarding compliance with DOT, EPA, OSHA, and CPSC regulations about HazMats? Is diamond-shaped HazMat signage in place? Do those handling HazMats were protective equipment?

- What incentives to avoid lost-time warehouse accidents does the company have in place?

This is not an all-inclusive list of questions for your warehouse walk-through ahead of pricing the engagement, but it is enough, I believe, for you to assess the complexity and time component related to the warehousing phase of operations. Make no mistake about it: if it's done slipshod, it has the potential to trash your time budget. Just think about the effect on valuation profitability of an SMDC with three warehouses, 30,000 SKUs, and no uniformity—in policies, routines, or operating architecture—among the three.

Pricing the Engagement

Assuming that the engagement is non-adversarial (i.e., no "opposing counsel"), you should quote a fixed fee for the engagement. Even in divorce, if you're expecting to be retained by the propertied spouse, you should consider going the fixed-fee route. I said "consider"; if the propertied spouse is one of those people who believes that everyone is out to get him, then it is probably best to do it hourly so he can absorb the cost of his world-view. I should also mention that, in two engagements representing non-propertied spouses, we were able to conduct due diligence that led us to quote a fixed fee . . . but with a provision to switch to hourly if the situation turned into mud-wrestling; neither one did.

---

3. The BLS website: www.bls.gov/iif/osheval.htm.
4. www.bls.gov/iif/oshwc/osh/os/ostb2439.txt.

There are two reasons to do fixed-fee pricing:

- The work is far easier to sell; and
- You don't want a high hourly rate to get in the way of essential communications—in other words, you don't want your client thinking, "Jeez, this phone call is costing me 6 bucks a minute!"

However, to avoid working for a pittance under a fixed fee, you *must* do the requisite due diligence. Moreover, if you get any hints from the business owner and CEO that the fee, even one dwarfed by its measurable value, could be an issue, you could, early on, say something like this:

> *Ummm, we are a 95-octane firm. That is because we aim to deliver value that hugely exceeds what we charge. We perform at a high level and do work of the highest quality. That is because we love what we do and want to do it as well as it can be done. Of course, some clients don't need that level of service. How do you feel about that?*

If the fee is going to be an issue, you'll know. And if it is an issue, then you're ahead by finding out now, before you invest five or 10 hours in due diligence. If the client asks what you mean by "95 octane," parry that question with one of your own: "Do you have a notion of what the work we're discussing should cost?" You want the client to quote a number first; if yours is first, it can only go down from there. Again, recall my earlier comments about there being some clients that we cannot afford to have. Let 'em go make your closest competitor's life miserable.

Let's assume that you are dealing with an SMDC and that you believe you have scoped the engagement well. The purpose is business and estate planning. The company has revenues in the $4 million range and one warehouse. You have a good sense of the SMDC, and its warehouse stood up decently in response to your questions during the walk-through. Subject to agreeing on price, the owner or CEO wants to retain you. How much is your fee?

Well, the only remaining question is the deliverable. Are you doing a *detailed report* or a *summary report*? If it's non-adversarial, the latter should be sufficient. If you're organized and disciplined in your work, you should be able to do it in 50 hours, maximum. A detailed report should take 70 or 80 hours. Multiply the appropriate figure by the hourly rate—your own or a "blended" one if you expect to use subordinates or subcontractors in some roles—and that'll get you to a fee. We tend to round down to the nearest hundred bucks; the nearest thousand looks too much like a round number.

If any of the five due-diligence metrics I cited a few pages ago is "deficient," you should consider raising your price at least 15%. The work is going to be messier, more difficult, and longer. In addition, if you do a value-map add-on, then it is going to demand more time. Price accordingly.

But you're not done yet. At least, we're not. As we all know, serious valuation practices have high overhead. Subscriptions, reference books, database access, CPE, conferences—it all comes to real money. Since the beginning of 2008, we have added a flat 5% to our fee quotations to cover some of that overhead. Not one client has complained about it. We add 5% to invoices for hourly work, too. In both cases, we put the add-on on a separate line labeled "Access to proprietary databases, etc." Sometimes we come out a little ahead, sometimes a little behind. It balances out.

If the engagement is more or less local—within 70 miles or so—we do not charge separately for driving back and forth. If we have to buy a plane ticket and a hotel room, though, those travel expenses are expressly provided for separately in the Engagement Letter. They are not included in the 5% add-on.

If the engagement is for calculations, we will usually budget about 25 hours. But that can vary according to the scope and the particulars of the work. We add 5% here, too.

If the work combines calculations and a value map, "the number" should be upwards of $20,000 . . . plus the 5%. Although the time we put in probably won't, in and of itself, justify the entire price, we base this pricing on value, not time. Clients *will* pay for value. And they hate paying for pure compliance because they see no value.

If the engagement is a combination of a valuation (detailed report or summary) and a value map, you should be able to increase the valuation-only price by 50%. And don't forget that 5%. Again, billable hours might suggest a lower fee, but you are delivering value. Charge for it. The client is getting a whole lot more than it is being asked to pay for. If your value map won't make or save the client at least 10x what you're charging, then either you shouldn't be doing a value map, or your value map missed some essential aspects. Value maps are win-win for both client and service-provider.

Always get the client's agreement to the fee **before you prepare an Engagement Letter**. Wherever possible, quote the fee to the client company in person. If you have to do it by phone, O.K. But *never* by e-mail, and *never* let a draft engagement letter be the first time the client has heard what the fee will be. If you're good enough to be charging what you should be charging, you don't have to hesitate about looking a client in the eye or saying with confidence via telephone what the fee will be.

In the fixed-fee context, which we try to do whenever possible (never in M&A, though), we explain that the fixed fee transfers pricing risk from the client to us. We also note that "the overwhelming majority of our work" is done on a fixed fee. Many SMDCs will say they have been burned by attorneys with ticking meters that the client didn't know was "on." The fixed fee finesses the issue and is a much easier sale.

Finally, let me say a few words about "bidding." Start with what any construction company owner will tell you: "Bid work is bad work." If we are asked "to quote on an engagement," we cut to the chase with our "95-octane soliloquy." If we conclude that the client has realistic expectations about price, we then ask about "the process": what is the primary criterion for the decision (if it's price, we wave good-bye); who will make the decision (if we can't talk to the decision-maker or at least someone who can sign the engagement letter, we bow out); to how many companies is the prospective client talking (if it's more than four, including us, we say, "Adios, amigo"); and so on.

Here's an example of what can happen if you don't attack the bidding situation aggressively at the beginning: A colleague in another state recently told me about an experience he had with bidding. He went through two rounds of it. He also shared a sample valuation report with the prospect (argggggg). He was one of two finalists. He made no attempt to try to find out who the other firm was. Even if the client had refused to tell him, he probably could have learned enough with some probing questions to get an idea of how to price. He didn't. He quoted $12,000. The other firm quoted $30,000. You know the rest.

How to Eliminate Collection Problems

Regardless of how you're working—fixed fee or hourly—your Engagement Letter should stipulate that you will submit an invoice via PDF when your "Incomplete Work Product—For Discussion Purposes Only" document is ready and that you will send the client that document after you are paid. This will eliminate collection issues.

If you're working hourly, you should ensure that your retainer is "evergreen": when the work you've done has consumed the retainer, the engagement letter should allow you "the option" of stopping work until it is replenished. As a practical matter, you will seldom decide to do that . . . unless you have other work that pays comparably well.

If the client is one with whom you have worked before, or if a law firm has guaranteed payment of your fees, then you have obvious flexibility. Even then, though, get your 50% retainer up-front before you do any work beyond the scoping activities that you've already done.

Incidentally, those activities *do* take time. No two ways about that. And sometimes you might have to wave good-bye to that time, either because you don't want the work or because price is an issue. You should be able to avoid most instances of the latter with the 95-octane conversation.

The Wrap

We have covered a lot of administrative, pricing, and negotiating ground in this chapter. Here are the key points:

- get the NDA signed before you invest any serious time
- scope the engagement

- there are some clients that neither you nor we can afford to have
- **define the domain**
- review the preliminary information you obtained
- if you're still interested in the prospect, then, wherever possible, do a "shake 'n' howdy" visit before taking the time to draft an Engagement Letter
- if you get *any sense* that the client is overly fee-sensitive (**all clients** are fee-sensitive at some level), roll out that 95-octane spiel and gauge the client's reaction—you might save yourself a lot of time and frustration
- be skeptical about bidding situations; if you choose to get into one, make sure you understand the process and, especially, the primary criterion for decision-making
- during the S&H, walk through the warehouse and ask about enough of the bulleted issues in this chapter to assure yourself about the time component the warehouse-related aspects of the engagement will require
- if a calculations engagement is appropriate, do it . . . but never provide a point estimate for a calculations price—always provide a range of value
- any time you can price on a fixed-fee basis and do so without your gut yelling at you not to, do it—the work is just easier to sell
- if the engagement is non-adversarial, you should know from the S&H whether the client needs a value map or not; if so, discuss it with the owner or CEO, preferably in person. We find that having that discussion over supper (at our expense) increases our chances for landing the engagement
- unless you have a heckuva good reason to do otherwise, get paid before you deliver the draft; don't find out the hard way that you're working *pro bono*

We are now ready to move into the valuation process itself. Chapter 3 deals with a subject that is near and dear to my heart, but also one that is, in my view, **the** issue in valuing SMDCs: unsystematic risk. Turn the page, and let's get to work on the work itself.

Unsystematic Risk in SMDCs

Introduction

Our community has a mountain of data—from Morningstar/Ibbotson and from Duff & Phelps—proving that smaller companies are, on balance,[1] far riskier than big ones. But size is only part of the problem of unsystematic risk. In most cases, at least where risk premiums are concerned, it's not even the biggest one. Our focus in this chapter is on the concept of unsystematic risk in valuing SMDCs.

Financial Economics and Unsystematic Risk

Scholars in financial economics, led by Harry Markowitz over 50 years ago, developed modern portfolio theory (MPT). One keystone of MPT is that unsystematic risk, which they call "diversifiable risk," can be eliminated through diversification. In fact, MPT posits that rational investors hold fully diversified portfolios. MPT wasn't a lot of help in 2008, though, was it? And MPT has an increasingly vocal cadre of critics, led by the legendary "Sage of Omaha," Warren Buffett. He argues that MPT leads to *over*diversification, which is both expensive and counterproductive. Even the CFA Institute, normally a bastion of sound thinking, is still dancing to the MPT tune.

From my perspective, the issue with MPT—indeed, with traditional financial economics generally—is that it is still wedded to the same-old, bad-old traditional approach to microeconomics: static analysis, the company-as-production function, homogeneous companies/consumers/products/services, innovation doesn't matter, entrepreneurship is irrelevant, and so on. We see it even in so-called "scoring" of proposed legislation by the Congressional Budget Office, that bastion of nonpartisanship (and economic ignorance); those geniuses always assume that changes in tax rates *do not affect human behavior*. They really don't get the idea of incentives, do they?

Financial economists threw up a serious roadblock to the valuation of SMDCs and small and mid-sized companies generally when they assumed away the issue of unsystematic risk. That assumption precluded research into unsystematic risk because, they said, it didn't matter. Try telling that to owners of the typical SMDC who have over 90% of their net worth locked up in the illiquid equity of their closely held company. To paraphrase legendary NFL coach Vince Lombardi, to them, "Unsystematic risk isn't everything. It's the only thing."

There is no research because there are no data. There are no data because there is no framework within which to collect data and test hypotheses. It reminds me of a definition of an economist: a guy with a Phi Beta Kappa key at one end of his watch chain . . . and no watch at the other.

1. Yes, you'll find an occasional exception.

Why Unsystematic Risk Matters in Valuing SMBs

Unsystematic risk matters in valuing small and medium-sized businesses of *any* kind because it is unsystematic risk that explains the differences among companies. No other risk component or group of risk components does that. Therefore, if you really want to understand the company you're valuing, you need to get your arms around its unsystematic risk.

That takes time. In the typical engagement, we spend two-thirds to three-quarters of our time analyzing, researching, talking about, writing about, and thinking about unsystematic risk. If one is valuing a 10th-decile company, as most of those in the line of work are, I will bet that if valuation activities related to unsystematic risk don't consume at least half of the engagement time, then the probability that the person who signs the report understands why the client company's performance metrics are what they are is between slim and none. And "slim" just left town.

Why Unsystematic Risk Matters in Valuing SMDCs

That goes in spades for wholesalers because their margins are under assault from all quarters—upstream (manufacturers), downstream (customers), and technology (Internet). In fact, as we noted in Chapter 1, technology is *the* major source of margin pressure in distribution. On the plus side for SMDCs, technology has the potential to produce supply-chain efficiencies that cannot be realized any other way. But it also empowers customers because they can price-shop nearly anything. Heck, start with eBay; that's the first place we go when we're wondering how much a bigger-ticket items might be worth.

But there's another factor that threatens SMDCs: manufacturers "going direct," either to retailers or, in some cases, straight to the end user, be it consumer or business. My favorite haberdasher, Larry Davidson, the third-generation owner of Roanoke, Virginia, retailer Davidson's, points out that the price of many custom-made suits has sunk to $600 nowadays vs. $2,000 just two or three years ago. That reflects the fact that most textile manufacturing has relocated to China, which, for now, has the lowest labor rates in the developing world. But it also mirrors the development of tools that enable you and me to go online to, say, the upscale rag merchants on London's Savile Row, input our measurements, and wait for the custom threads to arrive. In a riff on China, where the TV in your hotel room watches you, Larry says that he expects technology to turn clothing stores into artifacts within two decades. He believes that today's customers will just stand in front of their computer screens while sophisticated scanning devices take their measurements as they respond to automated voice commands emanating from the workstation. If that happens, the era of "mass customization" will truly be upon us.

I hope for Larry's sake and mine that that technology doesn't come to pass. He's the best men's-clothing merchant I've ever known, though, and I've done business with some fine ones. Ultimately, if stores like Larry's are going to survive—and this applies to SMDCs, too—they are going to have to convince their customers that they deliver value that is worth paying for.

That means a strategy of focus/differentiation (in SPARC parlance, the "Experimenter"). A successful Experimenter has lower risk than its rivals. Its higher margins also allow it to absorb some margin compression, if it must.

External Sources of Unsystematic Risk

When I began doing valuation seriously back in 1993, my first instinct was to create a "valuation program" kind of like the old audit programs that we followed at Union Pacific Corp., where I went to work after undergraduate school. I quickly fell back on my strategy knowledge, though, and realized that no "valuation program" or any other questionnaire could possibly anticipate all of the questions to ask and issues to check. It was impossible, even though I know talented professionals, even today, who assert that they have "*the* questionnaire." My response: "No way."

As many readers of this book know, unsystematic risk comes in two flavors: external and internal. At the external level, however, there are two levels of forces with which to contend. Luckily we have tools from organization theory and from industrial organization (a branch of economics) to help us organize our thinking about risk emanating from the ***macroenvironment*** (six forces) and from the ***domain*** (also six forces), respectively. Unless you work for a big firm that has only behemoth clients, I recommend that you replace the phrase "industry analysis" with "domain analysis." That is because few SMDCs or SMBs compete industrywide. Most are in strategic groups, which we talked about in Chapter 1. The word "domain" subsumes both scopes. The analytical process is the same, whether it's the industry or the strategic group. But, as we also noted in Chapter 1, a canned, off-the-shelf industry analysis is almost certain to be inaccurate when it is applied to a strategic group.

Internal Source of Unsystematic Risk

We know that the company is the internal source of unsystematic risk. But companies are so multifaceted, variable, and different from one another that getting an analytical framework that would work across domains was a big challenge. As a guy who does not subscribe to the NIH (Not Invented Here) worldview, I was sure that I could use something from my days as a Ph.D. student in strategic management. I started off with Michael Porter's value chain—that **black x** inside the dark **circle** is the client company, incidentally).[2]

I mean, Porter was[3] the strategy guru. His value chain provides a nice logical flow to line operations ("primary activities"); however, I never could figure out where R&D should be—probably in "Technology Development," though that would appear to make it a staff activity. The bigger problem was that his value chain didn't resonate with our clients. It didn't help that I also found it hard to work with.

2. Porter, *Competitive Advantage*.
3. And in some quarters, still is.

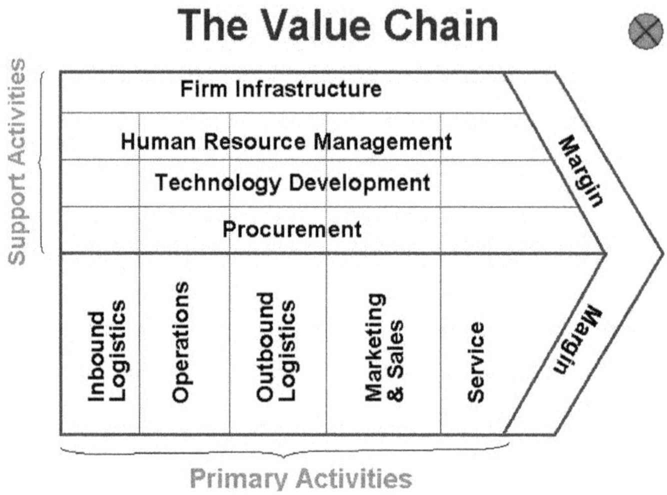

I then went to McKinsey's 7-S Framework, which I'd first seen in 1982 when Peters and Waterman's *In Search of Excellence: Lessons from America's Best Run Companies* took the U.S. business community by storm. McKinsey hires graduate MBAs from the best schools around the world. Unfortunately, that is no guarantee that the new hires show up with much other than a high level of intelligence and an upscale pedigree. That's why McKinsey's management decided to come up with something so simple that "even MBAs could remember it," as one wag put it. And now we have the alliterative seven S's:

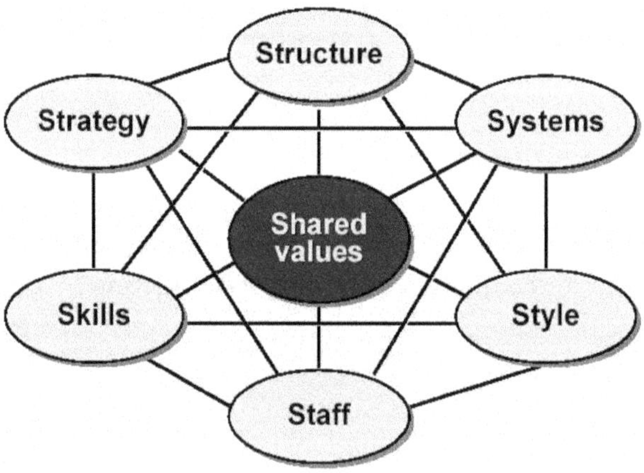

Truth be told, I liked the 7-S Framework. I still do. But I think the graphic is "busy." Clients thought so, too. So I continued to search. As I got deeper into valuation, I saw that the issues of coordination and incentives in closely held companies often differed in major respects from those in most public corporations. In the latter, at least in theory, the incentive is to maximize profitability. That should get the stock price up where the company is not an attractive takeover target. If that happens, managers can keep their jobs, and shareholders should be purring.

As I spent more time around smaller companies, however, I quickly saw that a lot of owners were obsessed with minimizing taxes. Even in the 1990s, it was hard to avoid taxes[4] if your company made money; it is even harder now. To be sure, I'm not keen on paying taxes that I don't owe, either. But then I homed in on another set of incentives: the one with which many tax professionals must contend.

I've seen it a bazillion times, and here's how it works: company owners play golf or fish or hunt together. And they talk about their businesses. Never mind that, where valuation is concerned, those conversations remind me of eight-year-olds talking about what it takes to make a marriage work. But those owners also talk about taxes. One owner says, "You know, my tax guy has figured out ways for me not to pay taxes on my S-corporation for almost 20 years now." And, of course, his cronies ask in unison, "Who's your tax guy?" That word-of-mouth often turns out be how tax professionals are rewarded and get new clients.

The problem, though, is one I've had to tell more than one owner who thought his company was worth millions, despite the fact that its non-existent profits said otherwise:

> Sir [*and it's always been a guy, not a woman, that I've had to say this to*], I have some bad news for you. You've already been paid for your company, but no one told you. You got paid on the installment plan during all those years when you showed marginal profits or none at all. With today's tax code, a company that doesn't pay taxes (or whose owners don't have pass-through income to report on their personal returns) isn't worth anything. I'm sorry, but you can't have it both ways: you can't beat the tax collector, and then turn around and collect a few million bucks from an eager buyer. Economic reality won't allow it.

I mean no disrespect to tax professionals who are reading this. You folks have to make a living, too. And it's not your fault that your clients want to minimize what they have to remit to the IRS. Heck, it's the American way. It always has been. I just wish you would tell your clients that own smaller businesses that, if they expect to have a big payday at exit, they need to start showing some significant profits at least in, say, the last five years or so before they ride off into the sunset. That means getting the son-in-law who can't make a living elsewhere off the payroll. It means putting the company plane into a separate entity. It means installing some governance with spine and getting a CFO who will tell you what you *don't* what to hear.

Of course, those views and three bucks will get me a latte at Starbucks. The problem with tax-minimization, though, is that it produces some goofy—irrational, even—decisions. Their impact often appears in "aberrant metrics"—performance measures that are well above or well below those of a public-company composite. Because financial economists have assumed away the whole problem of unsystematic risk, finance has nothing in the way of a framework to help us understand ***why***: *why* is the client company's DSO 107 days when its invoices have Net 30 terms? **Why**

4. *Avoid*, not *evade*.

does the accounting arm of the enterprise spend three weeks closing every month? **Why** did a company that says its employees are its most important assets issue 168 W-2s last year for a work force that averaged 36 FTEs? **Why** is its inventory turn one-fourth the average of the composite? **Why** is its productivity (measured as annual revenues ÷ full-time-equivalent employees) barely three-fourths that of said composite? **Why? Why? Why**, indeed?

I needed something that would help me get to *why*. If I couldn't explain why, I'd get the valuation where it should be only by accident. Except for preparing for the three levels of the CFA exam, valuing a business is the hardest work I've ever done. I didn't want to look like an audit partner I'd had breakfast with in a city in America's southwest in the mid-'90s. He'd had an audit client, which had become our valuation client, for almost 25 years. Over breakfast I asked him 35 questions that I thought were basic. He was an honest guy. Unfortunately, he said, "I don't know" to 34 of them. I didn't want to be that guy if I were ever on a witness stand and opposing counsel began asking me a ton of *why* questions about a valuation I had done.

My third run at a possible solution was Jay Galbraith's "Star Model":

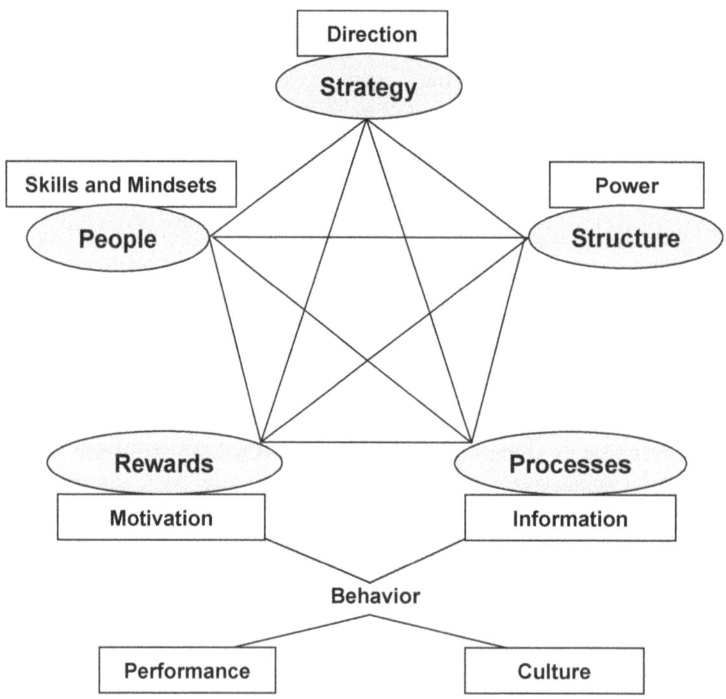

Despite the fact that it looks like a child's mobile, there is a lot to like about this model. But, like its 7-S predecessor, the Star Model is busy—too busy for clients, too busy for me. My pea brain needed something simple and intuitive. By the time I concluded that "the Star" wasn't for me, 2005 had arrived, and I'd been wrestling with this problem for a dozen years. That is a long time to be wandering in the wilderness trying to solve the same bloody problem. Many times I wondered if there was a solution or if I was so close to the problem that I'd never see the solution, even (especially) if it were right there under my nose. It didn't happen that way, thank goodness.

The Trilevel Unsystematic-Risk Framework

I decided to go back through all the valuations I'd been involved in during the preceding dozen years and try to attribute various aspects of the company level of unsystematic risk to one or more underlying causes. This took a *lot* of time—at that time, I had been involved in over 300 valuations. But I pulled up the reports—or, in the case of some early ones that I'd archived, dug them out—and began going through them. If you want to sharpen your sense of humility, read the first three reports you ever wrote. If you don't shake your head in disbelief at how you dodged malpractice bullets, let me know. You'll be the first.

As a strategy guy, I'm a believer in patterns. That's one definition of strategy: "a pattern in a stream of decisions."[5] To be sure, I don't subscribe to that particular definition, but the idea of patterns in economic phenomena is a real and useful thing to keep in mind. I was looking for some pattern—I didn't know what it might look like or even if there was one—in those underlying causes of company risk. I did the analysis manually with a pen and paper. Every time I thought I had a decent template to work with, I found out I didn't. Finally, I just started at the beginning and went through each engagement, making notes that said enough for me to be able to recall later what I meant.

Sure enough, it turned out that there *was* a pattern. The complete one didn't show itself in every valuation, of course, but five broad classifications of underlying causes emerged. I could attribute to one or more of them *every* loony-bin metric or risk factor I had encountered in my then-300-plus engagements. The pattern has continued without so much as even a close call.

We call that pattern the SPARC Framework—<u>S</u>trategy, <u>P</u>eople, <u>A</u>rchitecture, <u>R</u>outines, <u>C</u>ulture. In over 450 engagements, it has not failed to explain a single cause of aberrant performance. I first sketched what has become the Trilevel Unsystematic-Risk Framework on a cocktail napkin at Mr. K's, a wonderful Chinese restaurant located at 50th & Lex in Midtown Manhattan, for my good friend and valuation colleague, Jim Travis, in September 2005. We were in New York to attend a meeting of the Appraisal Issues Task Force. I showed him my drawing, and he said, "Cool. What is it?" As I explained it, he nodded.

We use it in every valuation engagement. In fact, I hate to think of where we'd be without SPARC. I know one thing: doing a valuation would take two or three times as long as it now takes, and the product wouldn't be half as good, despite all that additional time. The illustration is on the next page.

It is straightforward: two concentric hexagons for the two levels of external risk (note that the Macroenvironment is "farther" from the company at the center than is the Domain) surrounding a five-piece triangle circumscribed by "resources." You might have noticed that our company logo bears a distinct resemblance to the two hexagons and the equilateral triangle. Beckmill Research, LLC, is an **Experimenter**: our strategy is focus/differentiation. It always has been, it always will be, and that mirror image is part of why. Nothing else makes a lick of sense.

5. Mintzberg, "Patterns": 934.

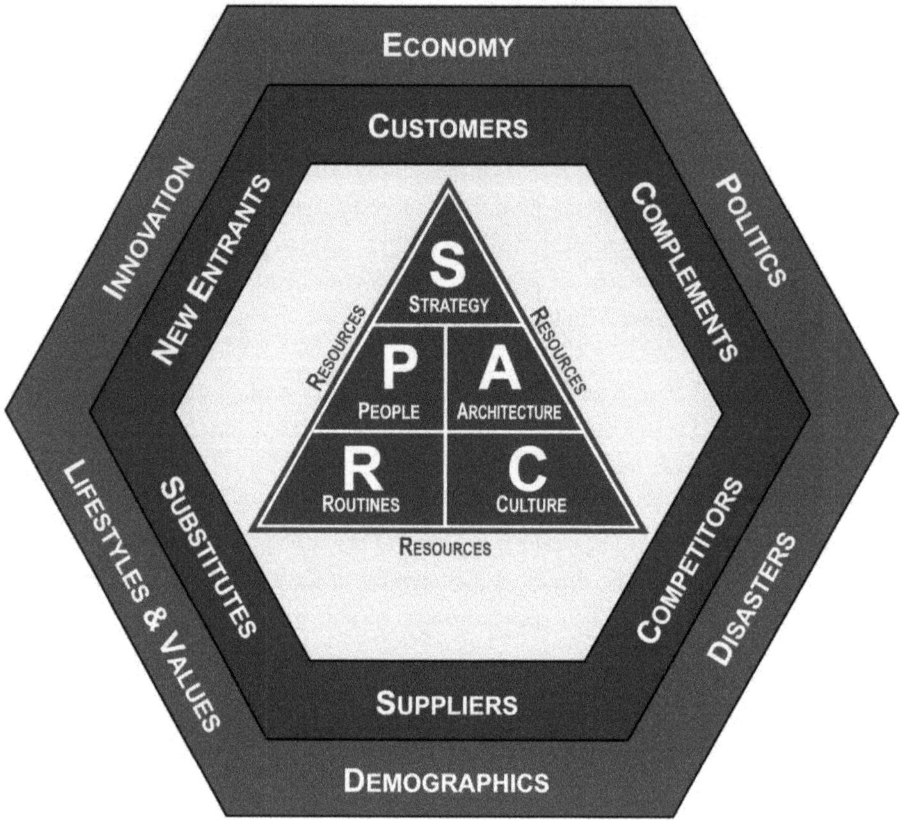

TRILEVEL UNSYSTEMATIC-RISK FRAMEWORK

MACROENVIRONMENT   DOMAIN   COMPANY

Published Research

Beginning with Rumelt's 1991 paper (the first one in the table below), ten articles have been published that measure external and internal sources of variation in rate of return at the company level. The scholars have used different datasets, different time frames, and different techniques, yet their conclusions are consistent. They are summarized in the table on pages 34–35.

One way to measure risk is through volatility (i.e., variation).[6] In the table, company-level sources of variation in rate of return (ROR) account for three times as much variation as do domain sources. The message from each paper is consistent: companies within a "domain" are more different from one another than are industries themselves. This is more evidence that the homogeneity that traditional microeconomics assumes is bogus.

6. In public companies, stock volatility = beta.

Models of Risk

The notion of risk in securities typically begins with the capital asset pricing model (CAPM).[7] It posits that the expected return for a security is a function of its risk. Here's the CAPM in its purest form:

$$E(R_a) = R_f + ([R_m - R_f] \times \beta_a)$$

where:

$E(R_a)$ = the required rate of return on security *a* issued by Company A

R_f = the risk-free rate of return (typically the yield to maturity on a government bond, short-, medium-, or long-term, depending on the facts and circumstances of the assignment at hand)

R_m = the rate of return on a fully diversified market portfolio

β_a = Company A's "beta"—its volatility relative to an underlying market benchmark; beta also purports to measure "systematic risk"

Arbitrage pricing theory (APT)[8] and the Fama-French three-factor model[9] are two other methods for quantifying the required rate of return on an asset. However, the CAPM and variants, including its sibling, the build-up method, which has the unfortunate acronym BUM, are the two most common, especially in the less rarefied environs of valuing private equity.

The Cost of Capital Model for SMDCs

In virtually every engagement, we use the build-up method. For reasons that will become clear in Chapter 5 of this *Guide*, we aren't any keener on individual published industry betas than we are on individual published industry risk premiums; however, there is some shelter in aggregation, as we shall see in this chapter. Therefore, we try to avoid the capital asset pricing model unless we're dealing with a bigger company *and* we can use at least 15 or 20 guideline public companies in our analysis. We want the DCF and GPC results to act as checks on one another.

7. Two scholars conceived the CAPM independently of one another: Sharpe, "Capital Asset Prices," and Lintner, "Valuation of Risky Assets." CAPM extended Harry Markowitz's pioneering work in modern portfolio theory a decade earlier.
8. A nice explanation of APT: viking.som.yale.edu/will/finman540/classnotes/class6.html
9. This has editorial content, but: www.travismorien.com/FAQ/portfolios/famafrench.htm

Selected Papers (1991-2007) – Sources of Variation in Rate of Return

Date	Citation[1] (pub/vol/pp)	Title of Paper (*Author[s]*)	Cohort	Sources of Variation in Rates of Return (ROR)[2]: Domain (DOM)					Company (CO)			
				IND	SG	Year	IND x Year	Total	Corporate	Firm	Firm x Year	Total
1991	*SMJ*, 12, 167-185.	How Much Does Industry Matter? (*Rumelt*)	A	8.3%	NI	0.0%	7.8%	16.1%	0.8%	46.4%	36.7%	83.9%
			B	4.0%	NI	0.0%	NI	4.0%	1.6%	44.2%	NI	45.8%
1996	*SMJ*, 17, 653-664.	Markets vs. Management: What Drives Profitability? (*Roquebert, et al.*)		10.1%	NI	0.4%	2.3%	12.8%	17.9%	37.1%	NI	55.0%
1997	*SMJ*, 18 (Summer Spec. Issue), 15-30.	How Much Does Industry Matter, Really? (*McGahan & Porter*)	1	8.1%	NI	NI	NI	8.1%	10.5%	35.0%	NI	45.5%
			2	18.7%	NI	NI	NI	18.7%	4.3%	31.7%	NI	36.0%
1999	*JIE*, 47, 373-398.	The Performance of U.S. Corporations: 1981-1994 (*McGahan*)	1	27.9%	NI	NI	NI	27.9%	-0.1%	37.1%	NI	37.0%
			2	10.7%	NI	NI	NI	10.7%	-0.2%	23.7%	NI	23.5%
			3	14.0%	NI	NI	NI	14.0%	-0.2%	27.0%	NI	26.8%
2000	*SMJ*, 21, 739-752.	Corporate and Industry Effects on Business Unit Competitive Position (Chang & Singh)	A	19.4%	NI	0.9%	0.9%	21.2%	4.3%	52.7%	NI	57.0%
			B	25.4%	NI	0.3%	1.8%	27.5%	8.5%	46.8%	NI	55.3%
2002	*MS*, 48, 834-851.	What Do We Know About Variance in Acct'g Prof.? (*McGahan & Porter*)	Hi	16.3%	NI	1.1%	NI	17.4%	23.7%	59.1%	NI	82.8%
			Lo	6.9%	NI	0.2%	NI	7.1%	8.8%	32.5%	NI	41.3%
2003	*SMJ*, 24, 1-16.	Is Performance Driven by Industry- or Firm-Specific Factors? (*Hawawini, et al.*)	1	6.5%	NI	1.9%	4.2%	12.6%	NI	27.1%	NI	27.1%
			2	11.4%	NI	1.3%	2.9%	15.6%	NI	32.5%	NI	32.5%
			3	8.1%	NI	1.0%	3.1%	12.2%	NI	35.8%	NI	35.8%

2003	*SO*, 1, 79-108.	The Emergence and Sustainability of Abnormal Profits (*McGahan & Porter*)	1	29.6%	NI	1.7%	NI	31.3%	30.0%	38.7%	NI	68.7%
			2	22.5%	NI	0.4%	NI	22.9%	22.8%	54.3%	NI	77.1%
2006	*SMJ*, 27, 571-590.	A New Perspective on a Fundamental Debate: A Multilevel Approach to Industry, Corporate, and Business Unit Effects (*Misangyi, et al.*)	1	7.6%	NI	0.8%	NI	8.4%	7.2%	36.6%	NI	43.8%
			2	7.4%	NI	NI	NI	7.4%	NI	45.0%	NI	45.0%
2007	*SMJ*, 28, 147-167.	Firm, Strategic Group, and Industry Influences on Performance (*Short, et al.*)	1	14.7%	6.4%	NI	NI	21.0%	NI	79.0%	NI	79.0%
			2	19.2%	15.0%	NI	NI	34.2%	NI	65.8%	NI	65.8%

	DOM		CO
MEANS	16.7%	⟷	50.7%
standard deviations	8.4%	⟷	19.1%

[1]– *AER = American Economic Review*
JIE = Journal of Industrial Economics
MS = Management Science
SMJ = Strategic Management Journal
SO = Strategic Organization

[2]– average R^2 if in a narrow range; presented separately if range isn't narrow

NI = Not Included in research

Mean R^2 of Company effects	50.7%
Mean R^2 of Domain effects	16.7%
Company R^2 ÷ Domain R^2 =	**3.0**

Here's a starting point for the BUM:

$$E(R_a) = R_f + (R_m - R_f) + U_a \quad [Eq. 3\text{-}1]$$

where:

$E(R_a)$ = the required rate of return on security *a*

R_f = the risk-free rate of return (typically the yield to maturity on a Treasury security, short-, medium-, or long-term, depending on facts and circumstances)

R_m = the market rate of return for large-cap stocks

U_a = unsystematic risk associated with security *a*

Longitudinal data from Morningstar and from Duff & Phelps confirm that size (however measured) and rate of return are negatively correlated. However, both datasets take us only as far as the size premium. After that, there are three components of non-size unsystematic risk:

- macroenvironment (six forces)
- industry/strategic group (six forces)
- company (risk is a function of alignment and the durability of value-creating mechanisms)

Expressed mathematically, unsystematic risk looks like this:

$$U_a = P_{size} + P_{mac} + P_{dom} + P_{com} \quad [Eq. 3\text{-}2]$$

where:

U_a = total unsystematic risk for firm *a*

P_{size} = risk premium for size

P_{mac} = macroenvironmental risk in *the industry/strategic group*

P_{dom} = domain (industry or strategic group) risk

P_{com} = company-specific risk

Now, expanding **Eq. 3-1** on the preceding page, we get:

$$E(R_a) = R_f + (R_m - R_f) + P_{size} + P_{mac} + P_{dom} + P_{com}$$

And, since $(R_m - R_f)$ = the equity risk premium (ERP), the equation simplifies to:

$$E(R_a) = R_f + ERP + P_{size} + P_{mac} + P_{dom} + P_{com}$$ *[Eq. 3-3]*

Solid data are available for the first three terms, but not for the last three. It is these latter factors which complicate the analysis and valuation of SMBs and SMDCs. That is why an analytical framework is so important. Lacking reliable data, we have no choice but to exercise judgment in estimating macroenvironmental, domain, and company-specific risk. The objective is "qualitative rigor." And that's *not* an oxymoron.

Done right, the analytical process endows us with insights and a comprehensive understanding of the business(es) of the subject company. One cannot understand an SMDC's business—*really* understand it—without an in-depth grasp of its unsystematic risk. Let's carry it to the final step. If we assume that no firm can have an equity cost of capital that is below the risk-free rate ($\mathbf{R_f}$), then:

$$(P_{mac} + P_{dom} + P_{com}) + (ERP + P_{size}) \geq 0$$ *[Eq. 3-4]*

If that's *not* true, then

$$E(R_a) < R_f$$ *[Eq. 3-5]*

which makes NO economic sense!

Therefore, there is a mathematical constraint on quantifying non-size-related unsystematic risk at the low end. That constraint will vary over time. ERPs change, and so do size premiums. At this writing (July 2011), there's not just one figure for each—Damodaran's "implied" (i.e., forward-looking) ERP is 5.20%, the historical ERP in the Duff & Phelps dataset is pegged at 4.40%,[10] the "supply-side" ERP is 5.96%, and Morningstar (nee Ibbotson Associates) says the ERP is 6.72%.[11] Like the ERP, the size premium varies depending on one's choice of cohort (10th cohort, 10a, 10b, 10w/x/y/z, microcap, etc.); of underlying index (S&P 500 or NYSE Composite); of measurement frequency (annual vs. monthly); and of beta method (sum vs. non-sum). Done one way, the constraint could be about –9 percentage points (5% ERP, 4% RP_{size}). Done another, it could approach –13 percentage points (7% ERP, 6% RP_{size}) or –19% (7% ERP, 12% 10z size premium). Or it could be something else entirely. It depends on the choices the analyst makes.

---

10. The D&P "forward looking" ERP is 5.5%.
11. Sources: www.stern.nyu.edu/~adamodar/pc/implprem/ERPbymonth.xls; 2011 Duff & Phelps, LLC, Risk Premium Report (p. 30); Stocks, Bonds, Bills, and Inflation [SBBI]—2011 Valuation Yearbook (Chicago: Morningstar, Inc., 2011), Table 5-6, 66.

Summing up—We are concerned that the sub-decile measures of the size premium at the small end of the market have a significant level of company-specific factors embedded in them.[12] That is especially true for the 10z cohort. In addition, more "degrees of freedom" (i.e., a bigger sample) makes for greater statistical robustness than fewer. Accordingly, we conclude that the aggregate constraint at the low end is **–900 basis points.** It consists of 5 percentage points for the ERP and 4 for the size premium. That constraint, then, is the maximum *negative* premium that can come from non-size unsystematic risk: $\Sigma\ \mathbf{P}_{mac} + \mathbf{P}_{dom} + \mathbf{P}_{com} \geq -9$ **percentage points.** See Appendix A to this chapter for an elaboration.

In the meantime, keep in mind that value is created when the actual rate of return exceeds the expected rate. In other words, when actual returns on assets exceed the cost of the funds required to finance them (interest-bearing debt + equity), economic wealth is the result.

Put another way, let's divide the traditional balance sheet, which is usually:

Assets = Liabilities + Equity

or

What We Have = What We Owe + What We Own

Breaking down several terms above, we can say that:

Assets = Current Assets + Fixed Assets + Intangible Assets + Other Assets

Liabilities = Current Liabilities + Long-Term Liabilities

and

Working Capital = Current Assets – Current Liabilities

We can now rearrange the accounting balance sheet into one that comports with economics:

Working Capital + Fixed Assets + Intangible/Other Assets

=

Interest-Bearing Debt + Equity

The cost of funding sources (interest-bearing debt and equity) on the right side of the balance sheet is called WACC (weighted-average cost of capital). The return on assets on the left side is called the WARA (weighted-average return on assets). When WARA > WACC, real wealth (which is not the same as accounting wealth) is created.

12. See Israel, "A Generous Helping."

The Wrap

We have covered a lot of ground in this chapter. In valuing SMDCs, unsystematic risk is the heart of the matter. In fact, in a typical engagement, we typically spend 60%–70% of our billable time researching, analyzing, talking about, and writing about unsystematic risk. It is mighty important stuff.

Here are what I believe to be the key takeaways from this chapter:

- External sources of risk come from two levels: the **macroenvironment** (more remote) and the **domain** (closer to the company)
- Each set of external risks comprises six factors
- The SPARC framework is used at the company level of unsystematic risk to identify underlying causes of aberrant performance metrics
- Ten papers published in "A" refereed journals over a 16-year period found that, on average, internal sources of variation in rate of return had 3.0x as much impact as external sources
- For reasons we proved algebraically a few pages ago, the lower bound for each of the three risk-premium ranges is -3%
- When WARA > WACC, economic wealth is created

Before we tackle the analysis of the three levels of unsystematic risk, we have to devote a chapter to what I call "nontraditional tools" from fields distant from our comfort zone. But we will be using them, so you need an introduction. Appendix A follows, and then Chapter 4.

Appendix: 'Industry' Risk Premiums (IRPs)

In its 2000 edition, Ibbotson Associates (now owned by Morningstar) began publishing IRPs, presumably in response to requests from the valuation community. The 2011 edition of its annual yearbook arrayed what it erroneously labeled "industry risk premia" (IRPs) for 503 two-, three-, and four-digit SIC codes; there are 71, 212, and 220 of these, respectively.[1]

Why "erroneously"? True, the data compilers do separate the data by industry SIC codes. But, as we have established before, all companies within a given domain have the same external risk premiums—the "opportunities and threats" in SWOT analysis. Therefore, these are *external risk premiums* because the analysis underpinning them did not separate factors in the macroenvironment from factors in the industry (a.k.a. domain).

Because of the importance of business diversification as a way to both reduce risk and enable growth, few public companies compete in just one SIC/NAICS code. For multi-business enterprises, Morningstar makes the questionable assumption that risk occurs ratably across business segments according to their revenues. By excluding privately held firms, most of which are SMBs, and by prorating risk according to segment revenue, Morningstar's IRPs are biased toward bigger companies; that results in understated IRPs. Nonetheless, there is strength in numbers—degrees of freedom: we don't use individual IRPs, but aggregated IRPs are statistically robust. See next section.

Moreover, these premiums are drawn from companies that are more likely to compete industrywide, rather than in strategic groups. Most closely helds, in contrast, compete in such groups because they don't have the resources to compete industrywide.

Here are some aggregated data from IRPs in the 2011 edition of *SBBI*:

The High End of the Premium Range

- Risk premiums usually fall in declining markets, which 2008 certainly was; they rise in up markets, which 2009 and 2010 turned out to be.
- Since 1926, market averages have risen in more years (61) than they have fallen (24).
- At the three- and four-digit SIC level, seven SIC codes comprising 123 business segments meeting Morningstar's criteria had IRPs ≥ 10½ percentage points. Their weighted-average IRP = 11.67%.

1. SBBI, 32-42.

- Using a similar method with *SBBI's* IRPs data in the 2008-2010 *Yearbooks*, the upper limit for *total external risk* was 12%.

- Therefore, we conclude that a *robust upper limit for total external unsystematic risk is +12%.*

The question now is how to apportion the 12% between the macroenvironment and the domain. One thing is sure: the high end for the domain will be greater than the maximum for the macro-environment. That means that the domain will have to be >6% and < –12%. We see no reason not to pick the middle of that range: **+9%**. Could it be closer to 8% or 10%? Yes. But in the overall scheme of the BUM, this particular breakdown doesn't matter. What matters for *computational* purposes is the 12%; the breakdown into smaller parts matters for *analytical and explanatory* purposes.

With +9% as our assumption for the domain's upper-end constraint, we subtract that from 12% and conclude a maximum risk premium for the macroenvironment of **+3%**.

The Low End of the Premium Range

- Similarly, six SIC codes had IRPs ≤ –5%. For these 63 segments, the weighted-average IRP was **–5.67%**.

- We obtained similar results from 2008–2010 SBBI.

- Rounding, we get **–6%** as the lower limit for total external unsystematic risk.

We have the same problem at the low end that we just solved at the high end: how to apportion the –6% between macroenvironment and domain. The choices are: 1% and 5%, 2% and 4%, and 3% and 3%. Here we chose –3% and –3%—the middle of the –6% range. Any other choice would have made the figure for the company level (see next section of this Appendix) look goofy.

Again using $\mathbf{P}_{dom}$ to denote domain (industry or strategic group):

–3% ≤ P_{dom} ≤ +9%

For $\mathbf{P}_{mac}$:

–3% ≤ P_{mac} ≤ +3%

P_{mac} + P_{dom}: –6% ≤ total external unsystematic risk ≤ +12%

Implications for the Company Level

Since we know that, at this writing, the maximum possible *external* risk premium is 12%, calculating the company level is simple. We know that variation in sources of rate of return at the company level is 3.0x what it is from external sources. So, we just multiply the maximum external risk premium (12%) by 3.0 and get 36%. We inferred on the previous page that the low end for the company is –3%. Here, then, is the total range for the company level of unsystematic risk:

$$-3\% \leq P_{com} \leq +36\%$$

If we assume a 4% yield to maturity on a 20-year T-bond, then the maximum risk premium from all sources is 61%. That's robust enough to "play" in the venture-capital space, and that's what this framework should allow its users to do.

In unusual facts and circumstances—valuations of start-ups and of distressed companies come to mind—the analyst may include situation-specific risk premiums that datasets with a survivorship bias (i.e., Duff & Phelps; Morningstar/Ibbotson) exclude. A key-person risk premium is but one example. We caution readers not to use such premiums in "ordinary" engagements, however, because of the risk of double-counting.

Here, then, are the various premiums that make up the two extremities of the range of estimates of the cost of equity capital in well over 99% of the engagements that most of us can expect to encounter:

The Range of Empirically Derived Equity Discount Rates – 2011

	Low	Both	High
Risk-free rate		4%	
ERP		5%	
P_{size}		4%	
P_{mac}	– 3%		3%
P_{dom}	– 3%		9%
P_{com}	– 3%		36%
Totals	4%		61%

Chapter 4

Nontraditional Tools for SMDC Engagements

Introduction

For gauging the variable aspects of SMDCs' unsystematic risk, the traditional tools of finance and accounting are inadequate. As some readers of this *Guide* know, I come at valuation using perspectives from other disciplines. First among equals is strategic management. As a strategy academic for a half-decade (1983-88) after I was a CFO and consulting guy, I was immersed in the strategy literature. Michael Porter was new to the scene then, but his work quickly brought discipline and rigor to a field that, until then, had lacked both. In fact, the strategy area, then known as "business policy," had served as a kind of dumping ground for retired executives who told war stories and used case studies as the sole basis for teaching. Now there is nothing wrong with retired execs, war stories, or case studies. But war stories are anecdotes. And the plural of anecdote is *data*, as Nobel laureate George Stigler once observed. Data are gathered within frameworks, frameworks mean theory, and theory demands hypothesis-testing. Financial economists denied us those things by assuming away the problem of unsystematic risk. Shame on them.

This chapter introduces you to what I consider the most essential tools from strategic management and four other disciplines. Because the analysis of unsystematic risk is top-down, I begin with the outer ring of the trilevel framework. I trust you will find this approach useful and productive. These are short explanations, but I add SMDC context for each one.

Strategic Management

We start here because, as you've inferred by now, strategy is my intellectual passion. It has been for nearly 30 years. Strategic management connects inside perspectives about a company (know-how) to outside ones (know-why). We who value SMDCs and other private companies need to be about know-why because the incentives in non-public enterprises are disparate from those of public firms. Here are three key tools from strategy.

Competitive strategies: In his first book,[1] Michael Porter introduced a typology of how companies compete. There were four effective ways, he argued, plus one self-destructive choice. The four alternatives for being successful could be divined from a 2x2 matrix built around two parameters: (1) scope of competition (industrywide or not) and (2) strategy emphasis (lower cost ["cost leadership" in the Porter lexicon] or uniqueness [a.k.a. "differentiation"]). I have extended that

1. Porter, *Competitive Strategy*, 34-46.

with what I call "SPARC Archetypes in Small and Medium-sized Enterprises."[2] The graphic below melds Porter's typology with four archetypes; to facilitate recall, each of them begins with the letter E. The graphic below intentionally repeats from page 7:

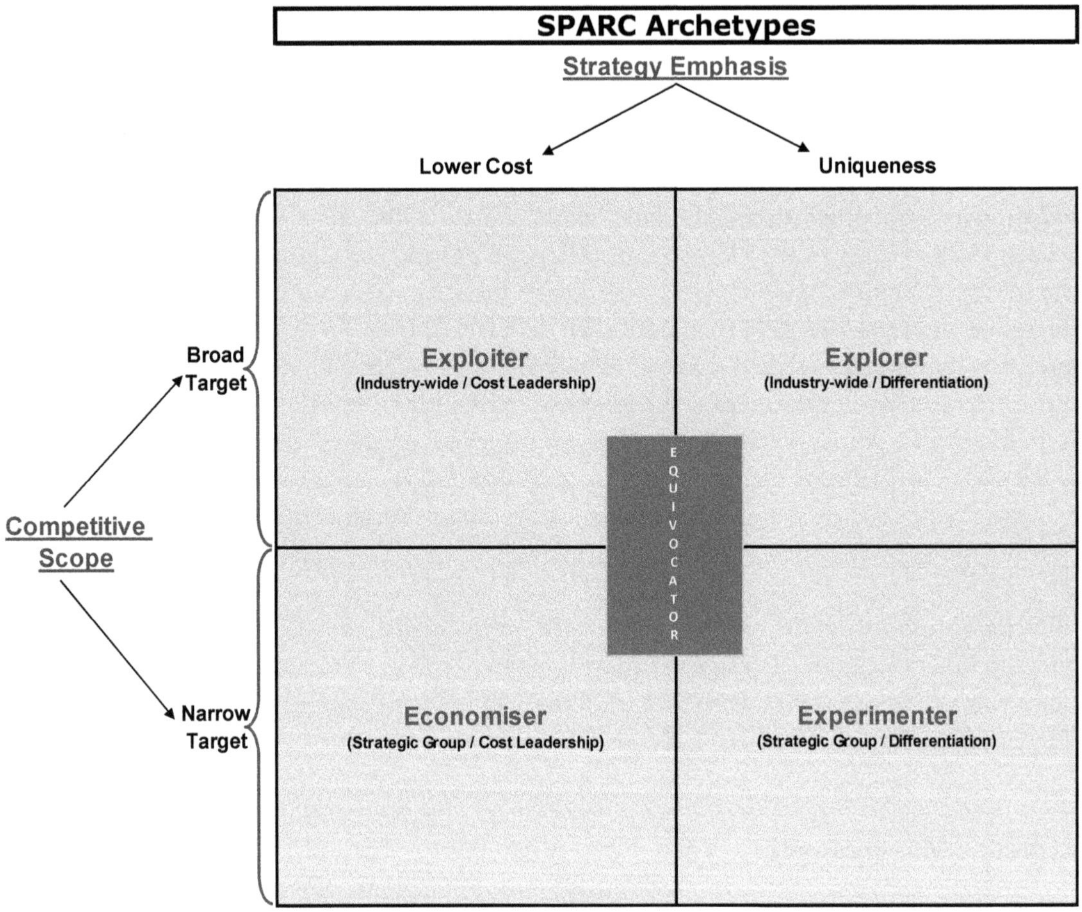

I'll have more to say about each of these five archetypes in Chapter 12. For now, let me make three observations:

- There can be only one low-cost producer in a domain. That should be obvious, but we continue to be bumfuzzled by smaller companies that think they can beat the big guys on price. The cost leader is usually the market leader, too. Every company is different, and each has a unique endowment of resources. It is not the resources themselves, but the *services* that those resources provide that account for the heterogeneity among companies in a domain:

2. Miller, *Value Maps,* 207-215.

> Strictly speaking, it is never *resources* themselves that are "inputs" in the production process, but only the *services* that the resources can render. The services yielded by resources are a function of the way in which they are used—exactly the same resource when used for different purposes or in different ways and in combination with different types or amounts of other resources provides a different service or set of services. The important distinction between resources and services is not their relative durability; rather it lies in the fact that resources consist of a bundle of potential services and can, for the most part, be defined independently of their use, while services cannot be so defined, the very word "service" implying a function, an activity. As we shall see, it is largely in this distinction that we find the source of the uniqueness of each individual firm.[3]

- Those running the company are responsible for configuring the services from resources into unique capabilities for which customers are willing to pay more because they perceive more value—the Experimenter archetype.

- "Equivocator" is our archetype for the (non-)strategy that Porter calls "stuck in the middle." This mindset is seldom seen in strong companies, although, when a competitive domain is in flux, it can rear its hydra head. The Equivocator tries to be all things to all people and ends up baffling employees, confusing would-be customers, and burning up tons of energy brainstorming . . . and committing to nothing.[4]

> ***SMDC context:*** *There can be but one cost leader in a domain. Any other SMDC that aims to compete on cost is playing catch-up. Therefore, the strategy* du jour *for the typical SMDC should be* ***Experimenter****. The sources of differentiation are limited only by management's imagination and its ability to persuade customers to pay more because they perceive they're getting more. It's harder than it sounds.*

Distinctive advantage: The phrase "sustainable competitive advantage" is overwrought and misleading. For one thing, it is used so much that it has an acronym: SCA. For another, "sustainable" implies permanent. In capitalism, the only permanence is the lack of it.

> ***SMDC context:*** *UCLA scholar Dick Rumelt estimates that the durability of competitive advantage is 10 years, max, even with a patent. That is why our phrase is "distinctive advantage." It is neither overwrought nor misleading. It also reinforces the thrust of the preceding paragraph: advantage comes from being different.*

VRINO (Valuable, Rare, Imperfectly imitable, Non-substitutable, Organizationally aligned): That last word tells you about this tool, which comes to us, courtesy of Ohio State's Jay Barney. We use VRINO to test for alignment of a source of differentiation, which we call a *capability*

3. Penrose, *Growth of the Firm,* 25.
4. See Ghemawat, *Commitment*

(see Chapter 7). The appropriate metaphor is a tug-of-war between two teams that are a perfect match, except that, a member of one team is pulling off-center. If the laws of physics apply, then the other team wins.

The textbook case of what happens when the "O" is missing from VRINO is Xerox's legendary Palo Alto Research Center. It originated the PC, the laser printer, Ethernet, and the graphical user interface (think Windows), among many others. But Xerox was not organizationally aligned to take advantage of those inventions, so the actual innovation—reaping the economic rewards of invention—was left to competitors.

Here's VRINO:[5]

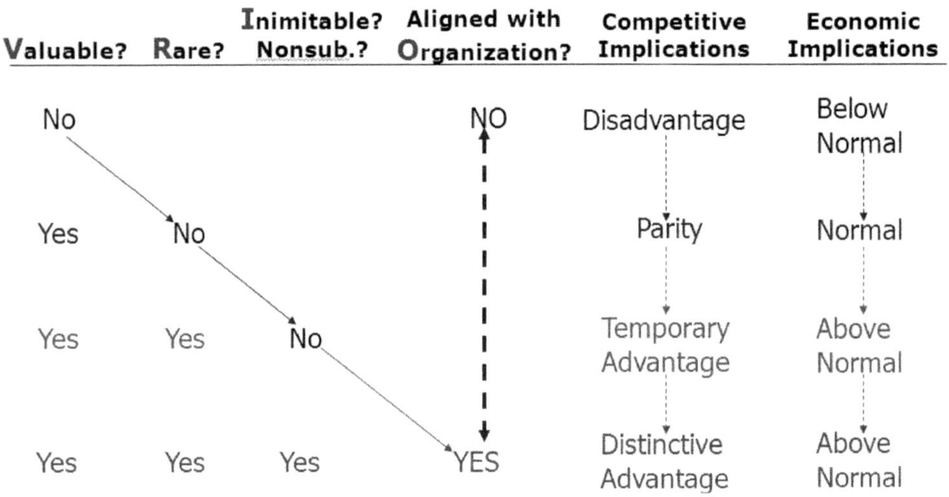

It's the same way in business, but with a wrinkle: alignment (a.k.a. "fit") is ever-changing. Look at the planet Saturn through a telescope some starry night. You'll see its splendid-looking rings. Then, take a five-minute break and come back for a look through the telescope again: Saturn is gone. You know why—the solar system is in motion. So it is in business: success is a moving target. Any coach will tell you that it is a lot easier to become #1 than it is to *stay #1*. That is because of human nature. When the heavens have opened up and money is flowing into people's bank accounts like a tsunami, the last thing they want to do is change anything. But competitors are moving, innovation is moving, and entrepreneurs are moving. If #1 doesn't move, it won't be #1 for long. Ask GM. Ask U.S. Steel. Ask Compaq. Ask Joseph Schlitz Brewing Company. Ask WordPerfect Corp. The nature of capitalism is change, and companies that don't change don't survive.

> ***SMDC context:*** *VRINO is a powerful tool for SMDCs because it makes the test for distinctive advantage straightforward. Of course, not every advantage needs to be distinctive. Sometimes, just parity will do fine because it buys essential time.*

5. Barney, *Competitive Advantage,* 138-162.

Organization Theory (OT)

Organization theory sees the enterprise through two lenses: macro and micro. Both come in handy in valuing SMCs. Like your Humble Servant, OT also does not embrace profit maximization. Oliver Williamson, the 2009 Nobel laureate in economics, is the leading contemporary OT scholar.[6] Herewith, three tools from OT:

Macroenvironment: These six forces form the outermost external hexagon in the trilevel framework. They are situated "further" from the firm itself to reinforce the notion that these six factors are nearly impervious to control or manipulation by an individual firm or industry. These are derived from OT's macro lens. The macroenvironment in detail is the subject of Chapters 5 and 6.

> ***SMDC context:*** *Few SMDCs have a disciplined approach to monitoring the external environment. I think that is because either it doesn't occur to them or they think it's complicated and expensive. It's neither. If, after reading Chapters 5 and 6, you disagree, I'd appreciate it if you'd drop me a line at* SPARC@beckmill.com *and let me know why.*

Coordinating Mechanisms: Coordination is the linchpin of organizational structure. The appropriateness of a coordinating mechanism depends on the complexity of the task(s) being coordinated. Here is a scalar:[7]

Low ←		Task Complexity			→ High
Mutual adjustment	Direct supervision	Standardization of work processes	Standardization of output	Standardization of skills	Mutual adjustment

As for structure itself, we've all heard of "org charts." Certainly the organization chart, including the name and title of each department head and supervisor *and* the number of people reporting to her or him, should be on your Document Request List (DRL). The more layers there are, the "steeper" the organization's structure is said to be. More steepness means greater centralization. That, in turn, means, slower decision-making, less innovation, and, often, lower-productivity employees (because higher producers head for workplaces where they can have a say and an impact).

Organization structure comes in four flavors:[8]

Simple—seen in companies too small to allow specialization of labor. Each individual reports directly to the owner. Thus, there are just two levels. The primary disadvantage of this structure is often chaos—everyone does everything.

---

6. See the Bibliography. The first chapter of *Economic Institutions* is "Transaction Cost Economics" (TCE). TCE and his observation that all contracts are incomplete because of the limits of human cognition won him the Nobel Prize.
7. See Mintzberg, *Structure in Fives*.
8. I was told in about 2000 that the organization structure of the American Institute of CPAs was circular ("C-form," maybe?). In other words, the CEO was at the center of the chart. That explains some things about AICPA that I, for one, have wondered about.

Functional—typically seen in organizations that are a little bigger, but that have one location. Work is organized by its type—manufacturing, shipping & receiving, accounting, sales, customer service, and so on. The functional structure brings greater efficiency, but it also can promote a "silo," that's-not-my-job mentality. In some organizations, the only lateral communication is between department heads.

Divisional—this structure, also called the "M-form," is used in companies that are decentralized either geographically or by product or service line. Sometimes a given division will be organized by target market; in the early 1980s, IBM's sales organization went to this structure so that a company would have only one rep, rather than several who didn't know what the others were doing. In the M-form, line functions are decentralized, but staff functions are often centralized at corporate headquarters to avoid duplication in jobs that don't create wealth.

Matrix—this structure is seen most often in firms whose employees have regular duties, but who also serve on project-oriented teams. So there is a vertical hierarchy and a horizontal one. If it's not organized and designed properly, matrix can descend into chaos.

> ***SMDC context:*** *Most SMDCs have functional structures, even if they have more than one location. We have seen several, however, with divisional structures, but their size was toward the upper end of the "SM" in SMDCs.*

In our on-site visit, we show the org chart that we were given as part of our DRL (p. 14) to each interviewee and ask, "Is this an accurate picture of this company's *real* structure?" In most companies, an informal organization structure makes things work. It often includes power brokers who are not even on the formal org chart. You need to know about the informal structure, how it works, and who the key players are. I've always wondered why companies don't make the informal structure official. Do the folks in charge know the informal one exists? Are they in denial?

Boundaries: This tool defines what the firm will do for itself and what it will outsource. In an increasingly competitive world, more companies outsource non-core competencies, especially IT. This frees up resources for the outsourcer to dedicate to wealth-creating processes and capabilities.

> ***SMDC context:*** *Outsourcing is a form of hedging, and one that SMDCs don't use nearly enough. My favorite example of something that should be outsourced by most SMDCs, but isn't, is the website. That should be built by a firm that does websites for a living. The result will be better and more effective in differentiating the company, although it will not necessarily cost less.*[9]

---

9. One look at the websites of too many CPA firms will tell you that they insourced something they should have farmed out. There are good ways to save money, and there are expensive ways. Doing one's own website almost always falls into the latter category.

Industrial Organization (IO)

This school of economics has two branches. One deals with antitrust policy, regulation, and monopolies. The other, which is the one in which we're interested, focuses on industry studies. Strategy guru Michael Porter got his Ph.D. in IO from Harvard in 1974. Following are three key tools from I.O.

Strategic groups:[10] a strategic group is a segment of an industry where rivals compete along shared strategic dimensions. What are some of those? Well, there is geography. Most SMDCs have a geographical constraint. The second shared dimension is often target market. But it could be a **specialized product line**, **distribution channel**, or **competitive strategy**. Strategic groups are separated by *mobility barriers*.[11]

> ***SMDC context:*** *Nearly all SMDCs compete in strategic groups because they lack the resources (or, sometimes, the knowledge and/or desire) to reach industrywide. The underlying economic structures of these groups of smaller competitors tend to differ from those of the industries of which they are parts.*

Domain analysis: This is our phrase for what is often called *industry analysis*. The problem is that most SMDCs—indeed, most non-public companies—do *not* compete industrywide. They compete in segments, which are the next I.O. tool. Porter's influence made domain analysis a staple of the strategist's diet, and it is the subject of Chapter 7.

> ***SMDC context:*** *Strategic groups face a different set of opportunities and threats from that of the industry as a whole, and that is why they are so important in valuing SMDCs. For instance, the strategic group of building-materials wholesalers that serves, say, the San Francisco MSA will have a domain analysis that differs in major respects from both the industry's and from a strategic group that serves the Miami MSA.*

Oligopolies: Just saying the word can be a mouthful. This form of industry structure is almost invisible nationally (exceptions: ready-to-eat breakfast cereals, auditing services for public companies). However, oligopoly is alive and well regionally and locally. Three forces have transformed a nation of cozy national oligopolies into one with more domestic competition:

- **Antitrust enforcement**—The U.S. Department of Justice and the Federal Trade Commission (FTC) have antitrust divisions, and they compete. FTC, in particular, directs more resources to anticompetitive mergers that used to be off its radar screen.

10. This phrase originated in the unpublished 1972 Harvard dissertation of Michael S. Hunt, "Competition in the Major Home Appliance Industry, 1960-1970."
11. Caves & Porter, "Mobility Barriers." Caves was Porter's thesis advisor.

- **Increased domestic competition**—In consumer electronics, home appliances, and automobile manufacturing, to name just three, overseas competitors have charged into consumer markets. Too many pundits and politicians talk about "our automobile industry" and ignore thriving non-U.S. players with non-union plants in Alabama (Hyundai), South Carolina (BMW), Mississippi (Nissan), Ohio (Honda), Texas (Toyota), and Tennessee (Nissan).

- **Innovation**—Forty years ago the "Big Three" television networks had a chummy oligopoly of the public airwaves in America and market share north of 90%. Today their share is south of 40% and sinking like a stone. The culprit (besides lousy content)? The use of fiber optics in cable TV transmission has given many Americans hundreds of TV channels from which to choose. But if you say "Fox News" to an Obama supporter, duck.

By definition, an oligopoly is a domain with few sellers and no dominant market leader. Two characteristics differentiate this structure: (1) *interdependence among rivals* and (2) *tacit collusion*. The latter gives rise to the First Five Rules of the Oligopolist in Good Standing: never, Never, NEVER, **NEVER**, ***NEVER*** compete on the basis of price. The classic example is two gasoline stations at an intersection. If one cuts price, so does the other. Who wins? Not the stations' owners. You and I win because we get lower gas prices. Oligopoly matters to us who value SMDCs because a well-functioning oligopoly should have lower risk embedded in the interdependence and tacit collusion cited above.

> *SMDC context: The oligopoly structure is alive and well locally and regionally. In a well-functioning oligopoly, the competitive dynamics differ big-time from those of other structures.*

Austrian Economics (AE)

This view of the world of economics is at sharp variance with conventional views. It eschews highfalutin' mathematics, static analysis, and the firm-as-production-function approach to economic analysis. Readers will not be surprised to read that where economics is concerned, I am an Austrian.[12] Three tools from AE are below.

Subjectivity of value: Readers might be thinking, "Well, *of course*, value is subjective." And it is. But *not* in traditional microeconomics. Remember, in that view, there is no differentiation. Customers base all buying decisions on price. They have perfect information. This subjectivity is key, I believe, to forging a successful strategy of differentiation—in the strategic-group context, the Experimenter.

12. See Miller, *Value Maps,* 105-125.

> *SMDC context: Because value is subjective, SMDCs must target customers whose idea of value comports with the value that the SMDC brings to the party. This implies that customers represent a strategic choice on the part of SMDCs.*

Incentives: Organizations that want to change the behavior of their employees should first change the incentives. Messing with employees' bank accounts focuses their attention like nothing else. It is not manipulative, at least in a malign sense. Incentives help align employee decision-making with shareholders' interests. This can be an effective way to address the age-old "agency problem" with which some prominent contemporary economists, especially Michael Jensen, grapple.

> *SMDC context: Too many SMDCs believe that cash is the only incentive. They forget that recognition, affirmation, and professional development also count.*

Ignorance: All economic knowledge is incomplete. Therefore, each of us is continually discovering new information. The price system is the most common and accessible source of such information. There *is* information embedded in prices and figuring out why a price is either higher or lower than the individual thinks it should be is part of learning and, thereby, reducing our ignorance. It's a journey, though, and one that never ends.

> *SMDC context: Austrians know that traditional microeconomics ignores the role of the entrepreneur. That is why microeconomic analysis is "static"—there is no innovation, there is no entrepreneurial discovery, there is no disruption. In the real world, there is each of those. That is why, for instance, Penrose's emphasis on the need for managers to find new uses for old resources, which I discuss in the next section, is so important, especially for smaller companies.*

Evolutionary Economics

This field came to the fore in 1982 with the publication of *An Evolutionary Theory of Economic Change* by Dick Nelson and Sid Winter. The book was a powerful attack on traditional microeconomics. The Nelson-Winter perspective had its roots in the 1940s and '50s work of economists Joseph Schumpeter,[13] Nobel laureate Herbert Simon,[14] and Edith Penrose, a much-overlooked and -underappreciated scholar.[15,16] Evolutionary economics challenges the notion that companies maximize; "bounded rationality" prevents that. Instead, they tend to make decisions, even big ones, by rote, using "routines."

13. Schumpeter, *Capitalism, Socialism, and Democracy.*
14. Simon, *Models of Man.*
15. Penrose, *Growth of the Firm.*
16. I heartily recommend all four of these books. Any valuation professional will benefit from a close reading of the Penrose book, in particular. It is remarkable.

In contrast to the perfect-equilibrium/static analysis assumption of the neoclassical paradigm in microeconomics, the evolutionary perspective embodies three key components that have antecedents in biology:

- *variation*—this refers to differences among competitors. It arises in the form of innovation
- *selection*—markets "select" surviving firms on the basis of usefulness of their innovations. Companies with low-productivity routines will eventually go out of business because they will run out of capital
- *retention*—retention occurs when the same innovation spreads among units of a company or competitors within a domain or more broadly

Herewith, three tools from evolutionary economics:

Routines: Routines are how work gets done and decisions get made in organizations. Big decisions tend to follow the same processes and touch the same bases as smaller ones. Routines are the DNA of organizations. Here's an excerpt from Nelson and Winter:

> Our general term for all regular and predictable behavioral patterns of firms is "routine." We use this term to include characteristics of firms that range from well-specified technical routines for producing things, through procedures for hiring and firing, ordering new inventory, or stepping up production of items in high demand, to policies regarding investment, research and development (R&D), or adversities, and business strategies about product diversification and overseas investments. In our evolutionary theory, these routines play the role that genes play in biological evolutionary theory. They are a persistent feature of the organism and determine its possible behavior (though *actual* behavior is determined also by the environment); they are heritable in the sense that tomorrow's organisms generated from today's (for example, by building a new plant) have many of the same characteristics, and they are selectable in the sense that organisms with certain routines may do better than others, and, if so, their relative importance in the population (industry) is augmented over time.[17]

> ***SMDC context:*** *Routines provide an efficient way for getting things done and making decisions. However, in margin-pressed SMDCs, there's a downside: they can act as a barrier to needed change. That is another reason that Personal Development Programs (PDPs) are so important to SMDCs: they provide essential, but pre-approved, disruption to the status quo.*

Resource-based view of the firm (RBV): In free markets, companies are heterogeneous, not homogeneous, because they comprise free-thinking individuals who see the world differently, do the same tasks differently, and bring different resources to the party. The RBV's two fundamental precepts are:

17. Nelson & Winter, *Evolutionary Theory:* 14.

- Each company has an endowment of *resources* (strengths and weaknesses)
- Resource endowments are immobile and non-portable

> ***SMDC context:*** *The RBV ties directly to the work of Penrose and Nelson & Winter. It has analogs to biology, where diversity is one of the keys to the survival of a species. Companies are similar. That is why having a diversity of background, perspective, and experience in an SMDC is so important. It has nothing to do with politics or political correctness. It's about survival.*

Path dependence: Understanding this concept is essential for anyone who wonders why things are the way they are in SMDCs (or any other business, for that matter). The first genetic roll of the dice in a new company comes from how the founder believes the world works. That establishes how the firm is organized and how it gets work done. She imparts her view to her new organization. As employees are hired, they adopt her view, if they didn't already have it. If they disagree strongly enough for long enough, they will end up working somewhere else. Path dependence sets an enterprise on a trajectory that is hard to alter. That is one reason that organizations such as General Motors and the U.S. Postal Service[18] resist change. It's not so much that they don't want to change. It's that they can't.

> ***SMDC context:*** *This concept is especially powerful in organizations that have been around for at least a decade, are more than Mom-and-Pop enterprises, and have enjoyed a modicum of business success. Those conditions describe many SMDCs. Again—and I know I'm doing my broken-record thing here—this is another good argument for PDPs. They provide an easy and inexpensive way for companies to manage growth and to be exposed to the need to make changes along the growth path.*

The Wrap

This short chapter focused on a limited number of "non-traditional tools" that you will encounter in the chapters ahead. From each of the five non-traditional disciplines—organization theory, industrial organization, Austrian economics, strategic management, and evolutionary economics—I selected three tools. In each case, I had a heckuva tough time limiting my choices to three. I could have easily listed twice that many. The fields and the tools I chose are below.

- Strategic management
  - generic competitive strategies
  - distinctive advantage
  - VRINO

18. I once attended a talk given by the late Nobel laureate in literature, Eudora Welty, where she referred to it as "the Postal Disservice."

- Organization theory
    - macroenvironment
    - coordinating mechanisms
    - boundaries

- Industrial organization
    - strategic groups
    - domain analysis
    - oligopolies

- Austrian economics
    - disequilibrium
    - incentives
    - subjectivity of value

- Evolutionary economics
    - routines
    - resource-based view of the firm (RBV)
    - path dependence

That's a wrap. The next several chapters are about the process and mechanics of assessing each level of unsystematic risk that we introduced in Chapter 3. You will find the tools from this chapter much in evidence in what lies ahead. The analysis of unsystematic risk is *always* done top-down (i.e., we start broadly at the macroenvironment and gradually home in on the company). Therefore, we begin with the macroenvironment, and that is the subject of Chapter 5. Read on, please.

Assessing the Macroenvironment of SMDCs

Introduction

More than a few valuation professionals believe that **macroenvironment** and **macroeconomy** are interchangeable. They are not. They are different phenomena. In fact, because the macroeconomy is one of the six forces in the macroenvironment, the latter *subsumes* the former. If we write only about the macroeconomy, we ignore five other factors that affect unsystematic risk. This chapter is about analyzing and quantifying these six forces. As we did in the last chapter, we will also "connect" the dots in this one with sidebars about the "SMDC context."

What *Is* the Macroenvironment?

We get the concept of macroenvironment from organization theory (OT).[1] OT sees the organization through its structure and its relationship with its external environment. The macroenvironment consists of six sources of risk:

- Economy
- Innovation
- Values & Lifestyles
- Demographics
- Disasters
- Politics

Each of these, in turn, has certain features for valuators to consider. SMDCs tend to be cyclical businesses, so economic trends and expectations are crucial. Regulatory issues might not be far behind economic ones for a given wholesaling domain. Demographic trends tend to matter, too. Before we discuss each of these forces individually, we need to deal with two essential issues: the unit of analysis and environmental scanning.

1. Oliver Williamson, one of the co-winners of the 2009 Nobel Prize in economics, is an economist and prominent organization theorist. He is also the father of the "transaction cost economics" movement. For more: http://groups.haas.berkeley.edu/bpp/oew/; there's a link on that page to a fascinating video interview with him.

The Unit of Analysis in External Risk Assessment

I'm now going to pound my spoon on my high chair again—and not for the last time, either—about a subject I was shrill about in Chapter 2: the unit of analysis. I repeat myself, not to insult your intelligence and be condescending, but to reinforce new and sometimes counterintuitive ideas. I know from my own experience in learning the craft of valuation that there needs to be plenty of repetition. Most readers of this *Guide* have at least several years of valuation experience, and that gives them a well-formed view of valuation. Part of what I need to do with them is rearrange a few aspects of that view.

In this particular case, the restructuring, if your view of valuation needs it, deals with "the unit of analysis." That is, when we look at a particular idea and the impact it might have, we have to give a precise description of the unit on which that impact will occur. In *all external risk assessments,* the unit of analysis—that which is on the receiving end of whatever opportunities and threats lurk externally—is ***the domain.*** Not the client company by itself, but the group of competitors that includes the client company. That is because the "OT" in SWOT analysis—"Opportunities" and "Threats"—are *external* to the client organization. Therefore, the magnitude of opportunities and threats is the same for every rival within a given domain. That means—repeating what I said in Chapter 2: **the external risk premiums are the same for every player in a given competitive domain.**

It is then up to each individual company to take steps to seize an opportunity or neutralize or hedge a threat. To the extent that it does or doesn't do so—in some cases, it might not even know that a threat or opportunity is out there—it is showing a strength or a weakness. As a general proposition, a strength lowers risk, and a weakness increases it.

As I have said several times already in this *Guide,* most SMDCs do not compete industrywide; instead, they are members of *strategic groups.* To repeat, a strategic group is a subsector of an industry. I can't think of any industry without such groups.

So, if you have gotten through the process of negotiating, issuing, and executing an Engagement Letter *without defining the domain* in which the client SMDC competes, do so now. Again—and I'm repeating from Chapter 2—ask two questions:

1. "Where do your company's competitors do what they do?" and

2. "How else do they make themselves your competitors?"

But, in wholesaling, what defines a competitor depends, in part, on how we define *competitive similarity.* For instance, is an SMDC that sells building supplies to retail outlets doing the same thing as every other SMDC in its area that sells building supplies to retailers? Again, it depends. The activities are likely similar, but just as likely not identical. One SMDC might specialize in certain types of building supplies—lumber, for instance; another might be an expert in venetian blinds and windows. Are they competitors? I would say that they do compete with one another because there is nothing to keep an SMDC in this domain with one expertise from encroaching on the turf of a rival's expertise. In fact, doing so might create *economies of scope*.[2] In wholesaling these days, such economies can be godsends.

To be sure, two rivals might not sell the same brands. They might even target, at least for now, different market segments to which they distribute. But, in the absence of written contracts stipulating otherwise, nothing keeps them from entering a new market segment where a rival had enjoyed a stress-free and lucrative business life with no competitors.

The economic activity of a strategic group is a given: it is the industry's economic activity. The strategic groups in which SMDCs compete are typically defined, first, by geography (Question #1). It might be a city, a county, a metropolitan statistical area (MSA—Census term) or an area defined by natural barriers (e.g., the San Joaquin Valley in central California).

The second parameter defining a strategic group can vary, but it is most often the target market. Other possibilities include, but are not limited to:

- technical know-how that customers find valuable enough to maintain the business relationship
- expertise in a particular type of product (hand tools, for example)
- product quality
- range of products
- price points
- customer service

The point, though, is to define the domain. Do so because it is going to drive your research at both levels of external risk. It will also focus your attention throughout the valuation process. Early on, you should be able to name your client company's three or four biggest competitors; it shouldn't be long before you can give a brief overview of each. If you can't do that, then you're not asking either enough or the right questions.

2. Teece, "Economies of Scope."

How Do SMDCs Monitor External Forces and Events?

Like many other smaller and mid-sized enterprises, an SMDC may have difficulty recognizing certain opportunities and threats. It might not recognize them because, truth be told, no one is looking. Instead, everyone is internally focused. An excess of such focus can leave a company blind-sided by outside forces. In some cases, the enterprise might go out of business or become so crippled that it has to be sold or liquidated piecemeal. Savvy SMDCs engage in what the literature calls "environmental scanning" by incorporating it into the development of their aspiring employees. After all, the bigger a company gets, the more resources, livelihoods, and assets are at stake, so the more that scanning is needed. But the little guys don't want to get stepped on by some lumbering economic Goliath, either.

Scanning knowledge can arise from a range of activities. It can come from participation in a trade group. It can come from reading periodicals, from a membership in the local chamber of commerce, from monitoring competitors' websites and reporting periodically on what they're doing, from tracking political developments that could help or hurt the domain, from watching for new IT packages, or from skimming pertinent journals for papers that convey knowledge that competitors might not be aware of. The possibilities for environmental scanning are many, but the takeaway is this: scanning is an important habit for an SMDC to get into. It can help an organization reduce risk over time. Or duck a haymaker. Or speed up collections in a customer segment that appears headed for rough financial seas. Assigning scanning activities is also a good way to see who picks up on its importance.

Macroenvironmental Analysis

I begin here by imploring you (again) to *do your research top-down*: macroenvironment first, then domain, and then (and only then) the company. Some valuators will want to start with the company because that's where their comfort zone is. They will reduce realization and productivity if they do. In assessing these three sources of unsystematic risk, top-down is the only way to go. Bottom-up will require you to start over and over and over.

The ultimate goal of analyzing the macroenvironment is to be able to make an informed judgment about the client company's ***alignment*** both externally and internally. Good alignment means being in a position to take advantage of opportunities and buffer, hedge, or otherwise protect against threats. As we go through this section of the chapter, I will draw your attention to alignment issues. I'll do it again at the domain level and yet again with the client company itself.

We now want to put some meat on the skeletal representation of the unsystematic-risk framework that we introduced in Chapter 2. See the diagram on the next page.

Economy: In cyclical domains such as the ones in which many SMDCs compete, economic factors—interest rates, inflation, GDP, and unemployment—are the big issues. However, keep in mind that unemployment is a *local phenomenon*. That is, unemployment might be sky-high in places with high

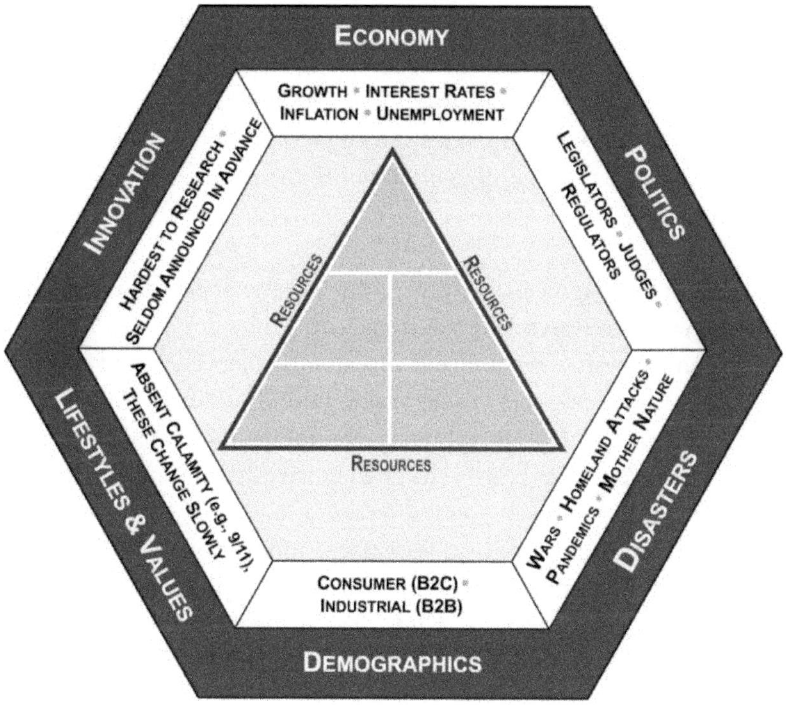

MACROENVIRONMENT

dependence on a weak sector (think Detroit and automobiles), while it is far lower in locales with more diversified economies (think Chicago, arguably the most diverse economy in the U.S.).

In some service sectors, a weak economy is great news. Outplacement services, pawn shops, bankruptcy specialists, and therapists come to mind. A weak economy is also good for automobile repairs because people choose to fix up the paid-for old car rather than go in hock for a snazzy new one.

Readers might have seen—or might themselves have prepared—reports that include a copy-and-paste, off-the-shelf "Economic Outlook." So long as your client company is competing industrywide, that's not a hanging offense. The potential crimes, though, are two:

- Failing to give attribution for the source of the verbiage, and
- Failing to explain the significance of the verbiage *in the context of the domain of the engagement*

If your client company competes in a strategic group, however, you should consider gathering your data locally or regionally or from a professor who oversees a university "econometric model" that is in the business of predicting regional or statewide economic futures. Even then, though, make sure you provide attribution *and* explain the significance of the data for the domain in which your client company competes. Don't leave readers to figure it out for themselves—**always connect the dots for them.**

> *SMDC context: This one requires little elaboration. I know of no countercyclical domains in the wholesaling space, so no need to worry about that. However, if the client competes in a strategic group, be sure to examine economic conditions within that group, especially where "company towns" and unemployment rates are concerned. Excess dependence on a particular company or set of related NAICS codes increases risk just as lack of diversification does in an investment portfolio.*

Innovation: As words in the graphic on the preceding page proclaim, this is the hardest dimension of the macroenvironment to research. For one thing, companies don't want to cannibalize current sales by announcing an innovative replacement product. For another—and this is not something that most Americans are aware of—most of the major innovations in the American economy come from managers' new practices and insights about the businesses they run. Such innovation contributes big-time to the heterogeneity that gives the lie to much of traditional microeconomics.

SMDCs are unlikely to be in the business of product innovation. No IP R&D for them. But developing new software internally, devising new configurations of resources, and creating new capabilities from new services for those resources, the better to befuddle rivals and delight customers—ah, that is the stuff to look for within the domain and the SMDC itself.

Be sure to contact the appropriate trade association(s) when you are researching the impact of current innovation and expectations about future breakthroughs. Always ask to speak to the librarian at the association. Don't ask me why, but it appears that almost no one talks to librarians because, in my experience, they have pent-up demand to talk. To blab, even, about things that they probably shouldn't talk about. Librarians can be a wonderful source of great information. Not every trade association has one, of course, but always ask. I've footnoted a free searchable database of associations.[3]

If you find yourself strapped for information about the impact of unknown innovation on a domain, close your eyes and imagine the worst thing that can happen to the players in that arena. One not-great event would be the emergence of a substitute product in a sector that has never had to contend with substitutes. A domain-threatening development would be the invention of a product that, overnight, threatened an industry (think e-readers and independent bookstores). This outside-the-box envisioning might not come naturally, but it's still worth the effort. I have to stretch my brain to ponder far-out what-if scenarios.

> *SMDC context: Most of the innovation in SMDCs does indeed come from breakthroughs in managerial thinking. But keeping abreast of relevant changes in technology is essential, too.*

Lifestyles and Values: This factor comes into play mostly in B2C contexts; B2B domains tend not to be much affected by this dimension. Values change slowly, but they do change. For instance, women account for nearly half of the U.S. labor force today. Those who can remember the early 1960s, including your humble writer, recall a time when stay-at-home moms were the rule, not

3. www.asaecenter.org/Community/Directories/AssociationSearch.cfm

the exception. Divorce rates were much lower then because of economic dependency. As women became more career-oriented, they added a new component of demand to the U.S. economy: women's business attire, sales of big-ticket products to unmarried women (think Beemers and Rolexes), and "lite beer."

The latter happened after Philip Morris (now Altria) bought Miller Brewing Co. from W.R. Grace in mid-1969. The deal was a diversification move (and a darned savvy one at that) after the Surgeon General's 1964 report lambasting tobacco companies. Unlike most acquisitions that fail to earn back their cost of capital, the Miller deal made great sense and even greater economics: PM sold Miller in 2004 for 43 times what it had paid for it 35 years before—that's an 11.6% compounded annual return on its initial investment . . . not counting all the money it made in the meantime.

But Philip Morris brought something to the deal that the beer industry had seldom seen. It brought *marketing* to a domain that had been dominated by "gentlemen brewers" from the likes of Carling, Pabst Blue Ribbon, Schlitz, and Falstaff. There had also been little product innovation until Miller Lite hit the market in 1975. Targeting women, its overall market share eventually rose to more than 20%.

The short-term result was the demise of most of those gentlemanly breweries and the increasing dominance of Anheuser-Busch (Budweiser and Michelob). Coors became a national brand as other nationals went by the wayside. Obviously all of this had implications for beer distributors. As many of their upstream brewers went out of business, the distributors did, too. Distributors representing multiple breweries became far less numerous as the industry leaders insisted on absolute loyalty from their wholesalers. Budweiser itself was taken over by Belgian company InBev in 2008.

Beginning in the 1980s, as trade barriers came down, the pace of communication quickened, and the effects of information technology on businesses around the world went into overdrive, non-U.S. beers came to America. They arrived from Europe, Asia, and Mexico. April 1985 brought a new American beer, Samuel Adams Boston Lager, from a startup called The Boston Beer Company, Inc. "Craft" beers, microbrews, and "brewpubs" ensued in large numbers. The major brewers responded with a plethora of new beers—bock, doppelbock, malt, pale ale, brown ale, porter, and stout—further segmenting a market that had never really seen segmentation until the advent of Miller Lite. Non-alcoholic beers also expanded their number of brands and market share.

The effect of this rapid evolution in brewing and the competitive landscape had obvious effects on beer distributors, too. Many went by the wayside. But many more were born because of the product proliferation within the industry. Today, there are more than 3,300 distributors of beer in the United States.[4]

> ***SMDC context:*** *The illustration about the brewing industry is about as compelling a story about lifestyles and values as I can tell. It's important to note, however, that the turmoil resulted from the innovation that the Philip Morris acquisition of Miller Brewing triggered.*

4. http://nbwa.org/about/what-is-nbwa

Demographics: As we said early in Chapter 1, wholesaling comes in two broad flavors: B2B and B2C. Therefore, when you're thinking about demographics—which are the characteristics of a population—keep in mind that B2B deals with the characteristics of a population of *companies*, while B2C is about people data. Those are radically different types of research, though they share some parallels. Where B2C might monitor birth rates, B2B concerns itself with new companies starting up. B2C thinks about life expectancies of individuals, while B2B looks at business failures, which is a different form of mortality, but mortality nonetheless. B2C looks at how many people, and B2B looks at how many companies. Both are concerned with growth in demand in their sector vs. growth in GDP. Again, on the B2B side, trade associations can be a great source of data. Hoover's (www.hoovers.com) allows us to construct our own domains, and we find it extremely helpful. D&B Marketplace used to do that, but D&B finally trashed this acquisition.

Demographic changes impact SMDCs. Increases in the number of unmarried adults mean more, but smaller residences, which affects building materials. The rise in unmarried also affects the size and design of appliances (e.g., Keurig) and furniture (Ikea) as well as the packaging of food (there was no such thing as a self-contained cup of soup when I was growing up).

> ***SMDC context:*** *The good news here is that, absent a major disaster of some kind, demographics change slowly. In all but situations involving calamities such as 9/11 or plagues, changes can be foreseen and predicted with pinpoint accuracy. But the SMDC must be monitoring the external environment in order to be aware of what lies ahead.*

Disasters: This refers to those history- or life-changing events that sometimes happen. 9/11 is the best example I know of, but "the greatest generation" might point to the Japanese attack on Pearl Harbor. My late grandmother used to talk about the 1906 San Francisco earthquake, which tipped the Richter scale at 7.9 and flattened "Baghdad by the Bay." This quake and the Galveston Hurricane of 1900 are commonly thought of as the two worst natural disasters in U.S. history, at least where the loss of life is concerned; the California earthquake killed more than 3,000 people; more than 6,000 perished in the Galveston hurricane. The blowout of BP's Deepwater Horizon well spewed 4.9 million barrels of oil into the Gulf of Mexico for 86 days before it was finally stopped.[5] And, of course, in 2005, there was Hurricane Katrina's head shot to the city of New Orleans; this hurricane resulted in spills of "only" 190,000 barrels, less than 4% of spill volume from the BP blowout.

Pandemics are disasters, too—recall we have had a couple of false starts in recent years with the swine flu. Sooner or later, there will be the real deal, and it will have a devastating impact.

Deep economic downturns—the Great Depressions of 1920 and the 1930s are the two modern examples—are also included in this dimension. It is too early to say whether the "Great Recession" of 2007-2009 will qualify. Unless unemployment really heads into the stratosphere (it's 9% at this writing), I would be reluctant to include it with those two Depressions. Then again, Congress can usually figure out a way to snatch defeat from the jaws of victory.

5. Source: www.eoearth.org/article/Deepwater_Horizon_oil_spill?topic=50364.

> *SMDC context: 9/11 caused me to alter what other renderings of the macroenvironment may include; some have a force for "ecology" (or "environment"). Before sustainability gathered steam in commerce, other portrayals of the macroenvironment had "international" as the sixth force. It seems to me that "international" is redundant where the other five forces are concerned. Our nation's experience with 9/11 also led me to conclude that "disasters" is more attention-getting and, to the extent there is an exception, also covers the sustainability waterfront.*

Politics: The sixth and last force in the macroenvironment—politics—has four dimensions: legislation (local, state, federal), regulatory actions (principally federal, but can also be state and local), court decisions (the U.S. Supreme Court and, for valuation professionals, the U.S. Tax Court and the Delaware Chancery Court), and likely results of near-term elections. Developments in each or all of these can exert major impact on certain domains.

The seismic shift in representation in the nation's capital as a result of the 2010 off-year elections have big implications for SMDCs. For instance, Rep. Jason Chaffetz (R-Utah) has introduced legislation (H.R. 1161) that would have the effect of barring interstate shipments of wine. That is something that SMDCs in the wine sector would welcome, though those who buy their wine online likely wouldn't. The outcome of the 2012 presidential and congressional elections will have obvious implications for SMDCs in the healthcare space, among others.

The impact of such far-reaching legislation as the 2010 financial services reforms, the 2010 healthcare bill, the 2009 stimulus, and the 2008 bank bailout will not be known for many years. The so-called "card check," climate-change, and immigration bills pending in 2009 and 2010 seem dead in the water until 2013 at the earliest.

Regulators can have major impact on economic activity. Among SMDCs, pronouncements and legislative interpretations by the Department of Transportation, the Environmental Protection Agency, the National Labor Relations Board, and the Occupational Safety and Health Administration can affect opportunities and threats in variety of domains. In particular, EPA's efforts to regulate carbon emissions have huge implications for nearly all players in the distribution space, wholesale and retail. Readers should also know what, if anything, is going on with regulators at state and local levels, too, depending on how a valuator defines a particular domain.

With a stroke of the pen, a judge can turn things topsy-turvy. The Obama Administration tried twice in 2010 to impose a drilling moratorium on all rigs operating in water more than 500 feet deep. Gov. Jindal of Louisiana said a moratorium would cost at least 24,000 jobs held by his state's citizens. In the summer of 2010, the U.S. Department of Justice filed a suit against the state of Arizona's new immigration law. The expectation is that the U.S. Supreme Court will eventually decide both of those issues, along with the constitutionality of the 2010 healthcare legislation.

SMDC context: *It is fashionable these days to trash politics and politicians. However, it's not O.K. to ignore them and hope they'll go away. That isn't going to happen. It is also not sufficient for an SMDC to count on its trade association both to protect it and to inform it of pending developments on the political front. Making one aspect of the macroenvironment part of key up-and-comers' PDPs, and then rotating that aspect annually, is a great way to help keep an SMDC abreast of what's happening outside its immediate sphere of influence.*

Quantifying Macroenvironmental Risk

Let's begin this section by recalling from Chapter 2 the –3% floor for risk premiums at each of the three levels of the unsystematic-risk framework. The question is what the upper bound should be for each level. It sounds like a tougher question than it turns out to be.

We'll confine our answer here to the range for the macroenvironment. This set of forces, recall, is also called the "remote environment." It is not that it doesn't affect domain risk. Of course, it does. One problem is that, with two exceptions, a domain of SMDCs cannot by itself exert much influence over its macroenvironmental forces. One place where it can is in the political realm through trade-association lobbying. Another, but much less common, area it can affect is innovation.

The potential impact that any set of forces in the trilevel framework has increases with proximity to the company. Therefore, the risk premium range will be the narrowest for the macroenvironment and the largest for the company. For reasons that will become obvious in the next chapter, we fix the upper bound for the macroenvironment at +3%. As you will see in Chapter 6, we have solid numbers backing us up on this. So, thinking back to Chapter 3, we can say that

$$-3\% \leq \text{RPmac} \leq +3\%$$

How does one decide where in that range the premium for risk in the macroenvironment should fall? Well, for starters, we resist the temptation to get too granular about this stuff. In our practice, we round these premiums to the nearest full percentage point, up or down. In fact, I have an Excel worksheet, originally introduced in my book, *Value Maps*,[6] that does that automatically. It is available to buyers of this *Guide* at www.bvresources.com/wholesaledownloads.

As for the premium itself, there are two ways that we know of to make the call:

- Use your judgment or
- Use the template available for free download through www.bvresources.com/wholesaledownloads to buyers of this *Guide.*

6. www.amazon.com/value-maps-valuation-unlock-business/dp/0470437561.

Until I created the template, I used my judgment. Back then, I made the decision after writing a summary paragraph at the end of my discussion of each of the six forces. That summary was a good indicator, I thought, of where the premium should fall. A better way, I'm now convinced—and here comes a plug, though not a shameless one, I hope—is to use the Excel template that we and a group of talented subcontractors have created. Let me elaborate on that.

The template has 39 statements for users to express the level of their agreement or lack thereof through electronic "radio buttons" on a 1-5 scale. The template also recognizes that the relative importance of the six factors will vary across domains and over time. Therefore, we have designed the template so that it will not produce a premium until a user has weighted each of the six forces by choosing from a menu of percentages. Every factor must weigh at least 10%; therefore, none can weigh more than 50%. Their responses and weighting choices, in turn, drive an underlying algorithm that produces a premium. The template offers a straightforward way to gauge macroenvironmental risk, and I commend it to your consideration.

The Wrap

Chapter 5 is the first of three that together cover each level of the trilevel unsystematic-risk framework. Our focus here has been on the most remote of those levels, the macroenvironment. Here are the takeaways that I recommend from this chapter:

- The macroenvironment comprises six forces: economy, innovation, lifestyles & values, demographics, disasters, and politics.

- The **Economy** dimension is often the most powerful of the six forces in the domain . . . but there *are* exceptions.

- **Innovation** is the hardest factor to research.

- **Lifestyles** change more often than **Values.**

- Know the differences between the **Demographics** of B2B vs. B2C SMDCs.

- Don't blow off the **Disasters** facet. As all learned on the beautiful Tuesday morning in September 2001, anything can happen any time.

- In domains that rely on unskilled labor or do work that is dangerous, the **Politics** force is powerful. Think minimum wage, OSHA, and unionization efforts.

- Be sure you have defined the domain before starting your analysis; putting it in your Engagement Letter is even better.

- SMDC domains are cyclical, so, absent some extreme event in terms of either disasters or politics, the economy will be the most important force in this analysis; however, the fact that it is the most important might not give it the heaviest weight—that depends on how skewed the near-term economic future of the domain appears to be.

- When it comes, innovation among SMDCs tends to arise from software, logistics, and management insights and practices.

- Don't forget to ask to speak to the trade association librarian.

- Make sure you check out developments pending at the state and local levels that might affect the macroenvironment of your client company.

- The risk premium for the macroenvironment ranges from −3% to +3%.

- Don't get overly granular in estimating this premium—the nearest whole percentage point will work just fine.

- There are two ways to estimate **RPmac**: using your judgment or using the value map workbook template available through www.bvresources.com/wholesaledownloads to buyers of this *Guide*.

- If you're using your judgment, assigning percentage weights to each of the six forces is cumbersome (I tried it years ago), and it also encourages superfluous granularity.

- If you're using the template, you won't have any choice but to assign weights, but the template limits the choices in order to discourage excessive granularity.

That's it for this chapter. We continue our top-down assessment of unsystematic risk in the wholesale space with Chapter 6. It deals with market structure. See you there.

Assessing the Domain: Market Structure of SMDCs

Introduction

Before we get into the nitty-gritty of analyzing domain dynamics, we must learn about *market structure*. This entails measurements of structure, the types of structure, the importance of an oligopoly, and estimating market share. Much of what we are going to cover here comes from a branch of economics called industrial organization (IO), which we first introduced in in Chapter 3 and offered some of its tools in Chapter 4. IO has two closely related branches: antitrust studies and industry studies. We will concern ourselves in this chapter with the latter. As in the previous two chapters, we'll also include the "SMDC context" feature to help readers connect the dots.

Structure-Conduct-Performance (S-C-P)

The S-C-P paradigm is the basic model from the industry-studies side of industrial organization. Here it is:

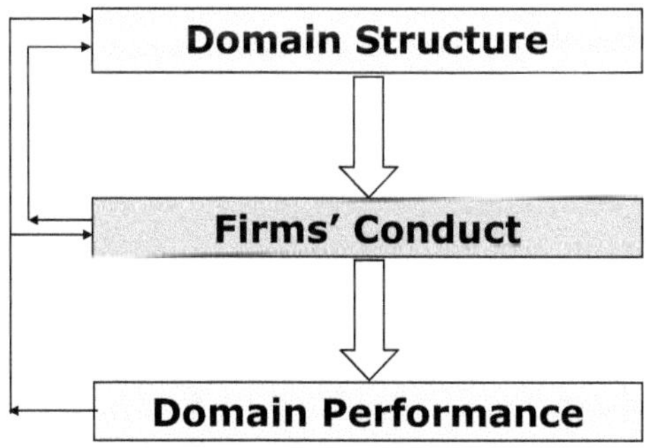

Now, lest anyone else say it, I will: the S-C-P model is an *equilibrium* model emanating from the same static economic perspective that I decried earlier in this *Guide*. Nonetheless, it is the cornerstone of IO, and it offers benefits to valuation professionals as I will shortly demonstrate. Ralph Waldo Emerson once said, "A foolish consistency is the hobgoblin of little minds." There are times to stand on principle. This ain't one of 'em.

As the model indicates, domain structure drives firms' conduct (think *strategy*), which itself drives *domain* performance. Note, too, the three feedback loops: from performance to conduct, from performance to structure, and from conduct to structure.

One other thing: market structure is *not* about any individual company. It is about the entire *domain*—the *group of companies that compete head-to-head.* I know I sound like a broken record, but I've taught for 28 years; I'm privileged that the last 16 have been with valuation professionals as my students. Please trust me on this repetition stuff. If you find yourself thinking, "There he goes again," good. That means you're retaining crucial ideas, and that is one of our goals.

Domain Concentration and Structure

Industrial organization is interested in the level of concentration in industries and strategic groups. In an economic context, *concentration* is about how widely dispersed market share is among firms as well as the relative level of equality in share. IO offers two ways to measure concentration:

- Herfindahl-Hirschman Index (HHI)
- concentration ratios

Concentration ratios are simple to compute and are sufficient for the purpose of most valuations. HHI is used by antitrust enforcers to decide which acquisitions to scrutinize. You will soon understand why the feds use it.

HHI. This method has been around for a while, but was used almost exclusively by academic economists until the Reagan administration took office in 1981. Its antitrust chief in the Department of Justice was William Baxter. He was a leader of the then-fledgling "law-and-economics" movement that has since risen to prominence. In administrations prior to Reagan, antitrust policy was loosey-goosey and not clearly enunciated. It seemed that some administrations would go after their enemies and coddle their friends, sometimes using antitrust enforcement or the lack thereof to do so. Baxter understood that not only were such practices unfair, but they also had the potential to discourage needed transactions. Therefore, he announced that Reagan administration policy would be to review announced acquisitions that overstepped a specific threshold of the Herfindahl-Hirschman Index. Before I disclose what that was, let's find out what the HHI is all about.

Unlike the Index's kissing cousin, concentration ratios (which are covered in the next section of this chapter), the HHI considers not just concentration but also how market share is dispersed among rivals. A short example will illustrate.

Let's assume that the four biggest companies in a domain have a combined market share of 100%; in tobacco manufacturing, it's actually 91%. The 100% figure is useful to know, but it has one gaping hole in it: the biggest firm's share can range from 25% to nearly 100%. I hope it is obvious to you that a domain whose four players have market shares of 97%, 1%, 1%, and 1% would function quite differently from one that had shares among its four biggest companies of 25%, 25%, 25%, and 25%.

In scenario #1 (97%-1%-1%-1%), the 1% players are what economists call "price-takers." They don't have the horsepower to set price, so they "take" whatever price the market leader decides on. Conversely, in the 25%-25%-25%-25% structure (#2), there is no clear market leader because the four competitors are evenly matched. If there's no leader, there are no price-takers. Competitive behavior in scenario #2 would differ big-time from that of #1.

For its part, HHI tells us about the dispersion of share because the HHI is the sum of the squares of each firm's market share. Not just the four largest, but all of them. Let's kick this around for a bit.

In a pure monopoly, the HHI would = 10,000 (100^2). With four rivals holding 25% each, the HHI is 2,500 ($25^2 \times 4$). The HHI for the 97%-1%-1%-1% distribution would be ($97^2 + 1^2 + 1^2 + 1^2$), or 9,412. Starting to get the picture? I hope so. Here it is, just in case, though: if share is skewed, HHI will tell you that because it will be much higher than what seems "normal."

The shortcoming of HHI is that one should know *all* of the market shares in a domain in order to calculate the index. Should know. Later in this chapter, you'll see why "should know" ≠ "must know."

Concentration ratios. These are calculated and published every five years by the U.S. Bureau of the Census. Unfortunately, there is usually at least a three-year lag between the date of publication and the date of the data. As of June 2011, most of the 2007 data are out. The rest are due out by year-end. That's our federal government oozing promptness and efficiency.[1]

SIC codes are slowly being replaced with NAICS (pronounced, "nakes") codes. The North American Free Trade Agreement in 1994 gave birth to NAICS codes. While they do take a little getting used to, they are, I think, a step up from the SIC code scheme. The latter, remember, was hatched in the 1930s when the U.S. economy employed many more people in agriculture, mining and extractive industries, and manufacturing than it does now. As anyone who values technology firms can attest, SIC codes have severe limitations.

The figures for 1997, 2002, and 2007 are organized by NAICS codes; prior to 1997, SIC codes govern.[2] Under NAICS, sector 42 is for wholesale trade; 423 is for wholesalers of durables, while 424 covers nondurables. In the SIC scheme, these were 50 and 51, respectively. NAICS has 37 six-digit codes for Wholesale/Durables and 32 for Wholesale/Nondurables; the comparable SIC numbers are the same, except SICs use four digits.

An *x*-level concentration ratio is the combined output of the *x*-biggest firms in an industry divided by its total output. Economists and regulators equate output with market share because they infer

1. See www.census.gov/econ/www/concentration.html.
2. www.census.gov/eos/www/naics/concordances/2002_NAICS_to_1987_SIC.xls is a searchable Excel file through which you can move back and forth between the 1987 SIC code scheme (that was the most recent one) and the 2002 version of NAICS. "ISIC" means International Standard Industrial Classification; it's not the same as SIC codes.

that companies are not going to produce more than they can sell. The Census reports concentration ratios in four flavors: 4-, 8-, 20-, and 50-firm. In our shop, we look at a concentration ratio only at the four-firm level (i.e., CR4) in valuing SMDCs.

It's worth pointing out that, unimpeded by substantive knowledge of economics, some in the media and politics assert that more-concentrated industries are more profitable. That is true in some cases, but it is not universal. A relatively high concentration in automobile manufacturing hasn't helped GM and Chrysler lately, has it? It hasn't helped the old "Big Three" television networks, either. Still, concentration ratios are useful to us.

> ***SMDC context:*** *In our shop, we "blend" HHI and CRs. We discuss the CR in our reports, but we also point out the presence of a dominant firm in a domain and note the outsized influence its decisions have on the other players. HHI is extremely helpful in detecting the likely presence of an oligopoly.*

Types of Structures

Most economics textbooks have *monopoly* at one end of the concentration continuum and *perfect competition* at the other. They are indeed polar opposites. Here's a quick graphic:

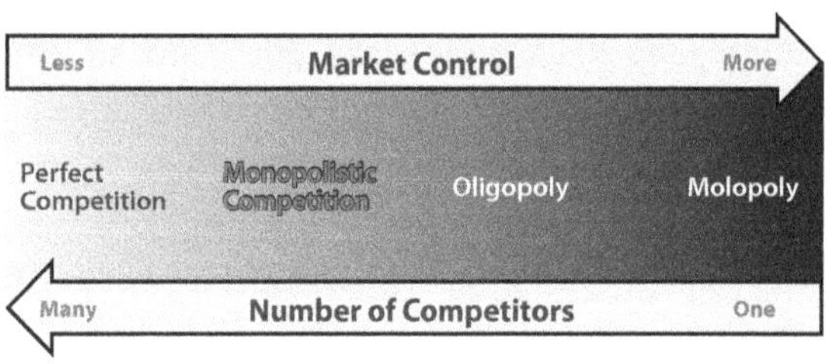

Many traditional microeconomists devote much of their research effort to the perfect competition structure. As the graphic above shows, next door to perfect competition is *monopolistic competition*. In this structure, many competitors sell, not homogeneous products, but differentiated ones, to buyers. Sellers have some pricing power because of branding. Examples of monopolistically competitive domains include restaurants, toothpastes, and craft beer. Both venues at the less-concentrated end of the chain are *fragmented*.

This takes us to the fourth and final market structure: ***oligopoly***. That refers to a market where a few sellers dominate *and* the barriers to entry are significant. How many is "a few"? My reading on this subject indicates that a consensus of economists appears to form around the number 8, max.

Why would we be concerned about oligopolies? Simple: they're alive and well in local and regional domains.

"So what?" you might think.

Consider this: a well-functioning oligopoly beats working for a living. By "well-functioning," I mean, first and foremost, that all of the oligopolists in a given domain observe the cardinal rule of oligopoly: NEVER compete on price. Oligopolists recognize that they depend on one another. This interdependence does not result in outright price-fixing—at least it better not because that is against the law. It more often produces *tacit collusion*: everyone knows the rules of the game, but no one talks about them, especially to rivals. Doing so would expose them to charges of market-rigging and price-fixing.

The efforts of the trust-busters at the Department of Justice and at the Federal Trade Commission have, along with technology and foreign competition, pretty much eliminated nationwide oligopolies. Some of us older folks can remember when the "Big Three" television networks had market share north of 90%; now it's below 40% and continuing to sink. The Big Three Detroit automakers once dominated world markets. Now they have a hard time dominating the markets at home. A few oligopolies do survive—brewing (CR4 = 90.8), cigarette manufacturing (95.3), and providing audit services to public companies (76.0 in the U.S. and, among the *Fortune 1000*, over 97.0[3]), to name just three.

My favorite is the ready-to-eat (RTE) breakfast cereal industry. Readers who doubt the pricing power of a tight oligopoly should wander over to the RTE cereal aisle the next time they're in a grocery store. Pick up one of those big boxes that seem to weigh little more than a feather and is about half-full. Then ask yourself: How the heck do they get 4 bucks for that box?

O-L-I-G-O-P-O-L-Y, that's how.

I saw this in some non-BV work I did for a well-known industrial-supply company in the early 1990s. The company was slow-growth and highly profitable, but it had an IT system that the Smithsonian would have coveted. Except for the CEO, the senior-management cadre was notably forgettable. Most days, people wandered in to work around 9 and left before 5. About the only outfit I've ever seen with a lower sense of urgency is Ms. Welty's "Postal (Dis)Service." Scratching my head about how a company with an antediluvian IT system and mediocre senior people could be so profitable made me wonder about its competitors. When I looked into it, I found that the CR4 in the client's domain was north of 90. Even better, all the players understood the implications of the domain's structure. No wonder no one had to work up a sweat.

What level of concentration qualifies as an oligopoly? A domain with CR4 ≥ 25 *might* qualify if market share among the four were divided evenly and the pricing discipline were high (i.e., they don't compete on price). When a domain's CR4 gets to 40, however, an oligopoly is almost a sure thing if share is divided comparably among the four firms *and* entry (or mobility) barriers are high *and* none of the big players cuts price. Price-cutting in an oligopoly is self-destructive behavior. News travels fast in this structure, so when one cuts, they all cut. Who increased

3. Francis, Michas, & Seavey, "Audit Market Concentration," working paper (School of Accountancy, University of Missouri, Columbia, 2010).

market share with that move? No one. Think of the classic duopoly: two gas stations at the same intersection. If one of them cuts price, the other will, too. Who wins? Hint: it's not the station owners.

The antitrust enforcers at the Department of Justice view a market with an HHI below 1,000 to be "competitive." They see a domain in the 1,000-1,800 range as being "moderately concentrated" and one over 1,800 as being "highly concentrated." Any deal that moves the needle by more than 100 points in a concentrated domain (HHI > 1,000) invites scrutiny.[4]

Oligopolies occur in mature economic environments. By definition, that means slow-growth domains. The only way to grow faster is through acquisition. But doing so risks attracting the attention of Justice or the FTC. No sane company seeks that. In the last decade or so, the FTC has paid increasing attention to anticompetitive transactions in smaller domains and market niches. Required filings under the Hart-Scott-Rodino legislation can get an obscure transaction on the FTC's radar screen; that agency seems to be more active than Justice in scrutinizing smaller deals. Nonetheless, oligopoly is alive and well in many local and regional domains. That is why it matters to BVers.

Why You Don't Need the Whole HHI Enchilada

It is a spooky thing, but, in my experience, CEOs who can't tell the difference between an operating budget and a balance sheet tend to have an uncanny grasp of market share in a domain. Ask the person running your client company to estimate the share of each of the four biggest companies. Then square each share and sum them. If you're north of 1,000, think oligopoly.[5]

Why does an oligopoly matter? Economic life in a functioning oligopoly is much less risky than it otherwise is. That has obvious implications for valuation and should be reflected in a lower discount rate.

Estimating Market Share

In our shop, we use the CR4 to give us an early indication of whether our new client SMDC might be part of an oligopoly. But how do we know what the "output" is for the four biggest competitors in our client company's domain? We don't. We do know from the Duff & Phelps dataset, however, that **number of employees** (a.k.a. ***headcount***) is a good measure of size. No, it doesn't have the statistical strength that the other seven measures have, but it's still a decent measure. And it makes sense intuitively that it would be: within a domain, there *is* a positive correlation between annual output and the number of people required to produce it.

4. See www.investopedia.com/terms/h/hhi.asp.
5. This is admittedly an incomplete calculation of the HHI. Think of it as a four-firm version.

What is so great about headcount as a measure of market share? It is an accessible number. Think about it: What if a stranger waltzes up to the owner of a $5 million SMDC and asks, "What were your company's revenues last year?" She's likely to give a polite version of, "It's none of your doggone business, dude!" But if she's asked how many jobs her company has created for the community, she can't get that number out of her mouth fast enough. It's also a figure that the local Chamber of Commerce has and countless business directories and databases have.

To be sure, few of us want to be calling companies and asking how many people they employ. Even if they would tell us—and these days enterprises are suspicious of strangers calling for "data"—it would take time. That's why we go to www.hoovers.com. There we add up the headcounts for the four largest companies and calculate the percentage of total employment in that domain that the combined headcounts represent. That is our proxy for the CR4.

Again, we are looking for an oligopoly. Its tacit and unspoken collusion might be like the family some folks grow up in: more than a few families have unwritten rules that family members just "know." Those who don't know get told by those who do. For instance, I have a friend in a wealthy family where any talk about money in any context is passé. He can't remember where or how he found out. He and every other family member just know.

Oligopolies are the same way. There are ways to send messages about unacceptable behavior in an oligopoly without picking up the phone. Out-price-cutting a wayward price-cutter would be a signal, wouldn't it? That kind of economic punishment can be effective. As old Sen. Dirksen of Illinois used to say, "When I feel the heat, I see the light."

> ***SMDC context:*** *We almost never see any discussion in any valuation report, whether for SMDC or any other entity, of market share. It's as if competition occurs in a vacuum. Yet headcount is an easy and accessible way to estimate share, and that, in turn, ties back to HHI and CRs.*

The Wrap

This is the first of two chapters about the ***domain***. The key takeaways in Chapter 6 are:

- The basic model of industrial organization is the structure-conduct-performance (S-C-P) paradigm. Structure drives conduct ("strategy"), which drives performance of the *domain*. The model has feedback loops from performance to conduct and to structure and from conduct to structure.

- The two ways to measure concentration in a domain are the Herfindahl-Hirschman Index (HHI) and concentration ratios.

- The U.S. Bureau of the Census publishes concentration ratios on its website every five years. Most 2007 figures are out now, and the rest will be by mid-2011. Since 1997, these have been arrayed under the NAICS scheme of defining economic activity.

- An *x*-firm concentration ratio (CRx) is the combined market share of the *x*-biggest companies in a domain.

- We use headcount as a proxy for output and compute CR4 accordingly. Over the years, this has proved to be remarkably sound.

- A domain's HHI is calculated by squaring the market share of *each* company in the domain and summing the squared shares. An HHI north of 1,000 alerts you to the presence of an oligopoly, and one larger than 1,800 is almost a cinch to be an oligopoly.

- Many CEOs have accurate insights into the distribution of market share in a domain.

- Valuators don't need to know all of the companies' market shares in order to estimate an HHI that will work for our purposes. All we need is the estimated share of the four biggest firms.

- Valuation professionals should care about the oligopoly structure because a well-functioning oligopoly has lower risk, all other things being equal.

- Finally, we used data from the 2010 valuation edition of *SBBI* to calculate the upper and lower bounds of the premium ranges for both the macroenvironment and the domain.

We now move to the second of the two domain chapters. Chapter 7 is about the mechanics of domain analysis and how to quantify your assessment. See you on the flip side.

Analyzing and Quantifying Domain Risk of SMDCs

Introduction

In some circles, only the phrase "the industry" is used. That works fine if the client company competes industrywide. But few SMDCs do. In fact, few small and medium-sized enterprises do. Companies that do not compete industrywide compete in strategic groups, as we have mentioned several times earlier in this guide. To finesse the nomenclature of the industry/strategic-group dyad, we call the client company's competitive arena its "domain." Defining it is, as we have also pointed out a few times already, a top priority. It should be done before the "S&H" and certainly before the Engagement Letter. Failing that, it should be done before one begins assessing the macroenvironment.

For nearly 20 years, Porter's "five-forces framework" held sway in industry analysis. That began to change with the publication of the Brandenburger-Nalebuff book, *Co-Opetition*, in 1996. As the dot coms' run-up in the market exploded in the late 1990s, complements were all the rage. Even after the market implosion of the dot-bombs in 2000 and the Great Recession of 2008-09, complements have remained at the fore in our advanced industrial economy. Therefore, they must remain at the fore in valuing a business. We have taken the liberty, therefore, of extending Porter's five forces to six and representing it with a second hexagon. This one, as you will see shortly, is blue. Domain analysis within that hexagon is the subject of this chapter, which ends with an appendix about competitive analysis.

What Is the Domain?

It is the closer set of six forces that confront the players within a defined competitive arena. "Closer set" is in comparison to the macroenvironment, which is the less-close set. The six potential sources of mischief in the domain are:

- the threat of new entrants
- rivalry among existing incumbents
- the bargaining power of customers
- the bargaining power of suppliers
- the threat of substitutes
- the availability of complements

As with the macroenvironment, each of these forces has features within it to consider and discuss. We're going to show you how to do that in this chapter. Before we do, however, we want to emphasize that, at the domain level, unlike that of the macroenvironment, managers try to influence the evolution of the domain in favor of the strengths of the company they run. Exhibit A in this respect is Walmart, which for many years plied its wares out in the boondocks in small towns and rural areas. Out there it had no risk of being perceived as twisting the tail of the Sears tiger. Being below Sears's radar also gave Sam Walton and his top people the opportunity to hone their processes, bullet-proof their advantages, and drill their team until the time came to take on Sears. And when it did, those boys and girls from Bentonville, Arkansas, whupped the backsides of those complacent dudes from Chicago. Sears has never recovered and won't. That is the nature of what Joseph Schumpeter labeled the "creative destruction" that is both the genius and the bane of capitalism. He put it this way:

> The opening up of new markets, foreign or domestic, and the organizational development of the craft shop and factory to such concerns as U.S. Steel illustrate the same process of mutation that incessantly revolutionizes the economic structure from within, incessantly destroying the old one, incessantly creating a new one. This process of Creative Destruction is the essential fact about capitalism.[1]

The Unit of Analysis

Once more, with feeling: the unit of analysis in domain assessment is—drum roll, please—the ***domain***. Even after what might seem like monotonous repetition, though, you'd be surprised by how many appraisers will still conduct an "industry analysis" for a strategic group and then (No-no #2) discuss the client company right in the middle of it. When they do that, they are broadcasting their confusion about what they are doing.

To repeat yet again, the fact that the domain is the unit of analysis at both levels of external risk assessment has a clear implication: that the premiums for external risk are the same for all rivals in a given domain. They have to be—they are the "OT" in SWOT analysis (which in some textbooks is called TOWS analysis for reasons that remain unclear to me). How the "SW" in SWOT (or TOWS) is configured in response to the OT tells the story at the company level. But we'll get to that in Chapter 8. Let's deal with domain analysis first.

Domain Definition (Again)

Like its counterpart, the macroenvironment, analyzing the domain is usually a walk in the park. Usually. It should be every time. But sometimes employees cannot easily describe the domain in which their employer competes, believe it or not. Again, though, ask folks what its employer's

1. Schumpeter, *Capitalism, Socialism, and Democracy,* 83.

competitors do for a living and where they do it. That should be sufficient to define the domain. Sometimes you might need to add a qualifying phrase about the target market, as I did with the examples in Chapter 2. As with so much in the valuation space, it depends. You will also want to say how expected domain growth compares with that of GDP and with the industry at large.

Domain Analysis

Let me say (again) how important it is to do your research top-down. If you don't, you'll find yourself in a seemingly never-ending "DO loop," as FORTRAN programmers many years ago used to call it. You'll feel as if you're going around in circles because . . . you will be. Problem is, most of your time will not be billable or, if you're working on a fixed fee, as you should be, your margins will decline because of the time wasted.

Here is a more detailed version of the domain level of the trilevel framework that came forward in Chapter 2:

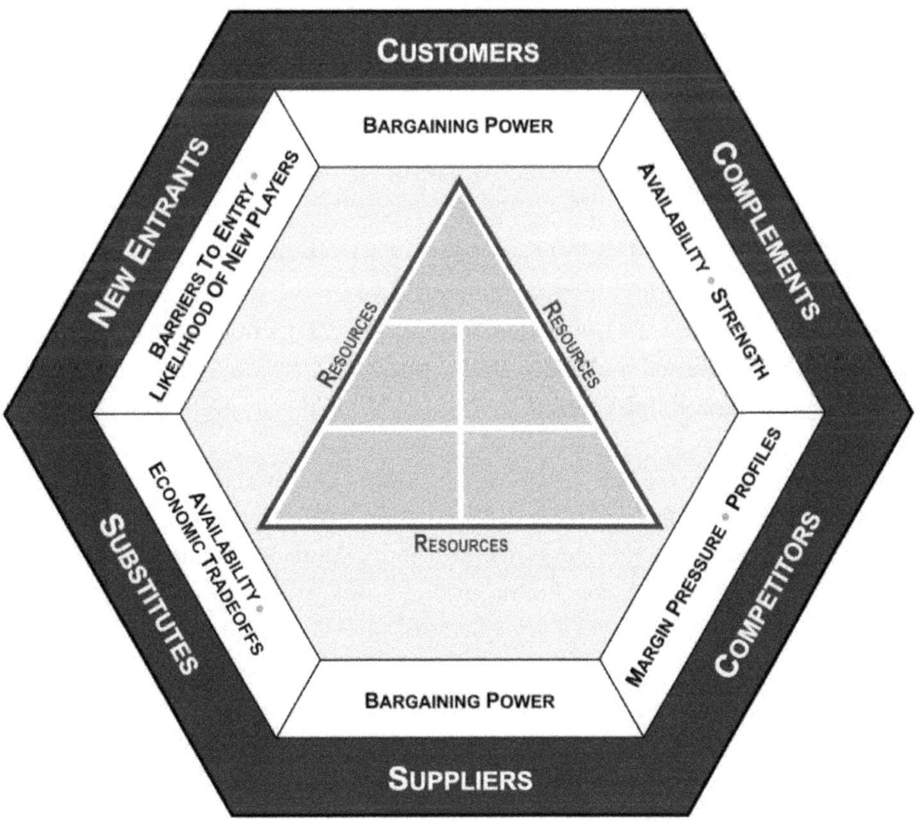

Domain

As it was with the macroenvironment, the aim of domain analysis is for the analyst to learn enough to be able to judge later the extent of the client company's ***alignment*** with its *external environment*, as well as the alignment *among its internal components* (Chapter 8). Well-aligned companies use fewer resources because they operate more efficiently through fewer employees and fewer routines and processes. We call it "elegant simplicity." In a complex world, simplicity is hard to come by, but when you see it, you'll love its understated elegance. Better alignment = higher free cash flow and lower risk attached to both the timing and the magnitude of those cash flows. That means higher valuation.

We turn now to a short discussion of each of the six components of the domain. We will start with *New Entrants* and then take on *Competitors* (opposite *New Entrants*). We will then move one notch counterclockwise from *New Entrants*—our next short discussion will be about *Customers*, followed by its opposite, *Suppliers*. We will wind up this section of the chapter with discussions of *Complements* and of *Substitutes*. Here we go.

The Threat of New Entrants: To the extent that entry is easy, risk increases for a domain's incumbents. How much it increases depends on that domain's expected growth and profitability. Of course, the higher the expectations are for growth and profitability (the latter measured as free cash flow either to the firm [FCFF] or to equity [FCFE]), the more likely it is that new entry will occur. If Paul the Plumber starts driving a Jag and tossing around C-notes, it won't be long before he has new competitors.

In order for a new player to enter, it must clear one or more barriers to entry. Think of these as hurdles. In some industries—oil and gas extraction, for instance—entry barriers are very high, principally in the form of cost disadvantages independent of scale and economies of scale. A new CPA must now have 150 semester hours of college credit in order to be licensed as a CPA; she or he must also have good character, a baccalaureate degree, and, in most states, at least one college course in auditing and one in business law.

It is a truism that the higher the barriers to entry, the more potential there is for profit. However, there are exceptions, principally high entry barriers in domains with too much existing capacity. In particular, if the capital investment is high (the U.S. auto manufacturing industry and the lodging sector during the Great Recession come to mind), fat profits are not necessarily gushing through a domain.

Where strategic groups are concerned, entry is accomplished by surmounting "mobility barriers." They are the strategic-group equivalent of barriers to entry. Mobility barriers also make it difficult, but not impossible, to move from one group to another.

Whether one is analyzing an industry (entry barriers) or a strategic group (mobility barriers), the process is the same. Here are the barriers:

Natural Barriers to Entry and to Mobility

- *economies of scale or of scope*—"scale" means falling cost per unit of output **within a given time frame**; therefore, it resets at the beginning of each period. Scale economies are traditionally thought of in terms of manufacturing. But larger companies can reap economies of *scope* in advertising, purchasing, and training, too, to name just a few. Scope economies arise from expanding the number of products or services offered, not from selling more of the same (that's *scale*). Market leaders in multiproduct enterprises typically enjoy scope economies.

- *differentiation*—buyers' perceived uniqueness of either a product or service. Differentiation is the source of so-called "brand awareness." It is why such companies as Lexus, Chanel, Budweiser, Ralph Lauren, Bose, Saint John, and Ritz-Carlton advertise in carefully-chosen venues. It makes no sense for them to do so in mass-market outlets to customers who cannot afford their products.

- *cost disadvantages independent of scale*—these refer to inefficiencies caused by factors beyond the control of the new entrant. Examples include proprietary technology, favorable access to raw materials, know-how, geographic locations conducive to higher profits, and the learning curve.

- *contrived deterrence*—these are investments that firms make to deter prospective entrants. Such investments have three characteristics: (1) they *force* a firm to fight if a new player enters; (2) they are domain-specific; and (3) they are made loudly and publicly. The most common example is highly specialized production or warehouse facilities.

- *government policy*—this one is less in evidence today than it was several decades ago. However, in some sectors, it remains a serious barrier. These include sanctioned monopolies (electric utilities, cable TV companies); prohibited entry (foreign airlines flying point-to-point inside the U.S.); tariffs/import quotas (sugar); non-tariff trade barriers (slot-machine manufacturing in Japan). Sometimes such restrictive policies lead to innovation: corn fructose syrup is now a widely used substitute for sugar.

SMDC context: *Don't overlook scope economies, either within existing players or as a way to reduce the relative slice of the economic pie that SG&A consumes within an SMDC. N.B.: "Contrived deterrence" affects retailers far more than wholesalers. In fact, I've never seen or heard of it being used in a non-retail domain.*

Competitive Intensity: This refers to the level of pressure on rivals' margins. Intensity can be ratcheted up in a number of ways:

- The *perishability of a product* (fresh produce in grocery stores) *or service* (the revenue not collected from an empty hotel room tonight or an unsold seat on a commercial airline tomorrow can never be reclaimed) can create intense pricing pressure. In some service sectors, there is no such thing as pent-up demand. There are only sales you get, sales others get, and sales no one gets.

- *Slowing growth* in a domain where growth has been brisk in recent years puts pressure on margins. High growth hides lots of sins (e.g., Krispy Kreme). Warren Buffett describes the problem of slowing growth in his usual pithy way: "It's not until the tide goes out that you can tell who's been swimming naked."

- *Undifferentiated products or services* encourage price competition and contracting margins. Until the Sarbanes-Oxley Act of 2002, many CPA firms had used audit services as a "loss leader" that allowed them to get their foot in a client's door to sell other (and profitable) services. The public outrage about the collapses of Enron and WorldCom, combined with the internal-controls provisions in SOX, however, gave the auditors of public companies pricing power that they hadn't in over 20 years. One of the purposes of a CPE course I have developed is to give auditors tools for differentiating their service offerings, especially to small and mid-sized clients, including SMDCs.

- *The absence of switching costs* can also put pressure on margins. Switching costs are the price we pay for switching from one seller of a good or service to another. There are significant switching costs in auditing, for instance, which is why many old-line public companies have had the same audit *firm* for over 30 years. Switching costs also come in the form of frequent-flyer miles and steep learning curves; where the latter is concerned, think of computer operating systems (Windows is dominant, but look out for the coming webOS onslought from Hewlett-Packard). There are also switching costs in moving from a long-time relationship as the area distributor of one vendor's products to another for a new vendor. Transaction cost economics then kicks in because all complex contracts are, by their very nature, incomplete:[2] not even the savviest lawyer can think of everything that needs to be addressed in a contract. That's why Oliver Williamson says, "All contracts are incomplete."

- *Exit barriers* keep marginal competitors competing when they should find something else to do. They often cut staff to the bone, and then they embrace low-ball pricing, just to ring their own cash registers. It's often one of those "lose-a-little-on-every-sale-but-make-it-up-in-volume" phenomena.

2. See http://groups.haas.berkeley.edu/bpp/oew/choicetocontract.pdf.

- *Diverse strategies* within a domain can also lower margins. Such strategies arise in domains where there is no consensus on how to compete. That can tempt a firm to be something that it's not, just because one of its close competitors is that other "thing." As this is written, the proliferation of product design and approaches in the "eBook/tablet" space (think Kindles, Nooks, iPads, TouchPads, and Xooms) is a great example. We saw this act in the shoot-out 20-odd years ago between the "Betamax" format for video tapes and the VHS format. Experts agree that Betamax was far superior, but VHS won the day, even though today, more than 20 years later, there seems to be no consensus on why.[3]

- *Players with roughly equal market share* is a condition that can intensify rivalry. That tends to be the case as the number of semi-equal rivals increases. However, if competitors are relatively few—say, eight or fewer—we are apt to be seeing an oligopoly, as we discussed before, but about which more later in this chapter. For now, remember the First Five Rules of the Oligopolist in Good Standing: Never, *never*, **never**, *never*, *NEVER* compete on the basis of price. In an oligopoly, that is as close to self-destructive behavior as anything in strategy gets.

  SMDC context: *You won't be surprised to hear that a lack of differentiation can be lethal to the personal financial statements of investors in SMDCs. Think "Experimenter."*

Bargaining Power of Customers: Customer groups need not be price-takers. That is, they don't have to be powerless in the relationship with sellers. Bargaining power here is the power to force down prices or to receive post-sales service, both of which reduce margins in the selling domain. Customer groups can exert bargaining power if they find themselves in one or more of the following scenarios:

- *Undifferentiated output from a domain* invites its customers to shop on price. For incumbent competitors in the domain, competing on price is a race to the bottom of the ocean . . . and the divers are wearing cement wetsuits.

- *Customers incur no switching costs, regardless of which competitor they buy from.* In other words, customers bear no penalty for buying elsewhere. It was to encourage loyalty that the legendary CEO of American Airlines, Bob Crandall (who was an accountant on his way up the corporate ladder), came up with the idea of frequent-flyer miles. Those created a switching cost. Of course, in the domestic airline industry today, trying to redeem miles for a plane ticket is not a battle for the faint of heart. The airlines have created other and easier ways for customers to get something for their miles, including hotel rooms, car rentals, theater tickets, and trinkets. Airlines must now report unused miles as liabilities on their balance sheets; that creates an interesting valuation issue—check www.eBay.com sometime to see how much (how little?) your miles are worth.

---

3. See www.mediacollege.com/video/format/compare/betamax-vhs.html.

- *Customers with access to full information* have bargaining power. The airlines have found this out the hard way, as have bricks-and-mortar booksellers trying to compete with online book purveyors.

- *Customer groups that are perceived by domain competitors as being credible threats to backward integrate—and, thereby, compete with the companies from which they currently buy—have more bargaining power.* For instance, the willingness of supermarket chains to create house brands to compete with high-budget offerings from Nabisco, Kraft, and Campbell's Soup, have increased the bargaining power of the low-margin stores buying from higher-margin food distributors.

- To the extent that *the domain's product is unrelated to the quality of the customer group's output*, the bargaining power of the customer group is enhanced because it is sensitive to the price of non-critical inputs.

- Similarly, *if the domain's output is a major portion of the customers' cost structure*, the latter group has incentives to shop for alternatives and bargain hard with the domain.

- Finally, *red ink on customers' bottom lines* creates incentives for them to push back in situations where, if their profits were robust, they might not be so price-sensitive.

> ***SMDC context:*** *Any of the seven bullets above can matter in a given SMDC valuation. As an ongoing thing to keep in mind, the creation of switching costs is both subtle and helpful. Customer service is often a primary source of such costs.*

Bargaining Power of Suppliers: Note that we did *not* say "vendors." That is because neither employees nor providers of capital (debt or equity) are "vendors," yet both are "suppliers." The choice of "suppliers," therefore, is intended to convey breadth. Suppliers can raise prices, reduce quality, or lower customer service, any one of which will reduce the domain's margins (think "Wintel" in PC assembly). Situations that increase suppliers' bargaining power include the following:

- *Suppliers have a credible option to forward-integrate.* The bargaining power of chip-maker Intel over its customers has always been significant, even with chip alternatives such as Applied Micro Devices out there. The fact that Intel, which already spends a lot of money on "Intel Inside" TV ads, and other chip manufacturers could easily assemble workstations under their own brands only enhances their pricing power with their semiconductor products.

- *There are no substitutes for the supplier group's output.* This means that there is no obvious price ceiling, and that increases its power over its domain customers.

- If the *supplier group's output is differentiated*, its bargaining power goes up. That is one of the beauties of differentiation and is further evidence of why we strongly recommend a strategy of focus/differentiation (i.e., "Economiser") for SMDCs.

- *Supplier groups that are more concentrated than the domains to which they sell* have power over the domain's competitors because the imbalance makes it harder for the domain to play off suppliers against one another.

    SMDC context: *For wholesalers, suppliers are apt to swing a bigger stick than customers. That is because the upstream manufacturer(s) that are the source of SMDCs'* raison d'être *tend to require constant care and feeding. Smart SMDCs have many bridges and contact points between them and each manufacturer of their inventory.*

The Threat of Substitute Products/Services: One has to be careful about how one defines a "substitute." N.B.: a competing product is *not* a substitute. The textbook definition is a product or service that uses an entirely different technology[4] to satisfy the same end-user need. My favorite example is TurboTax, a product that encourages otherwise sane individuals to believe the fable that they really can do their own tax returns. Hogwash. Or, as we used to say in Texas, "Heifer dust." Congress keeps insisting that it's "simplifying" the *Internal Revenue Code*, yet the percentage of taxpayers who get our returns prepared by third parties keeps increasing. The last number I saw was 58%—the majority of us are either incapable or don't have the time (or the stomach) to be exposed to a sewer of rules intended to ensure the re-election of political incumbents.

The existence of one or more substitutes for a product or service creates a price ceiling for the output of incumbents in the domain. A short list of substitutes includes the following (and there are many, many more):

- cell phones vs. landlines

- cameras vs. cell phones with cameras

- beer vs. wine vs. distilled alcoholic products

- tickets to sports events vs. pay-per-view

- dining out vs. carry-out vs. cooking at home

- flying vs. Amtrak vs. driving vs. taking a ferry (think Hingham, Mass., residents who commute to downtown Boston)

- resorts vs. timeshares

4. The word "technology" here does not refer explicitly to "high tech." Instead, technology in the context of a company's mission means the process by which inputs are converted into salable outputs.

- eBooks vs. printed books
- iTunes vs. compact discs
- e-mail vs. the U.S. Postal "Disservice"

> ***SMDC context:*** *In my view, the greatest threat to SMDCs is rooted in technology. To the extent that manufacturers can obtain end-user data and market persuasively and directly to those users, they have the potential to eliminate both wholesalers and retailers. I think it's unlikely that that will happen across a broad spectrum of the retail sector, but I also think it's a real threat to wholesalers. Walmart laid down that marker several decades ago when it decided it would no longer buy from distributors or other intermediaries.*

The Availability of Complements: Sometimes called "Complementors," Complements are the opposite of Substitutes: whereas a substitute can reduce output in the domain, a complement increases it because demand for their product is joined at the hip with demand for the domain's output. In other words, an increase in the demand for the one increases the demand for the other. That means that the best complement is the least expensive one. Try free. That would help explain why IBM has marketed Linux software so aggressively: it can bundle the quasi-free Linux with its not-quasi-free servers. The popularity of complements in the U.S. economy has driven the quantum jump in the number of strategic alliances. Here are some examples of complements:

- cellular phones and cellular minutes
- men's business clothing, neckties, dress shoes, belts, dress shirts, cuff links, collar stays
- automobiles, gasoline, mechanics' services, insurance, tires, financing alternatives
- swimming pools, swimming-pool chemicals, swimming-pool maintenance services, swimsuits, sunscreen, beach towels, iPods, pool furniture, sun umbrellas, outdoor grills and barbecue equipment
- fly rods, flies, fishing vests, waders, reels, landing nets, headwear, sunscreen, guides' services, fly boxes, magnifying glasses, needle-nose pliers, fly-casting DVDs, fly-fishing books, fly-fishing magazines, demand for SUVs, gorp
- razors, razor blades, shaving brushes, shaving cream, after-shave lotion, styptic pencils

> ***SMDC context:*** *In all candor, I've seen few strategic alliances and other complementary mechanisms in the SMDC space. That's not to say that there couldn't be, but I suspect it's the "captive nature" of the wholesaling beast—the relationship between an SMDC and its upstream manufacturer(s)—that makes complements unlikely in wholesaling.*

Quantifying Your Analysis

As I wrote in Chapter 5, I know of only three ways to quantify the various levels of unsystematic risk:

- use your judgment
- use our template
- use a "black box"

Before I designed the template that is downloadable by buyers of this *Guide,* I chose judgment. In those days, when I finished analyzing the six dimensions of the domain in the SMDC engagement, I wrote a short paragraph summarizing my findings. It contained one (1) sentence for each of the six forces. When I read that paragraph aloud, I believed I had a keen sense of where the premium should be. Of course, "I believed" ≠ "I knew."

Now I use the template. At the domain level, it has 54 statements with scaled radio-button responses ranging from 1 (Strongly Disagree) to 5 (Strongly Agree). There is no "N/A" option. The statements are generic and apply across all domains. As with the macroenvironment portion of the template, the forces at the domain level must also be weighted from a pre-selected menu; each one must have at least 10% assigned to it, which means the maximum weight is 50%. The underlying algorithm is linear and assumes, at the beginning, equal weighting. But the user must still assign weights. If she doesn't or if the weights do not total 100%, then the template will not calculate a premium. It also will not calculate one if all of the statements have not been responded to.

Of course, I still write that summary paragraph. But I've found that the template and my gut hunch after writing the summary are invariably in sync. So the template and my judgment act as the same kind of triangulating device that using both eyes, instead of one, to gauge distance provides.

A final comment: If you use your judgment, don't use fractions of a percent. That conveys a level of accuracy and science that is fallacious. It *is* about judgment—your judgment. Our template doesn't give you a choice. It rounds to the nearest whole percentage, up or down. You should, too.

The Wrap

There is a lot to chew on in this chapter. Here are the key takeaways:

- Early on, be sure to define the domain in writing. Then commit it to memory. If you have doubts about your definition, check with the owner or CEO. If that is unsatisfactory, please feel free to e-mail me at sparc@beckmill.com. No charge unless I start getting dozens of e-mails from you. Please include the details of the domain as you see them.

- Domains with high barriers to entry usually have higher returns on assets than those that don't. But there *are* exceptions.

- Be sure to indicate whether the domain is expected to grow faster, slower, or at about the same rate as the industry as a whole *and* as GDP in your country. That says something about the attractiveness of an investment in the domain. We include this "relative growth statement" in the domain definition in our reports.

- In your discussion of each force, you need not address every bullet point in this chapter. Talk about the ones that matter. And if none do, give a few examples so the reader will know what you're talking about, say they don't matter, and be done with it.

- Do *not* talk about individual SMDCs in the six-forces portion of your analysis.

- You can and should, however, talk about them in the competitive analysis section—see the Appendix that follows these takeaways.

- Whether or not you use our template, be sure to write a summary paragraph with one sentence for each of the six forces.

- Use a whole percent between –3% and +9% as your domain risk premium. Our template will do that for you.

Before heading off to Chapter 8, where we begin to tackle issues at the company level, take a look at my comments about competitive analysis. They begin on the next page, and I'll think you'll find them quite helpful.

Appendix: Competitive Analysis

Let me lead with a quote from *Value Maps*:

> It is a source of never-ending amazement to us that competitors are seldom mentioned, much less explicitly analyzed, in valuation reports. It is as if the client company competes in a vacuum. Competitive analysis is an essential component. Among other reasons, market share (part of the ***S*** in **S-C-P**) has implication for the ***C*** and the ***P*** in **S-C-P**. Such analysis is a crucial aspect of strategy-making more generally. It is an important aspect of conventional business valuation and one that is usually overlooked.
>
> Competitive analysis is also a key consideration in devising exit strategies for business owners. That makes it a critical aspect of value enhancement. A company's closest rival often can (and will) pay the highest buyout price in the shortest time frame with the least hassle. Competitor profiles offer the client company choices with which to position itself for sale later on. For instance, it might choose to buy and install a software system that one or more desirable purchasers are already using. That reduces risk, makes due diligence much easier, and eliminates conversion expense for the buyer, all of which increase the price for the seller.[5]

Much of what follows comes from a chapter in Porter's first book.[6] Competitive analysis need not be long or complicated. There are key bases to touch, however, and we want to cover those here.

Analyzing Competition: The key contribution here is to help the client anticipate what a rival is likely to do if the client makes a big competitive thrust. Porter's chapter offers four components under two broad headings (which I've **bolded** below) in competitive profiles:

- **What Drives the Competitor**
  - Future Goals—what it aspires to be
  - Assumptions—about itself and how the domain works

- **What the Competitor Is Doing and Can Do**
  - Current Strategy—cost leadership or differentiation? Industrywide or strategic group?
  - Strengths and Weaknesses—what are they? How does the rival hedge or otherwise protect itself from undue exposure to its own weaknesses?

5. Miller, *Value Maps,* 167.
6. Porter, *Competitive Strategy,* 47-74.

Porter's book and my own have plenty of details to support and flesh out bullet points. I will make only a few brief comments here.

Future Goals. Discuss risk tolerance, organizational structure, key managers, known aspects of a rival's system of internal incentives, and contracts that could indicate its capacity to act, or not act, in a given situation. In our experience, a lot of SMDC owners have much of this locked up inside their heads. Get it out.

Assumptions. Will Rogers once said about Herbert Hoover, "It's not what President Hoover doesn't know that bothers me. What bothers me is what he knows that ain't true." When we're talking about assumptions, we're talking about belief systems. Those are a key aspect of culture, of which here is our favorite definition:

> A system of shared values (*what is important*) and beliefs (*how things work*) that interact with a company's people, structure, and control systems to produce behavioral norms (*how we do things around here*).[7]

The older and larger the company, the more likely the assumptions (and the culture) are to be in concrete. Exhibits A in that regard these days: General Motors and Chrysler. Ford has avoided their fate, at least so far, perhaps because (a) the Ford family still has a major stake in the company and can make a lot of things happen that dispersed ownership at GM and Chrysler impede and (b) the Ford family and the Board "went outside" a decade ago for a CEO and have continued that with their latest recruit, Alan Mulally from Boeing. Mulally has led a stunning turnaround.

Companies that have enjoyed a major degree of success are likely to have trouble changing, too. For example, successful SMDCs might not understand why, as they get larger, they need to move up the outside-advisor food chain. Any company that thinks it might do an IPO or sell to a public company in the next few years would do itself and its shareholders a favor by getting audited by a firm registered with the Public Company Accounting Oversight Board. It need not be a Big Four firm or even one from the Big Twelve. But the choice should be a CPA firm that has a number of public clients, preferably in the distribution space. Such a firm will help the company prepare for the IPO in ways that are unlikely to dawn on a non-PCAOB-listed firm.

Current Strategy. You know the drill here. And you also know that *strategic group/differentiation* is the strategy of choice in all but the case where the client company really is the big gorilla in its space. Even then, it had better reinvest in state-of-the-art equipment and processes to keep its costs down.

---

7. Uttal, "Culture Vultures."

Capabilities. Again, I'd like to borrow from my book, which borrows from our pal, Prof. Porter:

> [Goals, assumptions, and strategy give us insights about] the *likelihood, timing, nature, and intensity* of a competitor's reactions. Its strengths and weaknesses will determine its *ability* to initiate or react to strategic moves and to deal with environmental or [domain] events that occur.[8]

At the end of the day, it's all about our client SMDC having a handle on the alignment, or lack thereof, in the businesses of its head-to-head competitors. Knowledge about each rival's future goals, assumptions, strategy, and capabilities gives the client insights into when to fight which fights and when to duck and fight another day. Every successful military general in history has gotten into the head of his rival general. Successful SMDC CEOs do the same thing.

> ***SMDC context:*** *Smart wholesalers are the eyes and ears in their marketplace for their upstream manufacturers. To the extent that they can embed "environmental scanning" in their way of doing things, SMDCs can enrich their relationships with those upstream and derive additional benefits in a variety of ways that will raise their bottom lines.*

8. Miller, *Value Maps,* 168-169, quoting Porter, *Competitive Strategy,* 63. Italics are in the original.

Chapter 8

Internal Analysis & SPARC

Introduction

We come now to the key implement in your valuation toolkit: SPARC. Make sure you understand this chapter. I believe it is straightforward and unambiguous, but heck, you'd expect me to say that: I wrote it.

We developed SPARC from analyzing our own valuation experience going back to 1993. We found that the cause(s) of **every outlying performance metric** in **every engagement** resided in one or more of the five SPARC elements.

Starting at the bottom right of the SPARC triangle with Culture, I am going to work my way to the top of the SPARC pyramid. I won't spend as much time as I otherwise might on Routines because it is the subject of Chapter 10. For now, I will explain each of the five SPARC components and what it comprises. None of these is more important than any of the others, not even Routines. That is why my software template does not allow weighting of any of these components; however, as we noted earlier, it mandates weighting in analyzing both levels of external risk. Recall that the Appendix at the end of Chapter 3 (pp. 40-42) documented the rationale for the range of the risk premium for each of the three levels of unsystematic risk. A shorter version shows up near the end of Chapter 13.

SPARC

SPARC consists of five components circumscribed by 11 functions found in many companies; the functions are themselves surrounded by Resources. The five elements of SPARC are Strategy, People, Architecture, Routines, Culture. Here is the graphic:

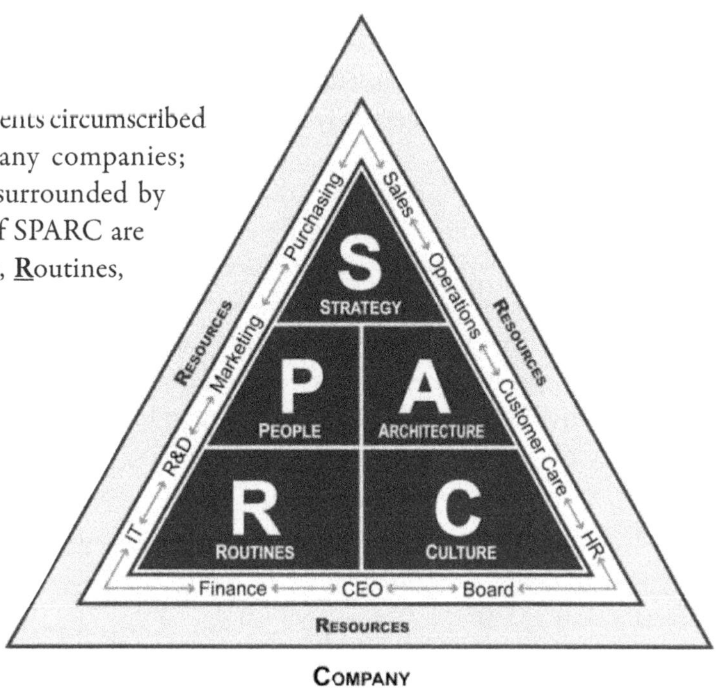

Resources

As she often did, Penrose said it best when she defined a company as "a collection of productive resources."[1] She added:

> Strictly speaking, it is never *resources* themselves that are the "inputs" in the production process, but only the *services* that the resources can render. The services yielded by resources are a function of the way in which they are used—exactly the same resource when used for different purposes or in different ways and in combination with different types or amounts of other resources provides a different service or set of services. The important distinction between resources and services is not their relative durability; rather it lies in the fact that resources consist of a bundle of potential services and can, for the most part, be defined independently of their use, while services cannot be so defined, the very word "service" implying a function, an activity. As we shall see, it is largely in this distinction that we find the source of the uniqueness of each individual firm.[2]

Resources are *all* of the strengths and weaknesses of a company. Top management is responsible for creating new strengths, building on existing ones, and hedging weaknesses (e.g., through outsourcing, insurance, substitution, etc.). How the SMDC accesses them—by ownership, lease, loan, or rent—matters only to the extent that the access is continual. Since most resources can be had by more than one company, it is the job of those who lead an organization either to use them differently—obtain Penrosean *services* from them that others have not thought of—or to combine them into routines. One or more routines can then be configured into combinations—capabilities—that deliver value to customers. Here is Sid Winter's definition:

> An *organizational capability* is a high-level routine (or collection of routines) that, together with its implementing input flows, confers upon an organization's management a set of decision options for producing significant outputs of a particular type.[3]

Unique capabilities are the heart of a differentiation strategy for Explorers and Experimenters. The good news is that the sources of differentiation are limited only by the imaginations of those inside the SMDC. The not-so-good news is that differentiation is harder for wholesalers because adding value to a buy/resell-to-sellers business model is tough. Most SMDCs we know add value through prompt delivery, product knowledge, and customer service. And they measure, measure, measure. The value of whatever source(s) of differentiation an SMDC chooses should be confirmed by periodic customer satisfaction surveys. In your analysis of your client SMDC, keep differentiation at the forefront.

---

1. Penrose, *Theory of Growth,* 24.
2. Ibid., 25.
3. Winter, "The Satisficing Principle," 277.

The most important resource is *the experience of the top managers working together as a team* of those running the company. That experience, or lack of it, is also a constraint on growth. Think of it as you would an athletic team that has been together for years—they know one another's moves and where they are supposed to be and at what moment—vs. one that is just getting acquainted. As Penrose again points out:

> [N]ot only does existing management limit the amount of new management that can be hired (after all[,] the services of existing management are required even to greet, let alone to install and instruct, the new personnel) but the plans put into effect by past management limit the rate at which newly hired personnel can gain the requisite experience. Extensive planning requires the co-operation of many individuals who have confidence in each other, and this, in general, requires knowledge of each other. Individuals with experience within a given group cannot be hired from outside the group, and it takes time for them to achieve the requisite experience. It follows, therefore, that if a firm deliberately or inadvertently expands its organization more rapidly than the individuals in the expanding organization can obtain the experience with each other and with the firm that is necessary for the effective operation of the group, the efficiency of the firm will suffer, even if optimum adjustments are made in the administrative structure; in extreme cases this may lead to such disorganization that the firm will be unable to compete efficiently in the market with other firms, and a period of "stagnation" may follow.[4]

Or the SMDC might just grow itself right into bankruptcy. High growth is risky, especially for SMDCs with thin and/or inexperienced management. Meteoric expansion has impoverished far more companies than it has ever enriched. SMDCs wanting to grow fast must invest in their people so that their skills and knowledge increase at least as fast as the revenues of their employer. Assembling a "Council of Advisers" can be a great tool for having experienced outside advice at affordable prices. Without adequate human infrastructure, the result is tantamount to constructing a 20-story building on a two-story foundation. It will fall down.

Few Resources are on the balance sheet or the P&L; in fact, the most important intangibles (teamwork, reputation, transparency, etc.) are not there. Take a gander at the Microsoft balance sheet: Where is Windows? Office? Internet Explorer? Nowhere.

Below, Barney's four types of capital—financial, physical, human, and organizational—are pitch-perfect.[5] To his list, we added our own measures.

4. Penrose, *Theory of Growth,* 47.
5. Barney, Competitive Advantage, 134.

Financial Capital

(funds from investors and lenders)

Examples of Resources	Measures
Borrowing capacity	1. debt ratio vs. industry avg. 2. debt-equity ratio vs. industry avg. 3. free cash flow to the firm (FCFF)
Liquidity	1. quick ratio 2. current ratio 3. DSO vs. industry avg. 4. inventory turnover vs. industry avg. 5. credit rating 6. gross cash flow ÷ net cash flow to equity
Ability to raise equity capital	1. ROE vs. industry average 2. net profit margin vs. industry avg.
Sustainable growth rate	1. ROE x (1 - dividend payout ratio)

Physical Capital

(the physical endowments a firm owns, leases, or can otherwise access)

Examples of Resources	Measures
Productive capacity	1. annual revenues ÷ FTE employees 2. annual revenues ÷ production sq. ft. 3. "Line" sq. ft. ÷ as a % of total sq. ft.
Investment service	1. CapEx vs. depreciation expense 2. accumulated depreciation ÷ gross fixed assets
Dedication to maintenance	1. maintenance exp./revenues vs. industry average
Flexibility of fixed assets	1. market value of equipment ÷ book value
Technological commitment	1. avg. RAM per computer 2. avg. age of PCs 3. avg. age of software applications 4. # of computers ÷ FTE employees
Access to suppliers	1. weighted avg. distance from which goods are rec'd

Human Capital

(characteristics of the individuals in the firm—knowledge, education, etc.)

Examples of Resources	Measures
Education	1. total years of education ÷ FTE employees
Training	1. training hrs./yr. ÷ FTE employees
Knowledge	1. total educational reimb. ÷ FTE employees
Employee commitment	1. % of absentee days vs. industry avg. 2. sick leave taken ÷ sick leave available
Leadership ability	1. weighted avg. Manager rating by FTEs
Trust	1. annual number of workplace thefts 2. # of complaints to HR (or ombudsman)
Experience	1. total years **with Company** ÷ FTE employees

Organizational Capital

(attributes of the company itself—teamwork, reputation, networks, etc.)

Examples of Resources	Measures
Loyalty	1. employee turnover vs. industry avg.
Teamwork	1. total cost of rework ÷ FTE employees 2. Total years with Company ÷ # of managers 3. performance of Co.'s sports teams
Reputation	1. overall customer satisfaction 2. % of revenue from repeat customers 3. average length of customer relationship
Product innovation	1. total # of patents 2. revenues from patents and copyrights 3. R&D $ ÷ revenues vs. industry avg.
Process innovation	1. % of employees making suggestions/yr.
Speed	1. # of organizational levels

Certain resources—R&D, teamwork, and know-how—are "indivisible." That is, the resource itself is the unit of measure. That applies, for instance, to each person and each stand-alone machine. Says Penrose:

> [The significance of indivisibility] lies in the fact that a large number and variety of indivisible resources are used. None of these need be very large, but if each is capable of rendering not only different amounts, but also different *kinds* of services, a combination that achieves the full utilization of all of them may perforce call for an output much larger and more *varied* than can be organized by a firm in any given period of time.[6]

Let us recall from a Penrose quote early in this chapter that it is the *services* that Resources provide that really matter. Different people at competing companies will view the services to be had from a given Resource differently. That heterogeneous view accounts for the unique character of each SMDC. If a company grows successfully, as we hope client SMDCs will, then the experience that employees get from the growth creates in them new perceptions of services from existing Resources, either individually or in combination.

Functions. SPARC's 11 functions consist of seven line (counting IT), two staff (HR and Finance), one leadership (CEO), and one governance. In some SMDCs, IT remains a staff function, but in many others, it has a key seat at the line table. The 11 functions enclosing the five SPARC elements are familiar to all readers of this *Guide* and do not require elaboration here.

Culture. There is much in print about "corporate culture." Most of it is "noise." I hear CEOs and consultants talk about "we need to change the culture" as if they will get it done after lunch today. No way. Show me a company that is more than a decade old and has 20 or more employees, and I'll show you a multi-year project of cultural change requiring endless repetition that will exhaust most professionals. Remember that pithy definition of culture in the Appendix to Chapter 7? It's worth repeating:

> [Culture] is a system of shared values (*what is important*) and beliefs (*how things work*) that interact with a company's people, structure, and control systems to produce behavioral norms (*how we do things around here*).[7]

As I noted in *Value Maps*:

> We subscribe to the notion of T^3: Truth + Transparency = Trust. It is simple, but not easy. Honest and transparent founders tend to beget honest and transparent organizations. It is easy to get preachy about these traits, but I am not aware of research that shows that such companies are any more or less successful than their neurotic and dysfunctional counterparts.[8]

---

6. Penrose, *Theory of Growth*, 69.
7. Uttal, Culture Vultures.
8. Miller, *Value Maps*, 197-198. For a riveting book devoted to the subjective of dysfunction, see Kets de Vries & Miller, *Neurotic Organization*. Kets de Vries, now at INSEAD in The Netherlands after a long stint at the Harvard Business School, is a trained psychoanalyst.

In Chapter 4, I touched on "path dependence" as a key valuation tool from the field of evolutionary economics. Think of it as "the genes of the founder." Sometimes, though, it might not be the founder, per se, but one who runs the place soon after the founder leaves. That is certainly the case at General Motors; it wasn't the founder, William C. Durant, who put it on its long-standing trajectory, but his successor, Alfred Sloan. What led to progress almost 90 years ago is impeding it now.

In our experience one of the most problematic cultures for SMEs is one where the founder was, or the successor is, a conflict-avoider. Don't misunderstand: conflict-avoiders are interesting clients. But the cultures of firms headed or founded by such individuals are, well, challenging, to say the least. For one thing, the inmates are often running the asylum; that is, subordinates often seem to be in charge because the conflict-avoider is only as good as his—we've never had a client with a conflict-avoiding woman at the top—most recent conversation. The result is that no one trusts anyone, and everyone walks on egg shells. The conflict-avoider never understands that he creates infinitely more conflict by failing to belly up to the bar and resolve issues than he would ever create by taking them on, one by one.

Segue: A few years ago we had a client run by a charming man who was also one of the world's pre-eminent conflict-avoiders. I mean, this guy had zero tolerance for conflict. His company, then generating about $40 million in annual revenues, was a zoo, a study in distrust. One day the CEO, the CFO, the lead HR guy, and I were going to go to lunch. The CEO got clotheslined by an unexpected phone call, so I took the CFO and HR guy aside and offered to bet each of them $20 with the following conditions:

- The CEO would order first.
- The guy ordering next would order something different from what the CEO had chosen.
- The other two of us would follow suit and order what our colleague had ordered.

"I have a twenty-dollar bill for each of you," I said, "if David [not his real name] doesn't change his mind and get what we get." The other two guys couldn't say "You're on!" fast enough.

We did, and he did. After lunch, I tucked two crisp new twenties into my money clip and grinned like a Cheshire cat. Truth be told, I wish I had lost. But I knew I wouldn't. This fellow just couldn't stand the level of conflict implied by ordering something different from his three dining companions. You can imagine what his then-400-employee company was like.

> ***SMDC context:*** *I have always wondered why more SMDC executives don't try to make their workplaces more fun-oriented, especially in what can be the dreariness of a warehouse. For instance, an SMDC could have a "funny costume" contest on various workdays—the first day of each of the four seasons comes to mind. Like anything else that's unusual, though, those at the top would need to lead the way with their own costumes. An SMDC could invite*

> *its best customers to lunch on its premises and have them judge the contest. The top three costumes could then go up on YouTube, there to remain immortalized forever. It sounds hokey, but I'll bet dollars to donuts that it'll work.*

Routines. These are the greatest cause of value destruction in SMDCs. Because they often think that a given Routine is obvious and requires no elaboration or formalization, few owners appreciate their value. In more than one conversation, when I have addressed a deficient Routine, the lead guy's response dissed them as trivial. That is a huge mistake. The way a successful $20 million SMDC conducts its daily activities differs in major respects from how its $2 million predecessor did, and vice versa: what worked at $2 million is unlikely to be effective at $20 million. Think of that 20-story building on the two-story foundation that I mentioned earlier in this chapter.

In SMDCs, the Routines that create the most chaos (a) affect inventory, operations, and billing/invoicing; and (b) are undocumented, especially low-value-added ones. Documentation, repetition, and stomping out variation in low-value-added tasks are key. Show me an SMDC where the monthly closing takes longer than three (3) business days, and I'll show you an SMDC with undocumented low-value-added Routines.

We have seen SMDCs where new hires were tutored in Routines by employees drawing on their memories. In a sector where efficiency is everything—that would be wholesaling—that is an expensive practice. It can produce disruption later because few people can remember everything, either teaching or learning. That is why documentation, esp. of low value-added tasks, is so important. In several SMDCs, we encountered department heads that gave *tests* on such tasks to new employees after they have worked at the company for 30 or 60 days. These functions are trying to get the right DNA into the new person. Hear, hear.

I suspect that most readers of this *Guide* hail from financial backgrounds. Therefore, I believe you should be comfortable poking around in finance-related Routines. Start with this:

> An accounting system is an information system. It serves three masters: (1) the GAAP master; (2) the IRS/tax master; and (3) the management-information master. In SMDCs, (3) tends to get the short end of the stick because most charts of accounts come from either outside CPAs or accounting software vendors . . . who are advised by CPAs.

If the chart of accounts does not reflect management-information needs, the result is data, not information. It is a chart of accounts with insufficient detail and inadequate use of sub-accounts to create the information that decision-makers need to run the business. That, in turn, gives rise to the proliferation of Excel spreadsheets. It is an affliction that I've christened "Excel-itis." There ought to be a 12-Step Program for it. It doesn't take long before what is in the spreadsheets conflicts with what is in the G/L. And it's all downhill from there.

Now, I'm going to contradict myself. It *is* possible to use Excel and get great information out of accounting software if the needed reporting capabilities are not built into it. David Ringstrom, CPA, of Atlanta-based Accounting Advisors, Inc. (www.acctadv.com) is the best we know at doing that. In one situation, using various G/L account numbers, I configured the reports a consulting client wanted, and he wrote templates in Visual Basic. From there, it is a simple matter of exporting the trial balance to Excel and running the macros in the templates. But if Excel isn't functioning on this sophisticated level, well, it is going to be a train wreck trying to get good information with which to value the SMDC. And that just mirrors the train wreck of bad information that top managers get every month.

Start by looking at billing and invoicing, payroll, payroll taxes, the monthly closing cycle, and the annual budget. Except for templates such as the ones I just described, processes should be done *inside the accounting software*. If they are not, Routines have a problem. In particular, look for account analyses being prepared on the fly in Excel with information that has to be keyed in rather than exported in. These are indicative of an inadequate chart of accounts and a failure to use either someone like Ringstrom or the report-writer function found in many accounting software packages.

Finally, if the SMDC's software is an "industry package," duck. We have yet to see industry-specific software whose financial applications—reporting, payroll, etc.—were anything other than a disaster.

> ***SMDC context:*** *Of the five SPARC components, Routines have the potential to generate the most mischief. That is because, under continual margin pressure from the Internet and other technological innovations, all employees must continually be on-guard for better, faster, and more-efficient ways of doing things. It's especially crucial to document low-value tasks and processes so that people don't get creative trying to do them.*

Architecture. Architecture deals with such questions as organization design and structure, coordination, dispersion of ownership, reporting relationships, financing choices, incentives, liaison across functions and/or divisions, and governance. But it also includes "soft" aspects such as informal networks within the SMDC. Sometimes these extend across internal boundaries and then go outside.

Four dimensions of Architecture show up most often in identifying cause-and-effect relationships in SMDCs. We discuss each of these in the paragraphs that follow.

Incentives: The longer I study organizations (28 years and counting), the more impressed I am by the power of incentives on the choices people make. That might sound trivial to the point of being self-evident, but, in my view, it is an increasing problem in issues of public policy. Washington politicians seem resolutely out-to-lunch on the impact of *their choices* in writing legislation on the choices of the rest of us. There's an old saying: "If you tax it, you'll get less of it, and if you subsidize it, you'll get more of it." We seem not to understand that simple sentence in the context of capital formation, agricultural output, healthcare, and the recent financial meltdown. It is as if the politicians aim to suspend the one constant through all of history: human nature.

There are three balances to strike in designing any incentive program:

1. between short-term and long-term,

2. between the individual and the group, and

3. between the division and the SMDC [which is an extension of (2)]

As a general proposition, the further up the SMDC's food chain an individual is, the greater should be the weight on (1) longer term, (2) the group, and (3) the SMDC. In addition, we believe in deferring portions of bonuses for senior managers. This has three benefits:

1. It extends their decision-making horizon.

2. It is a "golden handcuff" because, except for death, disability, or involuntary termination, they have to be on the payroll to collect the deferred portion(s).

3. It raises the cost to a competitor of hiring someone who is going to leave money on the table by leaving their current employer. Win-win.

In my view, *the* key to incentives at the level of the individual is Personal Development Programs (PDPs). I conceived this tool many years ago when I was the CFO in a high-growth distributor. I believed that, to avoid depressing my troops by bringing in outsiders above them later on because of the growth trajectory upon which my employer was then embarking, people had to grow their skills and knowledge at least as fast as the SMDC's revenues. Otherwise, we'd end up with the economic equivalent of that 20-story building on the two-story foundation that I cited earlier. That was in 1979. Since then, I've seen the pernicious effect of not having PDPs over and over: it jumps off the page almost every time an SMDC's revenues are going north and its bottom line is headed south. That is the first indicator that the size of the SMDC exceeds the abilities of the people in charge.

PDPs are simple, yet powerful incentive instruments. Participation in a regimen of PDPs is voluntary . . . yet those who opt out are putting a ceiling on their future *and* must be informed of that each year that they opt out. Here are the steps in launching PDPs:

1. Each employee is asked to make a list of at least three, and no more than five, enhancements in his or her skills or knowledge that he or she intends to make in the next 12 months.

2. These objectives *must be unambiguous*—that is, they have to be definite and objectively observable. Therefore, words such as "improve" and "better" are non-starters.

3. Not all improvements are equally important. Therefore, they should be weighted, and the total should be 100%.

4. If the individual's writing of the objectives is not precise and could lead to disagreement as to whether or not one or more was achieved, then that person's supervisor must coach the subordinate until each goal is crystal-clear and unambiguous. Otherwise, there is the risk of conflict and ill will a year hence.

5. The SMDC supports each PDP in whatever way is necessary; however, tuition and books for an evening class should be reimbursed, depending on the grade received (B or better). Learning motivation should go up if the employee has skin in the game. Some might argue that the knowledge is more important than the grade. Fair enough, but measurement is crucial, and that's why we recommend reimbursement based on the grade. Higher-ups should also be available to answer questions that may arise in the learning process.

6. No PDP should include attendance at off-site seminars that occur during the workday. We see these as junkets that should *not* be encouraged.

7. To the extent possible, work on a PDP should be done outside work hours. This forces everyone once again to confront the trade-offs we all have in their own lives about how to allocate the ultimate resource: time.

8. Under *no conditions* should a bonus be tied to a PDP. If it is, the Law of Human Nature kicks in: some may try to create objectives that are low-hanging fruit. We see this all the time at SMDCs that tie bonuses to actual performance vs. budget: everyone tries to game the system with low-ball numbers. Michael Jensen, founder of the Social Science Research Network (www.ssrn.com) and principal at Monitor Group, has written extensively on the perils of budget-based bonuses.[9]

Anyone who thinks constructing a PDP is easy hasn't tried it. For a new PDP program, those at the top should do theirs *first*. That way (a) they will appreciate the difficulty, (b) they can say that they've already done it and that they know it's no walk in the park, and (c) they can share theirs. In fact, we encourage *all* managers and supervisors to post their PDPs both online and on bulletin boards in break rooms and around coffee pots and water fountains. Constant reinforcement is essential. If you need help launching a PDPs program, e-mail me via SPARC@beckmill.com.

Let's assume, for instance, that an employee wants to increase his typing speed. So that objective in his PDP says: "Increase my typing speed." Obviously that's a non-starter—he should specify the target speed.

Another example: "I will learn Excel 2010." What does *that* mean? My idea of learning Excel—truly learning it—is to be able to write and debug a macro based on a fact pattern presented to the person, to create "pivot tables," to use the OFFSET command effectively in Excel. N.B.: *Any* objective related to Excel should include a requirement to *document every spreadsheet* so that

9. http://hbswk.hbs.edu/item/2647.html

others will quickly see how it works. Otherwise, if the individual moves up the food chain (or leaves the SMDC) without having documented them, the successor will have to invest hours and hours in trying to figure out how each spreadsheet works. The more sophisticated the spreadsheet design, the longer it will take the newbie to figure it out. Documentation avoids that.

If the owner or president of an SMDC wants to launch a PDPs program, then she or he should lead the way by creating her or his own PDP and then posting it on the SMDC's intranet for all to see. Ditto for department heads and supervisors. This is one of the few exceptions to usual bottom-up problem-solving. Successful change initiatives should be top-down. Done right and applied consistently, PDPs are the best way I have found to encourage people to take responsibility for their careers and grow their skills and knowledge. The alternative to PDPs is having long-time employees in key jobs where they are in over their heads. That means hiring outsiders, which is costly and risky. And, if trust is the linchpin of a culture, bringing in outsiders undermines that trust.

Boundaries: Most small companies try to do too much for themselves. They fail to distinguish between activities that must be performed repeatedly (which gives them an opportunity to become proficient) vs. those that are done infrequently (they don't get much practice here). Because more than a few readers here are CPAs, let me describe an example to which they might be able to relate: CPA-firm websites. Some outfit—I don't know its name—appears to have made a small fortune selling the same banal, off-the-shelf website software to CPA firms because so many of them have exactly the same brain-dead format. A website today is what a Yellow Pages listing was two decades ago: it's where people are likely to look to get a first impression about a company's seriousness of purpose and legitimacy.

SMDCs mistakenly believe that they can "save money" by doing things like website construction in-house. In most cases, that is an awful choice. It is far better to outsource the technical aspects of that task to an outfit that does websites for a living. Of course, the SMDC must participate in the design of the site, provide content for many of the pages, etc. So it is a collaborative effort. Luckily the right website company need not be local.

Examples of other projects or functions that many SMDCs should consider outsourcing: HR, IT, janitorial services (why can't people clean up after themselves?), designing business cards, creating policy manuals, and so on. There are good ways to save money, and there are expensive ways, especially in margin-pressed SMDCs.

Structure: Few SMDCs give much thought to how they're designed. When new layers are created on the fly, as they often are, the org chart eventually will not reflect how things actually work in the company. Reporting relationships will be contorted and sometimes illogical. We saw a distributor recently where the IT guy was also responsible for warehouse operations, including shipping and receiving. It was an $8 million outfit that could afford otherwise, but it was one of those things that "just happened" because no one else stepped up, and the company never got around to fixing it. I'm not preaching in favor of bureaucracy here, but division of labor is a key aspect of profitability and growth because it allows the specialization that produces efficiencies that rivals might not have. Such efficiencies go straight to the bottom line. At least annually, an SMDC's top people should review its organization design—both the one on paper and the one that exists in reality—and bring them into sync and rationality.

Structure should also deal explicitly with coordination. This topic receives short shrift in the literature for reasons I don't understand. Maybe research about coordination is cumbersome or difficult. One scholar who has written about it is UConn's Dick Langlois:

> In fact, a firm must be organized to undertake one, several, or all of the following activities associated with the profitable production of a good or service: conception, design and development, manufacturing, provision of inputs, marketing and distribution, and many others. A design that is outstanding in the sense that it meets the performance attributes that potential purchasers desire, however, may for that very reason cost more to produce than those same purchasers are willing to pay; or it may be impossible to produce at all. Thus, one reason for organizing such diverse activities is to provide coordination between aspects of production so that a plausible outcome results in the form of a good or service that can be produced (a) with non-cost attributes attractive to potential buyers; (b) at a price that is also acceptable to those buyers; and (c) that allows for an acceptable return on the productive resources involved.[10]

Alignment: In the context of organization theory,[11] "alignment" means "good fit" between the SMDC and its external environment. Good fit means that the company is positioned to take advantage of opportunities *and* shield itself from threats. Companies lacking alignment are called "misfits."[12] The key is to match structure and processes with the level of volatility in the two levels of external environment.

An SMDC, for instance, that is facing rapid change externally must have a fluid and flexible organization that is quick on its feet and responds rapidly. It should have little formality because the rate of change doesn't permit it. Incentives should encourage teamwork, agility, and quick adjustments. Despite their fluidity, such organizations can be tightly integrated internally.

The textbook cases—not SMDCs of course—of external stability are public utilities and most civilian agencies in government. In their situation, formality is high, as is rigidity and processes. About the only thing that isn't high is employee turnover. Many years ago, when I lived in Tulsa, Oklahoma, the average tenure of an employee at the electric utility, then known as the Public Service Company of Oklahoma, was 19½ years.

10. Langlois, "Coordination Problem," 33.
11. As opposed to, say, strategy, where alignment is assessed, in part, through the VRIO Framework.
12. Miles & Snow, *Hall of Fame*.

> ***SMDC context:*** *Incentives, boundaries, structure, alignment—each of these is a "big thing" for the typical wholesaler. Hate to sound like a broken record, but the issue is margin pressure. Anything that is a better motivator, or reduces costs, or speeds up throughput, or enhances alignment* ***must be done.***

People. The United States has one of the freest labor markets in the world. That is a major reason that our economy's history is that it grows faster than those of many other developed nations. There is labor mobility here that rarely exists in other countries, especially those in Europe. That is a major reason why those countries tend to have slower growth than the U.S. and also permanently high unemployment. Capital is comparably scarcer in Europe because governments in most countries there consume more than 40% of GDP.

In the U.S., longer-term employees self-select. They embrace a company's culture (shared values, beliefs, and behavioral norms) because it is attractive to them. Incentives and opportunities for personal growth are other factors that can attract people or drive them away. Therefore, there is interdependency among People, Architecture, and Culture. That is common in the SPARC Framework.

Key issues about "People" include:

- What kind of skills, knowledge, and talents do they tend to have?
- What do they need in terms of a tradeoff for taking risk?
- What is their relationship to the SMDC? Are they mostly owners? Employees? Independent contractors?
- What is their work ethic?
- What rewards do they expect in return for that work ethic?
- What is "the deal" between the SMDC and its People? What implicit contract is there? Does it lay people off or does it encourage shared sacrifice through across-the-board pay cuts where senior people take relatively larger reductions?

The 2010-2011 case of struggling Silicon Valley icon Hewlett Packard Co. is instructive in the latter respect. From the company's inception in 1939 until the two founders retired from active management in 1978, HP never laid anyone off. There were occasional (and temporary) pay reductions that were later repaid, but there was not a single reduction in force. When Carly Fiorina decreed the first downsizing in the company's history, it traumatized long-time employees. She said later that she didn't appreciate just how deep the impact of her decision was.[13]

13. money.cnn.com/2006/10/09/magazines/fortune/fastforward_fiorina.fortune/index.htm—accessed on August 22, 2010

To make matters worse, HP, under ex-CEO Mark Hurd, installed sensors in work areas to measure how much time people spent at their desks. In departments where the at-the-desk component is judged to be inadequate, HP will send the employees home, have them telecommute (and pay for their own broadband connection, incidentally), and gradually shrink the work space for which it pays. That is about as far from Bill Hewlett's and Dave Packard's "HP Way" as a roman candle is from a Roman holiday. Hurd's replacement, Leo Apotheker, certainly has his hands full.

> *SMDC context: More than most SMBs, SMDCs should recruit and hire with care. In periods of high growth, especially, they cannot, and they must not, "throw people" at problems. That will haunt them when growth goes away. High employee turnover makes for increasingly stiff premiums for state-level unemployment insurance. We recommend conducting detailed reference-checks, subjecting would-be hires to interviews with potential co-workers (not just with managers), and, wherever possible, asking the potential employee to take a week of vacation from his/her current job to work at the SMDC. That gives everyone, including the prospective employee, a closer view of future reality.*

Strategy. We explained the "Strategy" side of the SMDC world earlier. But I think it's useful to repeat the graphic:

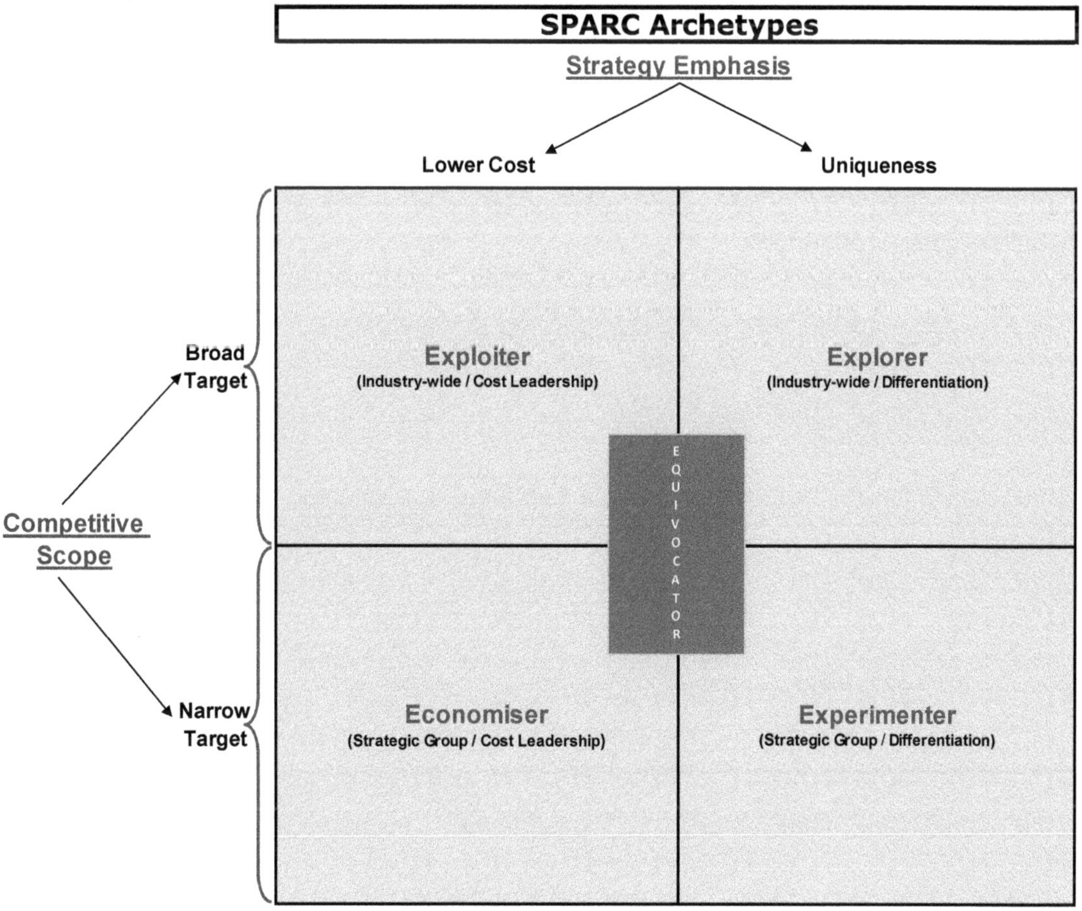

As I wrote earlier, the strategy of choice for the vast majority of SMDCs is the Experimenter in the lower right quadrant: **Narrow Target/Emphasizing Uniqueness.** So long as customers do not perceive the price disparity with the Economiser as untenable, the Experimenter archetype is the better choice. That assumes, of course, that the SMDC in question is delivering something *perceived* as unique and valuable for which customers are willing to pay more. This strategy, like any other, *must* be monitored by periodic customer-satisfaction surveys designed to elicit the relative importance and value of various aspects of the SMDC's products and services.

> ***SMDC context:*** *You know the drill: the Experimenter is the strategy for almost all wholesalers. Superior performance lies in being different, not being a catch-up copycat.*

The Wrap

This chapter dealt with the five SPARC components. It is important for you to understand each one so that you can identify causes of outlier performance metrics during your on-site interviews. As we noted early in the chapter, pay particular attention to Routines—they are the #1 source of outliers. In fact, we believe that the topic of Routines is so important that we devote all of Chapter 10 to it.

Before we get there, though, we take a detour through a short chapter on what we call the "preliminary financial analysis" of the client SMDC. Done right, it should get you over 90% of the way to where you will end up valuation-wise. The remainder of the path will come after your on-site interviews. Now, though, please move on to a subject with which most readers will be both familiar and comfortable.

Preliminary Financial Analysis of SMDCs

Introduction

Analyzing the financial aspects of an SMDC is, with a caveat or two (e.g., "What percentage of revenues come from drop-ships?"), straightforward and not difficult. However, SMDCs also have some unique characteristics to which valuation professionals should attach great significance. Those relate to technology, marketing, and inventory control. Operational analysis can be a challenge. That it is invariably interesting, though, makes it more fun than real work. Besides inventory control, marketing, and technology, this chapter will address key performance metrics, sources of normalizing adjustments, and other financial issues to look out for in valuing SMDCs.

I call this a "preliminary financial analysis," however. That is because the final version will not occur until after the on-site visit. We'll get it as close to final now as we can, of course, but keep in mind that there will be some loose ends flapping in the breeze. We can nail those down only after the on-site interviews.

Managing Inventory Levels

Let me start with this: Every SMDC I've ever met had too much inventory. The law of large numbers tells me that there are exceptions out there, but I have yet to spot one. In my experience, excess inventory occurs for one or both of the following reasons:

- The client company has never analyzed the trade-off between a back order and the cost of carrying a given item—a task that must be done at the SKU level. Start with the most expensive SKUs and go down the pricing food chain. At some point, the tradeoffs will be obvious.

- The SMDC's owner/president/CEO has a sales background.

You should be prepared to go "deep into the weeds" with the Purchasing function at most wholesalers. Be sure to ask for the lead purchasing person's resume as part of your Document Request List. In fact, our DRL for SMDCs singles out the resumes of the lead people in IT, sales, marketing (which is often lumped in with sales), and purchasing, besides the "usual suspects" (CEO, CFO, HR). Where the purchasing gal or guy is concerned, we want to see one professional affiliation above all: the Institute for Supply Management (www.ism.ws). Even if the purchasing leader is not a CPM (Certified Purchasing Manager or Certified Professional in Supply Management), if she or he is a member and goes to the regular monthly meeting, that is a good sign.

It is not enough for those doing the purchasing to rely solely on the algorithms in the software: one must *understand* what those are and how they work. One must also know how and when to adjust those algorithms should it become necessary. We like to shake hands with the purchasing person during our initial S&H. We keep it low key, of course, but we want to get a first impression. We casually ask how long the person has done purchasing. At some point, I slip in this question: "How often do you folks override the purchasing algorithms in the software?" If the answer is either "Never" or "All the time," then I worry, though I save the issue for follow-up later.

I also ask another question, not immediately, but in a couple of minutes, again casually: "How much do the EOQs vary among the SKUs?" More often than not, I get the thousand-mile stare in the four-foot room because the individual has no idea what I just asked. But if he doesn't, my expectation about company-specific risk just went up—think "Routines."

Savvy Marketing

Many SMDCs do not see much difference between sales and marketing. It is the difference between a class ring and a wedding ring. The disparity is huge. Most readers of this *Guide* have had at least one course in marketing. We were taught about the *marketing mix*, which comprised "the 4 P's":

- Product (or service)
- Price
- Promotion (a.k.a. advertising, including social media)
- Place (a.k.a. distribution channel)

With those four, we see right off the bat that marketing is broader and deeper than selling. Now before any latent sales superstars in the readership get sideways, I hasten to add that selling is both art and science. Those who are good at it will never want for work or income. I enjoy selling. But I enjoy marketing more. I find it much more creative and interesting, though selling creates the "cha-ching." Of course, fashioning valuation deals can require creativity, too. Either way, it's often about courtship.

In the SMDC space, though, with escalating margin pressure from the Internet and manufacturers getting stars in their eyes about "eliminating the middleman" (a la Walmart) and "going direct," wholesalers *must* be about marketing. It is not enough to have a product that other businesses want to buy. The savvy SMDC recognizes that it must create the desire for those businesses to buy *from the SMDC*. In other words, marketing and branding must be more about the SMDC and why the customer is better off with this SMDC and not its closest competitor.

In SMDC World, branding really matters. In most domains, manufacturers provide significant branding and other marketing support to their wholesalers. Be sure to ask about "co-op programs" wherein manufacturers reimburse wholesalers (and sometimes even retailers) for advertising and promotional outlays, including website updates and the creation of videos. Some SMDCs even create closed Groups on LinkedIn.

Yet few SMDCs have the capability, the time, the knowledge, or the creativity to do all of their marketing themselves. Remember "boundaries" from Chapters 4 and 8. They are much better off with an ad agency, preferably a small one where they have direct access to the owner(s). We have that for our own practice, and it's one of our most valuable relationships.

However, it is not enough to spend the money. The SMDC must continually monitor its customers, seek and get feedback, and conduct customer satisfaction surveys. Done right, the latter require significant knowledge of statistics, wording of survey instruments, and pre-testing—again, manufacturers might be able to help. Zoomerang, Survey Monkey, or others on the web can do the rest. I'll have more to say about this in the next chapter.

Marketing requires repetition, repetition, and more repetition. To the extent that a logo and/or tag line can offer visual/verbal reinforcement of a repeating message in other venues or media, so much the better. It is not inexpensive, but it is great stuff when it is done right. And it fits perfectly in the **Experimenter**'s strategy.

Commitment to Technology

A commitment to technology means more than a server with a snazzy distribution ERP package. I mean commitment ***throughout the organization***. It starts with a visible and durable commitment by the CEO, president, or owner to embrace technology anywhere and everywhere that she can. From a Blackberry or smart phone to an iPad or Xoom or TouchPad to a hands-free, voice-activated speaker (www.myblueant.com) or speakerphone in the car (a safety practice worth having employees emulate) to an iGoogle (or other individual) home page, to LinkedIn, Facebook, Twitter, and YouTube, the leader has to be seen as tech-friendly. She had better type fast, create her own files, and attach them to e-mails when warranted. If she can use a nifty tool such as Snagit to Copy/Paste into e-mails to employees or customers, that is way cool. Or kewl.

If she has a blog and posts to it using HTML commands, so much the better. To the extent that she can use Skype or Google video to communicate with field personnel and branch offices, more pluses accrue. Bottom line: if the lead person isn't hip on technology, no one else will be, either. The age of that leader does not matter. It is *not*—repeat ***not***—an excuse for being a Luddite. Grandchildren have gotten more grandparents online and into digital photography and streaming video than Apple ever will.

I cannot overemphasize the importance of the commitment to technology. It is simple economics: continual margin pressure from Internet sources of the same kind of products that the SMDC is selling means substituting capital (IT outlays) for labor. That commitment shows up in higher productivity (measured as annual revenues per full-time equivalent employee).

Key Performance Metrics in Valuing SMDCs

SMDCs create free cash flow by turning inventory faster, collecting receivables sooner, and shortening their operating cycles. That *sounds* much easier than it is. Remember Mr. Walton: "We have to have the *right* amount of the *right* SKU at the *right* place at the *right* time at the *right* price." That's a fifth-order challenge—he said "right" five times. So, besides efficient inventory levels and prompt collections, an SMDC needs to have its marketing and technology heads screwed on straight, too.

Inventory: Let's start with the usual activity-ratio suspects: **inventory turnover** (cost of goods sold ÷ average inventory) and **DSO** (accounts receivable ÷ [revenues/365]). A caveat about inventory turnover: Be sure to ask what percentage of the SMDC's revenues come from "drop-ship" transactions—shipments from the manufacturer directly to the SMDC's customers. If the drop-ship component exceeds 10%, subtract that drop-ship component from revenues and remove the related costs from COGS. *Then* compute inventory turnover. If you don't do this, your calculation of inventory turnover will look better than it actually is because the COGS component of drop-ship transactions spent about a nanosecond in "inventory."

Marketing: Tracking marketing outlays can be a challenge. In the chart of accounts, such outlays are apt to be found in a variety of places: Advertising, Conferences, Flyers, Website, Promotion, Trade Shows, Conventions, Booth, Mailings, Business Cards, Direct Mail, Google expenses, and so on. A savvy SMDC marketer should be spending at least 2% of gross revenue on marketing.

More than one SMDC client has told us, in essence, "No way. With a 23% gross margin, I can't afford 2% on marketing. That's crazy." My response is, "You can't *not* afford it. Look at marketing as an investment in higher future margins. It *is* an investment, even though, from an accounting standpoint, it's treated as a period cost." Remember AOL in its early days: it amortized its advertising expenditures over 24 months.

Technology: Start with this: What percentage of gross revenues come from e-commerce transactions through the SMDC's website? There are additional technology-related metrics, though. We like these:

- IT CapEx ÷ IT Depreciation (ratio s/b > 1.0)
- Average age of PCs/workstations
- (# of Sales Dept. laptops + tablets) ÷ # of outside sales reps (should be > 1.0)

- Average RAM per PC/laptop/tablet
- # of monitors ÷ # of PCs (I have four 22-inch monitors at my own workstation)
- (total # of PCs/laptops/tablets) ÷ FTEs

Ultimately the commitment to technology also shows up in one of my favorite metrics in any valuation engagement—productivity:

Annual revenues ÷ full-time-equivalent employees

You will also want to confirm the presence of an up-to-date Disaster Recovery Plan. That was one of the lessons of Hurricane Katrina. Like most lessons, "students" learned it the hard way. Another example: in July 2010 in downtown Lexington, Va., a prominent restaurant caught fire and was a total loss. The business that really got hammered, though, was a retailer a couple of doors away: it had no recovery plan, **and** it carried no business interruption insurance. Ask about this. Better yet, make sure "Copy of Disaster Recovery Plan" is a standard item in your Document Request List.

Adjustments to Financial Statements

Let me say at the outset that, in our shop, adjustments are a function of the "level of value." Here is our representation of Chris Mercer's wonderful graphic, used with permission:

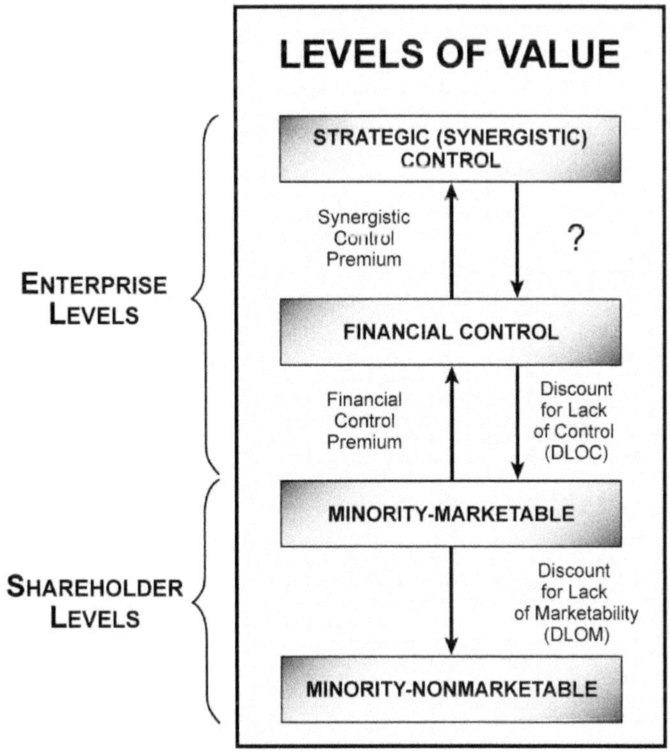

Adapted from www.mercercapital.com/media/Image/LEVELS_OF_VALUE/LOV-1.png

Except for the pass-through-entity premium, we prefer to avoid discounts and premiums wherever possible. That leads us to resist making control-type adjustments in engagements whenever we're valuing a minority interest. However, remember that valuation is always about "facts and circumstances."

We had an exception to our no-control-adjustments-for-minority-interests mindset 11 years ago. We were working alongside a CPA-firm client valuing a 25% minority non-marketable interest in a high-end divorce. The owner of that interest was the propertied spouse. The corporation's by-laws allowed board members to carry proxies of absent directors . . . and there were three directors. Because he traveled heavily, the in-spouse always signed over his board proxy to his brother. It didn't hurt that, between them, the two had a supermajority of the shares outstanding (the brother had funded the venture's start-up). Because of the proxy, the 25% holder enjoyed all of the benefits of control. Therefore, we collaborated with our client to make control-level adjustments because our client's client's spouse (did you follow that double possessive??) was clearly enjoying the benefits of control ownership. The judge agreed, and it stood up on appeal.

Readers are familiar with the typical sources of normalizing adjustments. Here is a basic, non-inclusive list:

- obsolete inventory
- inventory cost based on LIFO (probably understates profits)
- compensation (excessive or insufficient)
- payroll taxes and benefits related to compensation
- perks
- related-party transactions
- rent
- depreciation under MACRS and under Sec. 179
- notes receivable and payable
- advances from (or to) shareholders
- one-time vendor refunds
- one-time legal fees for a non-litigious company
- disaster recovery expenses

- non-operating assets
- excess cash/marketable securities
- land (if adjusted upwards, don't forget the capital-gain liability)
- bad debt reserve (direct write-offs aren't GAAP, and reserving isn't tax-deductible)
- expenses that should be amortized (e.g., E&O insurance, vehicle insurance, other insurance paid six to 12 months in advance)
- contingent assets (e.g., possible collections from being a plaintiff)
- contingent liabilities (e.g., earn-outs, environmental exposure)
- warranties
- routine maintenance that is deferred
- deferred taxes (if a C corporation)
- accruals
- expensed website outlays (e.g., adding e-commerce capabilities and/or creating a mechanism for customers to check/track their orders)

In SMDCs, consider these additional possibilities:

- **notable variation in gross margin**—most often, this comes from not getting "clean cut-offs" when taking inventory, usually at year-end. If the inventory was not "observed" by an outside CPA firm, inquire deeply into inventory-taking routines, how long taking it requires, where incoming merchandise is stored while inventory is going on, etc.
- **office supplies**—we're not in the paperclip-counting business, but we know of an SMDC that spent nearly $10,000 at year-end on printer toner that it immediately expensed. Because our DRL asks for P&Ls for each of the 12 months before the valuation date, the spike in the last month jumped off the page at us.
- **expenses for last year (or for next year) booked during the year ending on the valuation date**—this shows up most often in airfare, overpaid legal expenses, and conference registrations; again getting monthly P&Ls for the 12 months running up to the valuation date will help you spot these.

- **personal use of company vehicles**—check W-2s to see if a portion of the overall cost of operating/maintaining vehicles is charged back to employees, esp. the owner(s).

- **health insurance premiums in pass-through entities**—these should appear on 941s and on W-2s.

- **capitalization policy**—we know a $150 million company that expensed everything costing less than $2,500. Besides computers and laptops developing "legs," the IRS picked up on the policy during an audit and socked the company with back taxes and penalties; my comment to the chairman was, "George, think about the incentives that even obscure accounting policies can create."

- **advertising**—if the SMDC does recurring advertising that aims squarely at its target market, the advertising outlays might have "legs"; that is, advertising might not be a pure period cost. It depends on the content of the media, its catchiness, and its "stickiness."

Again, this is not a be-all/end-all list of possible sources of normalizing adjustments. But I believe that there is plenty here to get you going. Understanding the unsystematic risk of the client company will help you uncover additional possibilities.

Constructing a Composite

We are not keen on industry composites assembled by anyone but us. That is because we want to know *exactly* what companies comprise the composite. The only way we have found to accomplish that is to do it ourselves. Luckily there are some scale economies in doing so.

The best possible list, I believe, comes from the finalists in your guideline public company (GPC) analysis. Because our GPC template automatically size-adjusts valuation multiples (we can set an Excel flag for either Morningstar or Duff & Phelps premiums), we typically get a final group ranging from 10 to 30 companies. So, your finalists also double as the basis for your composite.

What about the megacompanies on such a list? Aren't they likely to have some economies of scale? Probably. The best way to get insight into that is by calculating annual revenues per full-time-equivalent employee. Even with some disparities between those numbers and the one for our client company, we usually use the finalists from our GPC analysis as the foundation for our composite . . . so long as they're not *all* behemoths. And we've never had an SMDC valuation where they were. That is one of the beauties of size-adjusted multiples: a large group of finalists makes for robust statistics and minimizes the likelihood of material error.

Spotting Outlier Metrics

As I said at the outset, pay particular attention to inventory turnover, days sales outstanding, productivity, and IT measurements. If the client has notably lower productivity than the composite, a big reason might come from those IT measurements. You should be able to use those as the springboard for a number of specific questions during your on-site interviews.

Take a close look at gross margin, too. In our valuation of SMDCs, we use gross margin as a key test of similarity. We try to avoid having a range of variation of gross margin of ± 5 percentage points. That means, for instance, that if our client company's gross margin is, say, 28%, we will lean toward excluding GPCs with margins outside a range of 23% to 33%; if GM is below 20%, our range narrows, too. Before you get too locked on this metric, though, make sure that the client's inventory numbers are reasonably solid. Remember, too, that, while LIFO is acceptable for GAAP (but not for IFRS), not every SKU must be costed on the basis of LIFO. Companies can pick and choose what method of valuing inventory that they want to use for which SKUs. SMDCs typically don't do that, but public companies might. And be sure to look for LIFO layers in the GPCs.

The favorite metric of too many investment bankers—EBITDA—is seldom a major concern in SMDCs. That is because few of them are capital-intensive. That means that the "DA" part is unlikely to differ much from the EBIT margin itself. I hasten to add that that does not preclude MVIC/EBITDA being a good valuation multiple. N.B.: Let the coefficients of variation be your guide, unless there is an industry tradition that companies in your client company's space are almost always valued on an EBITDA basis . . . by professionals (*not* i-bankers) who know what they're doing.

We do take a hard look at the operating margin (i.e., EBIT percentage). However, to avoid undervaluing a business using MVIC/EBIT as the (or a) basis for valuation, we have to make sure that our normalizing adjustments are thorough. Ask lots of questions and proceed in Socratic fashion. There isn't a checklist for this stuff. You're above-average in intelligence, or you wouldn't be a valuation professional in the first place. Just use that good brain of yours, and go where the facts and the data lead you.

The Wrap

This chapter purposely omitted a detailed discussion of the nitty-gritty of financial analysis because that topic is well-covered by all of the leading reference books in valuation. If your GPC template does what it should do, the financial analysis is fast, straightforward, and uncomplicated. However, the template won't do the normalizing adjustments or exercise the judgments that only you, the professional, are capable of.

We noted that three areas tend to tell much of the story in the valuation of most SMDCs: inventory, marketing, and deployment of technology. Those three should be foremost in your mind in every engagement involving SMDCs. The next chapter will offer additional depth and proportion to them, too.

When it comes to normalizing adjustments, there are no sure things. Just go through the bulleted items in the chapter and keep looking for additional opportunities. The financial statements of *every* SMDC we have ever valued required adjustments. Inventory is the first place to look—LIFO, obsolete inventory that shouldn't be on the books in the first place, and clean cut-offs when the physical inventory is being taken.

Reap the scale economies of constructing your own composites. Kick the RMA, Integra, or other habit and do it yourself. It should be a natural extension of GPC analysis. And if you do not regularly use the guideline public company method, well, you're either valuing Mom-and-Pops, or you're overlooking a valuable and important valuation tool. Such an omission *will* come back to haunt you.

Finally, what constitutes "aberrant" (as in "aberrant performance metrics") is a matter of judgment. The more SMDCs you appraise, the better your judgment will become. Pay particular attention to gross margin, inventory turnover, and DSO. If you run into serious questions, though, it's OK to send an e-mail to me at SPARC@beckmill.com. Since I have never asked to be paid for providing assistance, please be patient. I'm good about answering e-mails, but I do get a lot of them.

As promised in Chapter 8, Chapter 10's focus is Routines because they are the repository of the most causes of aberrant performance metrics. They also tend to be low on the list of top-management priorities. I will cover them in considerable detail, function by function, in the SPARC Framework, which makes them even more important from a valuation perspective.

Appendix: Book Value, Capitalization, Asset Accumulation Method

It's important to make some comments about three methods of estimating value. Too many in our community use the first two—book value (or its sibling, "adjusted" book value), and capitalization, either of "earnings" or of cash flows; too few use the last one—the asset accumulation method.

Book Value: To start with, this accounting construct should be called "book cost"; *value* has zilch to do with it. Its variant, adjusted book cost, usually adds an adjustment to reduce accelerated depreciation allowed by the U.S. Internal Revenue Code. Except for SMDCs that are young and haven't had time to create intangible value, book cost offers the professional no protection against making a mistake if the only other method that she or he uses is from one of the other two approaches. That is because book, or adjusted book, for a successful company that has intangible value is so far below the estimate an income or market method produces that comparing the two may well be a waste of time. What's the point of having an estimate of, say, $1.5 million under an income method and $400,000 under adjusted book value? We can state the obvious: the latter excludes intangible value and the former includes it. So what? Then what? Give it up. (See ***Asset Accumulation Method*** later in this Appendix.)

Capitalization: It is important to remember that capitalization is a unique form of discounted cash flow. If readers doubt that, please run this computation: increase free cash flow by the same growth rate for, say, five years, just as if you were doing DCF. Do the discounting and then compute the present value of the terminal value. The DCF result should be identical to your capitalization result. If it's not, then you made a mistake somewhere.

As a unique form of DCF, capitalization has two key assumptions: (1) that a company's free cash flow grows in perpetuity at a constant rate, and (2) that that rate is known. Think about that. Isn't it true that, by their very nature, smaller companies tend to be riskier than larger ones? And by "riskier," don't we mean that there is greater uncertainty that the expected cash flows will occur (a) in the magnitude expected and (b) in the time frame expected? Well, if that's the case, why use capitalization at all?

For years, I've thrown down the gauntlet as I teach valuation classes and as I make presentations to conferences by challenging audiences to "call me collect if you find a small company that's that stable." I'm still waiting for that first phone call.

Those who rely on capitalization tend to argue that the client company isn't sophisticated enough to do multi-year projections. I disagree. Teach 'em. We developed a simple Excel template that we give to clients; it is formatted to enable them, with a little company-specific tweaking, to create their own P&L projections. We spend a few minutes talking to them about CapEx, about the distorted *economic* picture that accelerated depreciation presents, how to determine economic depreciation, and then how to think about CapEx vs. economic depreciation in the context of a growing business: CapEx should > economic depreciation.

Remember, too, that, at some point, an SMDC will outgrow its current facility and will need either to expand the current one or to move into a new one. Either way, the result is a large increase in rent, in amortized leasehold improvements, and in equipment depreciation. Therefore, it's essential for you, as the appraiser, to ask what increment of capacity utilization the current run rate consumes. For instance, a company that's at 75% of capacity and is expecting to grow its revenues at, say, 15%, 12%, and 8% for the next three years will exceed its 100% capacity. If capacity is figured using only one shift, then perhaps the large increase in fixed expenses can be delayed by adding a second shift for the warehouse at night and a few more delivery vehicles for the day shift. Or maybe the company can move to 10-hour days instead of eight-hour ones and thus increase capacity by 25% (to 50 hours/week), even with just one shift.

You can also teach the client company about non-cash working capital—that's working capital that excludes cash and cash equivalents *as well as* current installments of long-term debt and the line of credit (if the latter rolls into installment debt and is thus a permanent part of the company's capital structure)—and how non-cash working capital tends to vary with changes in revenue. The company will learn how to guesstimate what the downward impact on cash flow of an X% increase in revenue is likely to be from the increase in working capital. Besides, if you don't exclude those cash-type items, you'll end up double-counting.

One final comment about capitalization: if there's a reason to use capitalization of "earnings" (a.k.a. net income) rather than "cash flow," I've not seen it. "Earnings" is an accounting measure, not an economic one. Investors care about cash. In a growing business, free cash flow will invariably be less than net income . . . unless that business can come up with a business model such as Dell's "reverse cash conversion model," wherein customers pay before vendors are paid, and there's never any finished-goods inventory. Remember, net income is an opinion; cash is a fact.

Asset Accumulation Method: This is an underappreciated and underused method under the cost (a.k.a. asset-based) approach. It requires the appraiser to construct an economic balance sheet, *including intangibles*. If you do purchase price allocations (PPAs) under ASC 805, you've got this one in your hip pocket. You already know how to value individual intangibles. Use the WACC in your DCF as the "anchor" for your rates of return on different assets. Working capital will have a much lower rate of return, and intangibles much higher rates; the latter will vary according to the riskiness of the intangible. Don't overlook internally created intangibles, such as software.

If some of the assets are collateral for loans, you need to assess the likelihood that the collateral will be forfeited to the lender(s). If payment patterns and company performance are such that, in your professional opinion, the likelihood is that the lender(s) will seize the assets, then you must omit them from the *economic balance sheet* you are constructing.[1]

Before I try to estimate any value for goodwill under the asset accumulation method, I'll write a paragraph about what the components of goodwill are in the SMDC circumstances facing me. Obviously, assembled work force is in there. But another part, going-concern value, is, too . . . assuming that my analysis doesn't result in the exclusion of fixed-assets debt collateral. For a successful company, teamwork, creativity, and know-how should be two more intangibles embedded in goodwill. Location is sometimes a part, too. In essence, I'm looking for intangible value that I haven't already estimated and that it is reasonable to believe exists in the specific SMDC situation. If I can't write a persuasive paragraph about these components of goodwill estimate, then I discard this method. But most of the time, I can.

Once I have that paragraph behind me, I then multiply each asset by its rate of return to get the components of free cash flow without goodwill. I sum them and compare that total free cash flow that I expect the assets to produce to economic income under the income approach. If the latter is larger, as it should be, I infer that the additional increment of economic income is attributable to goodwill. We capitalize that increment at a rate that is usually at least half again higher than the second-riskiest intangible. From the total assets, which now include goodwill, I subtract funded debt, and voila: the difference is the market value of the equity.

I should add that one can use the asset accumulation method only when valuing a controlling interest. Without control, various discounts (DLOC, DLOM) intercede. Those make the process messy enough as to be unusable, at least in my experience.

One other thing: This method can be time-consuming, even for those of us experienced in doing PPAs under ASC 805. Time-consuming means expensive, so make sure you have the budget before you take a run at this. If you've not done purchase price allocations, then the learning curve will be steep enough that I recommend that either you get some back-up from someone who has the PPA experience or forgo deploying this method.

At the end of the day, unlike either of the "book cost" methods that led off this Appendix, the asset accumulation method can give you an estimate of equity value that is meaningful. Besides that, if you've used this method and an income method correctly, they should be within hailing distance of one another. You have also avoided using one of those meaningless book cost methods. And the asset accumulation method, unlike book cost, can act as a check on the accuracy of methods under the income and market approaches.

Nifty? I think so, but you be the judge.

---

1. I am indebted to Susan M. Saidens, ASA, CPA·ABV, Managing Member, SMS Valuation & Financial Forensics, LLC, Malvern, Pa., for her insightful views and willingness to share how she deploys the asset accumulation method. She introduced me to the need for the professional to make a "probabilistic determination of the forfeiture of collateral" and, from there, to construct the economic balance sheet accordingly.

Chapter 10

Internal Analysis (II): The Importance of Routines

Introduction

We know from the published research that the potential for good or bad things to happen is greatest at the company level. We have all seen clients that were their own worst enemies. Over time, the market process of selection weeds them out. Fifty years ago, the character Pogo in the comic strip of the same name said it best: "We have met the enemy, and he is us." Others stumble along and survive, but never realize their potential.

We now follow Chapter 8 about internal analysis with one that focuses on one key SPARC component—Routines—and on the Resources that circumscribe SMDCs. Deficiencies in Routines are the single largest source of risk and aberrant metrics in SMDCs. We start with Resources.

A Graphic Reminder: SPARC

Differences in incentives between public companies and private ones make the identification of cause-and-effect relationships a crucial aspect of what we who appraise private equity do. Those causes fall within five areas: Strategy, People, Architecture, Routines, Culture. Thus, we have the SPARC acronym and graphic:

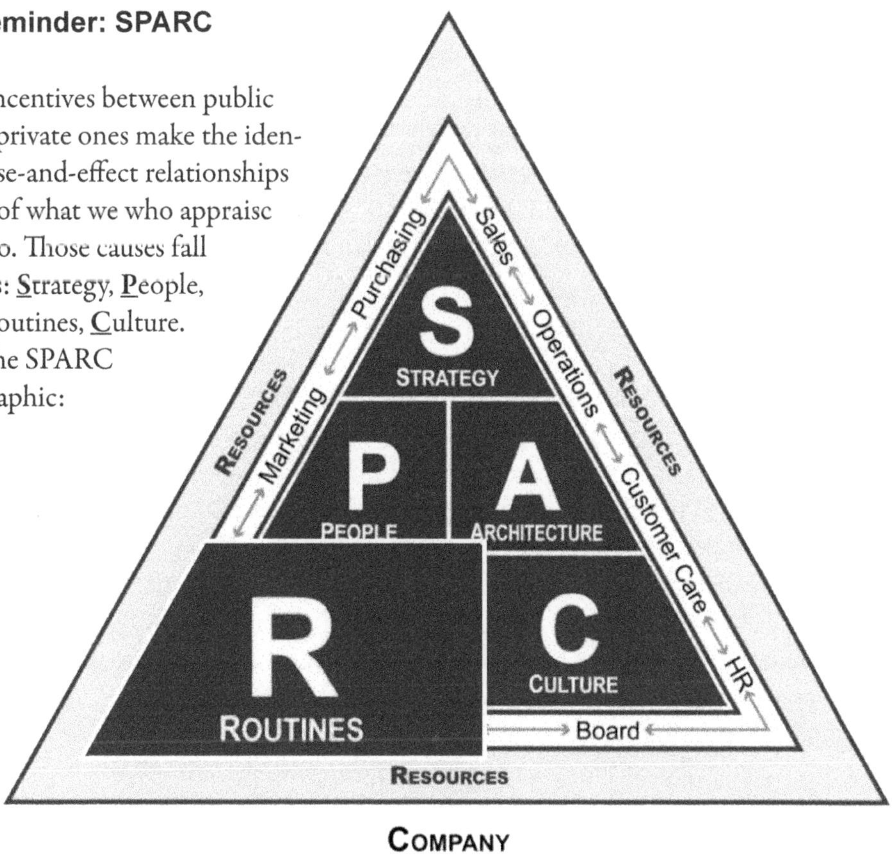

Cause-and-Effect Relationships

Let me begin here by putting a widely embraced urban legend to rest: financial ratios and other performance metrics are not—repeat, **NOT**—"value drivers." That is the greatest hoax since one-size-fits-all. These metrics are *symptoms* of underlying virtues and afflictions. In other words, they are *effects*; it is our job to figure out what causes them. Most often, that identification process occurs during the on-site visit, about which more in Chapter 11. For now, I want to introduce you to each of the SPARC components.

The design and configuration of the five SPARC elements for which top management is responsible determine value creation . . . and value destruction. The process of identifying cause-and-effect requires us (1) to identify an SMDC's value drivers (if any) and gauge their durability, and then (2) to find its value destroyers (if any) and determine whether they can be either eliminated or lessened, often through hedging (insurance and outsourcing are two examples). To repeat: financial ratios and other metrics are **NOT** value drivers.

In our experience, these drivers and destroyers most often pitch their tent in Routines. That is because Routines is the only one of the five SPARC components that resides at something other than a firm-wide level. There is also much more individual autonomy in the design and execution of Routines than there is in the other four elements, and that leads to much greater variation within them.

After Routines and in descending order of the frequency with which they are causes based on our analysis are Architecture, Culture, People, and Strategy. I believe that our coverage of SPARC in Chapter 8 is sufficient for getting at cause-and-effect relationships related to strategy, people, architecture, and culture. But Routines are a different issue because they are such a powerful source of underlying mischief in SMDCs.

Routines

Start here: Too often Routines are value destroyers in SMDCs. Because they often think that a given Routine is obvious and requires no elaboration or formalization, few owners appreciate their value. In many conversations, when I have addressed a deficient Routine, the lead guy's response borders on dissing them as trivial. That is a huge mistake. The way a $20 million SMDC conducts its daily activities and makes decisions differs in major respects from how its $2 million predecessor did. In other words, what worked at $2 million is unlikely to be effective at $20 million.

In SMDCs, the Routines that create the most disorder (a) affect inventory, operations, and billing/invoicing; and (b) are undocumented, especially low-value-added ones. Documentation, repetition, and stomping out variation in low-value-added tasks are key. Show me an SMDC where the monthly closing takes any longer than three (3) business days, and I'll show you an SMDC with undocumented low-value-added Routines. I'll also show you a company whose operations are in chaos: the financial side of the enterprise mirrors the operational side.

New hires are often tutored in Routines by employees drawing on their memories. That can produce disruption later because few people can remember everything, either teaching or learning. That is why documentation of low-value-added tasks is essential. We have even heard of departments that give *tests* on such tasks to new employees after they have worked at the company for 30 or 60 days. These functions are trying to get the right DNA into the new person. Hear, hear.

In the paragraphs that follow, I embed questions in comments about various functions of the typical SMDC. Before sitting down with selected individuals for one-on-one interviews, you should get a walk-through of each function in the SMDC, starting with IT. The questions I include are only starters. Based on responses to them, you can ask your own follow-ups. All phases of the on-site visit, including this walk-through, have Socratic features. Use your head, think on your feet, and you'll do fine.

IT: The first flag of inadequate IT Routines is a system that is down often. Few SMDCs are capable of running their own IT systems; instead, they should outsource it to companies that do that for a living. They will find lower costs and less stress. Customized programs written in-house are another flag; if one of them crashes, either the person who wrote it originally has to resuscitate it or, if that person is no longer around, the company is in a pickle. No software should be written in-house without full documentation. And security should be such that programs and applications cannot be changed without updating the documentation. Is there a Help Desk? If not, where do employees go for IT help? Is there a Disaster Recovery Plan? Is *everyone* computer-literate? Is software current? Where are back-ups kept? Who maintains the company's website? Are complaints to the webmaster forwarded up the food chain? Is the copyright on the website current? Is the website "brochureware"? Is there a reason for visitors to the website to register? Are registration data collected and analyzed?

R&D: Don't expect to find much in the way of R&D inside the typical SMDC. The R&E (Research & Experimentation) tax credit applies *only* to new products. By definition, SMDCs are not in that business. Even so, if the SMDC client does any R&D, even for services, it is a big plus because it's a strong indication that the SMDC is indeed thinking outside the box. It is perfectly legitimate to have an R&D account in the chart of accounts, even if it does not generate a tax credit. That does not obviate the need for R&D in services offerings; in how simple everyday tasks can be done faster, better, less expensively, and more accurately; or in better ways to gather, process, and disseminate information. There probably will not be an R&D Department, but there should be people, probably managers, spending a slug of their time on R&D-type issues, though they probably don't call it that.

Marketing: As we emphasized in an earlier chapter, this is one of the keys to successful SMDCs. Does the SMDC have a logo? A tag line? Is its logo crisp and simple? Is the tag line easily remembered? Does it reflect the values or skills or uniqueness of the SMDC? Does it appear to understand branding? Check through the website. Is it "brochureware"? Does it have at least one blog that is active and posted to at least weekly? Does the company have any advertising specialties (e.g., pens, golf balls, "sticky pads," etc.) to give to customers and visitors? Does it have an ad agency? Are its business cards printed on both sides (why give up 50% of card real estate)? Are key members of management registered and active through LinkedIn? Does the SMDC use any social media? Does the SMDC have a newsletter or other vehicle for communicating with its customers about the company aside from invoices and sales solicitations?

Purchasing: Ask about cycle counting in the warehouse—it is a wonderful tool for increasing the accuracy of inventory records. It also beats the chaos of an annual inventory. Be sure to ask what percentage of sales the 50% slowest-moving SKUs account for. Ask how vendors are chosen. Is the existence of a new vendor confirmed before it is "open to buy"? Are purchases made electronically? (If it is manual, and the company is anything other than a Mom-and-Pop operation, you can be sure that it needs fixing.) Do the purchasing people understand "EOQs" and "safety stock"? What percentage of orders requires a back-order? Again, ask about the ISM (www.ism.ws) and rigorous designations that I mentioned in Chapter 9.

Sales: The keys in sales are avoiding paper and relying on people's memories. That means pervasive deployment of IT.

The key IT application in sales is what used to be called the "Customer Master"; the process today is known as CRM—customer relationship management. Regardless of its handle, we need to get a handle on it. The CRM should have a running narrative about recent contacts with each customer, who made it, what was said, provisions for follow-up, etc. If there is no CRM, then ask how people know when to follow-up. The issue here is that the information related to each customer is the property of the SMDC, not the salesperson, and it needs to reside in the SMDC's "head," not just the individual's. Even in this enlightened time where SMDCs "get it" about IT, some companies will think they don't need to spend that money. They are dead-wrong. Having no CRM or comparable application (ACT!, for instance) is one of the most expensive ways I know of to "save money." And an SMDC looking to put itself up for sale without a CRM or something close to it is going to leave a *lot* of money on the table.

Do salespeople enter information into a CRM, or do non-Luddite clerical people? Why not, or why? Do they use technology for record-keeping, electronic "ticklers," submitting orders, etc.? Is the mix of salary and commission sufficient to motivate and stretch, but not break, the sales force? How is the sales group organized—by geography, distribution channel, target market, company size, etc.? Are there incentives to develop new customers? Is there a target percentage of new customers each year? Is there a target percentage of revenues from new customers each year? What is the churn? What is the "life" of the typical customer relationship? Do salespeople work by appointment or do they drop-in? If by appointment, who makes them? Do the salespeople have trouble seeing whom they need to see at the customer's worksite? Is the product catalog online or on CD? Is there streaming video online or on CD? Are training materials available online? Are there FAQs for more-complicated machinery and equipment online? What rate of warranty claims has the SMDC experienced (if applicable)? Does it own its salespeople's vehicles, or do they? If the former, do the vehicles stay at the SMDC or the individuals' homes overnight? If the latter, is there either withholding or a 1099 issued for a "personal component of vehicle use"?

Operations: In an SMDC, the flow within Operations varies. I'm going to discuss several different functions within it. The actual structures you encounter will vary, but the functions themselves are essential.

Inbound Logistics—How often do orders from vendors arrive? Are they unpacked and put in locations at the same time orders are being picked, or is the stocking done during off-peak times? If incoming and outgoing orders are processed at the same time, do changes in inventory hit the system in real time or are they batched? What features prevent a SKU from going to the wrong location? How are overflows handled? Is there a warehouse map "on every street corner"? If not, how do they know what's where? If SKUs are heavy, are employees tested for physical strength and agility?

Order Entry/Sales Desk/Order Processing—Start with where orders come into the SMDC from the field or from customers directly, whether by e-mail, snail mail, fax, phone, or off the website. The key in this function is to automate as much as possible and, especially, for inventory to be relieved in real-time, when the SMDC accepts the order, *not* when it's picked. Otherwise, orders will either be submitted (if off the website) or will be accepted for merchandise that is not there. That puts a strain on customer relationships and embarrasses the people who have to tell the customers when, in fact, the outage could have been spotted with affordable technology. If there is a sales order function, are the people staffing it motivated through incentives to sell more or encourage customers to upgrade to better products? Are pick tickets transmitted electronically to the warehouse or do they move as pieces of paper?

Order Picking—Are orders pulled in reverse sequence from that in which they will be delivered or shipped? Are they pulled based on a pick-ticket image viewed on an iPad or other electronic device? Is the heaviest part of an order pulled first or are the SKUs pulled according to the most efficient path in the warehouse? Is more than one order pulled at a time by the same picker? If so, how is commingling of SKUs avoided? Is each SKU that is pulled scanned and matched against the SKU number on the pick ticket in order to minimize errors? How is the productivity of pickers measured? Are there incentives to minimize picking errors? How is an exception on a pick ticket handled (i.e., a SKU shown to be in stock isn't)? If the picker rides a fork lift or other mechanized vehicle, does the vehicle move automatically from one SKU location to the next or does the picker have to drive it? Either way, how is congestion avoided or minimized in the picking process?

Outbound Logistics—For orders that are delivered by the SMDC, are they aggregated on a dock to which delivery vehicles (or third-party trucks) have easy access? Are orders placed on delivery vehicles in "LIFO sequence"? Is the delivery route predetermined through automation according to the deliveries to be made? What about the personal appearance, cleanliness, hygiene, etc., of delivery personnel? (Drivers for FedEx and UPS are the models here.) Does the same person drive the same vehicle each day? How are "rush orders" handled? Is there a shuttle van to deliver emergency orders? Have there been customer complaints about a driver or a delivery and, if so, what is the process for handling each type? Do the delivery vehicles have GPS-tracking devices with real-time traffic-monitoring to help them avoid congestion? If the SMDC makes deliveries, are its drivers' records checked annually? Do drivers have company credit cards to purchase gas and oil? If so, are the charges for each credit card aggregated on a monthly billing? Has the company considered outsourcing management of its vehicle fleet? Why or why not?

Warehouse Operations in General—Pay close attention to where inventory is stored and to labeling of bins or containers. If they are not labeled or bar-coded, low inventory turn relative to an SMDC industry composite is certain. Do employees wear hardhats and adhere to good safety practices? Is the Operations area clean and well-organized, or is junk spread around randomly? Do the walkways have boundaries defined by colored tape or paint? Are statistics for mis-pulled merchandise kept and tracked? Are picking errors analyzed for patterns to determine whether responsibility for them rests with the design of the system or with individual pickers? What is the SMDC's EMR (experience modification ratio)? Are there incentives to minimize lost-time accidents? If not, are there signs posted in the warehouse that track how many days have elapsed since the last lost-time mishap? Be sure you get a handle on what appears to be the nature and tone of the working relationships among the lead persons in Sales, Operations, and Purchasing—I have never seen an SMDC that did not have too much inventory; that suggests that the desires of Sales folks usually trump everything else . . . even at the cost of working-capital deficits.

Are there any underground tanks (e.g., for gasoline)? If so, has there been an environmental review and report? Are there any EPA exposures for disposal of scrap, solvents, lubricants, etc.? If so, are MSDS sheets posted and accessible?

How are bottlenecks in the warehouse handled? What is the "expedite rate" of incoming orders (higher is less efficient)? What is the turnaround time on a new order? What is the cut-off time for an order to go out the same day it is received? What percentage of pick tickets make it to the warehouse with at least one item that was supposed to be in stock but, instead, must be back-ordered?

Customer Care/Service: What is the rate of customer complaints per hundred or per thousand orders delivered or shipped? How much does it cost to resolve a customer complaint? How far up the SMDC's management food chain does a complaint usually go? Does the CEO personally conduct *all* interviews with exiting customers? Is Customer Care outsourced? If so, to whom, why, and how is it working?[1] Are customers assigned to particular Customer Care reps? If so, how is the decision made as to which rep gets assigned which customers? What are the incentives in Customer Care that motivate employees to resolve problems? Are those calling or e-mailing Customer Care solicited to rate their experience afterward? Are complaints to or requests from Customer Care tracked and aggregated as to type of complaint or request for help and/or the line of business of the customer in question? What feedback and liaison mechanisms are there between Sales and Customer Service?

1. There might well be a good argument for outsourcing Customer Care, but I have yet to hear it. It defeats the whole idea of being "close to the customer." Besides, those nearest a problem are best able to solve it, which is why outsourcing of Customer Care is a bad idea. SMDCs that outsource this vital function are making a loud and risk-increasing announcement about their business perspective.

HR: Many SMDCs are not big enough to enjoy the division of labor that would give them a full-time HR professional; don't be surprised to see this function handled part-time, either through Finance or the CEO's/Owner's administrative assistant. Now, I don't want to hurt any readers' feelings with what I'm about to say here, but in most SMDCs, the HR function is mostly about compliance, not policy. Therefore, the single most important question to ask whoever handles HR in-house is this: "Do you know the different headcounts at which various pieces of workplace regulation kick in?" If the individual cannot answer that one, then the SMDC, especially one that is growing and has fewer than 50 employees, has its backside stuck out in the sun.

Does the SMDC have an NSNDA (Non-Solicitation/Non-Disclosure Agreement) in place with *every* employee, including the owner(s)? These are crucial to hiring and keeping better people, we think. It doesn't carry the legal uncertainty about enforceability that a non-compete agreement has. Based on what we hear, we believe that NSNDAs are easy to enforce, if enforcement becomes necessary.

Beyond that question are these: How does the SMDC fill new positions? (If it is resisting unionization or has had a "de-cert," yet fills its positions from internal referrals, look out—it is only a matter of time before someone files a complaint with EEOC.[2]) Does the HR person know what the SMDC's IR (Incidence Rate) is? How often are performance reviews given . . . or are they?[3] Are employees given a right to disagree, in writing, with performance reviews? How closely is pay tied to performance? Are raises, even cost-of-livings, automatic? Can an individual employee access her/his HR records online? Is the Company Manual available online? How often is the manual updated? Does the current version *accurately* reflect current policy at the SMDC? Does the company use Personal Development Programs (PDPs) to prepare its people for higher levels of responsibility? What percentage of base pay are the typical employee's fringe benefits? Does the SMDC have an effective disciplinary program in place? Does it have people on its payroll that it should have fired? If so, why are they still there? (Remember to include payroll taxes, FUTA, SUTA, vacation, personal days, and holidays.) Does the firm have a company newsletter or other means of communicating HR benefits and choices to the families of employees? Does the firm use employee wellness to try to reduce healthcare claims and insurance premiums?[4]

Finance: I suspect that most readers come from financial backgrounds. That should make you comfortable poking around in finance-related Routines. As we said earlier, a chart of accounts is an information system that serves three masters: (1) the GAAP master; (2) the IRS/tax master; and (3) the management-information master. (3) always gets short shrift.

---

2. Equal Employment Opportunity Commission (www.eeoc.gov).
3. TQM guru W. Edwards Deming was an intransigent and outspoken opponent of performance reviews. See his book, *Out of the Crisis*, 101-120.
4. Burd, "Cutting Health-Care Costs."

> If the chart of accounts was not approached with the word "design" at the front of the mind of the individual responsible for creating it, well, it's a simple matter of garbage-in/garbage-out. Before the first account is created, the senior managers sould be pressed—hard, if necessary—to define just what kind of information they need to make decisions and run the company. I've asked that questions dozens of times over the years, and the response I often got was what I call the thousand-mile-stare-in-the-four-foot-room. It's a totally blank look, and then some. They are stumped. So I sat down with them and began brainstorming. I got a whiteboard or flipcharts and went hard after it. Sooner or later, they stumbled over what they wanted. But it always took several hours because (a) no one had ever asked them that question, and (b) they never thought that having that kind of information was possible in the first place.

If the chart is designed with*out* management-information needs in mind, the result is data, not information. It lacks sufficient detail. It likely makes inadequate use of sub-accounts to create the information that those at the top need to be able to run the business. That, in turn, gives rise to that paralyzing, energy-sapping, and time-wasting disease called "Excel-itis."

How long does it take for monthly financial statements to be published? Are there standard closing entries, including payroll accrual? What is the process for opening an account for a new vendor? For a new customer? Does the SMDC issue 1099s to unincorporated vendors and LLCs? Assess the usefulness of the Chart of Accounts. Are spreadsheets running amok in the finance function? Does the company have a lockbox? Does it send its invoices electronically? How often? Does it send monthly statements in addition to invoices (a terrible practice—companies pay from invoices, not statements—save the postage and the aggravation)? What do the finance people do when they get invoices and statements from the same vendor? ("Shred the statements" is the right answer, but ask.) Does it record invoices that offer a discount for prompt payment at "gross" or at "net"? Does the SMDC check credit before extending it? How past due does an invoice have to be to trigger a collection effort? How does the SMDC monitor bankruptcy filings? Are collection efforts noted in a CRM or other customer master file? Does the wholesaler accept credit cards? Nothing sexist here, but, in my experience, women are far better at collections than men. Trust me.

CEO or Owner: How does s/he spend her/his time? Does s/he appear to know when to delegate and when not to?[5] Does the CEO use technology to make her/his life easier?[6] If relatives are on the payroll, do they get treated differently from non-family members? Does the CEO publish his/her own PDP where all employees can see it? Does the CEO "understand the numbers"? How does the CEO hear criticism of her/his performance? Does the CEO get an annual physical? Is the CEO developing at least two (2) internal successors? At what age does the CEO expect to retire? Does the CEO have a blog? How does s/he communicate with customers? With employees?

5. An inability or refusal to delegate is a constraint on an SMDC's growth rate.
6. If not, not many other people in the SMDC will, either.

Board: Because of the cost of D&O insurance, savvy SMDCs rely on a Council of Advisors, rather than a formal Board mechanism. Councils are highly effective and deliver an impressive benefit-to-cost ratio if they're used properly.[7] How often does the Board/Council meet? Does it get meeting materials at least a week in advance? Does it get a chance to contribute to the Agenda? Does it review budgets? Capital expenditures? Succession issues? Litigation? How were members of the governing body chosen? For how long do they serve? Are term limits in place? How much are they paid? With what policy issues does the Board/Council grapple? Does the Board require credit and public-records checks on its key management and financial people to be conducted annually (with their permission, of course)? Do "rising stars" working for the SMDC make presentations to the Board/Council?

The Wrap

Understanding Routines is the key to valuing and advising small and medium-sized distribution companies successfully. That is why I devoted this chapter to Routines. Yes, we got far into the weeds on this stuff. But if we're going to understand—*really understand*—how the SMDC functions and, at least as important, *why* it works the way it does, we must do a deep dive into Routines. They are seldom the only cause of outlier metrics in SMDCs, but they are the big one.

As I said earlier in this *Guide*, the key areas of concern in valuing and working with SMDCs are IT, marketing, and inventory control. The latter two are relatively easy and straightforward to assess because they have a direct and obvious impact on easing margin pressure. IT, on the other hand, is both more pervasive and more pernicious. Much of what I wrote in this chapter about purchasing, sales, and various aspects of operations carried a heavy IT overlay. I'm not trying to make you into a geek because I don't have, nor do I want, that kind of in-depth knowledge myself. But one needs to be curious in order to be knowledgeable about the deployment of IT in wholesaling. It can be a source of value drivers or of value destroyers. Too often in SMDCs, it is the latter because owners choose to "save money" in the most expensive way possible: by throwing people at problems. That is a surefire way to go out of business.

That's a wrap. We now move to Chapter 11 where we will discuss SPARC archetypes in the context of SMDCs.

7. Contact me directly (SPARC@beckmill.com) to receive PDFs of a four-part series I wrote for the "Business & Industry Supplement" of the *CPA Letter*

Profiles of SPARC Archetypes in the SMDC Space

Introduction

This chapter is straightforward. We will begin with a short refresher of the SPARC archetypes first mentioned in Chapter 1 and then elaborated upon in Chapters 4 and 8. I will then profile dyads of the archetypes: the Exploiter/Economiser first, followed by the Explorer/Experimenter. I do these in pairs because the only difference between each archetype in a given dyad is the scope on which they compete; that difference helps define the Domain. A few comments about the Equivocator will bring us to The Wrap at the end.

Refresher

Before reconnecting with Porter's 2 x 2 matrix of "generic competitive strategies,"[1] which I used as the underlying rationale for the SPARC archetypes, I want to mention the work of MIT's Arnoldo Hax and consultant Dean Wilde on their "Delta Model."[2] The crux of their argument for a different typology is that Porter's perspective was rooted in *products*; the resource-based view of the firm, in their view, was *factor-driven*. They assert that their Delta Model is *customer-driven* because, as they write:

> We believe that a firm owes itself to its customers. They are the ultimate repository of all the firm's activities. At the heart of management and, certainly, at the heart of strategy, resides the customer. We have to serve the customer in a distinctive way if we expect to enjoy superior performance. The name of the game is to attract, to satisfy, and to retain the customer.

Their approach is rooted in what they call "customer bonding," which is a bit on the pop-psych side for my tastes, but decide for yourself. They provide three ways to accomplish such bonding:

- Best Product
- System Lock-In
- Total Customer Solutions

1. Porter, *Competitive Strategies*, Chapter 2.
2. Hax & Wilde, *The Delta Project*.

Space constraints preclude further elaboration. However, though I find Hax and Wilde's focus on customers intriguing, Hax and Wilde do not delineate between cost leadership and differentiation, which I think is essential. But I mention it in case you want to follow up.

Our adaptation of Porter's 2 x 2 matrix follows below. I know you've seen it earlier in this book, but, as I've said, there is value in replicating crucial ideas and constructs:

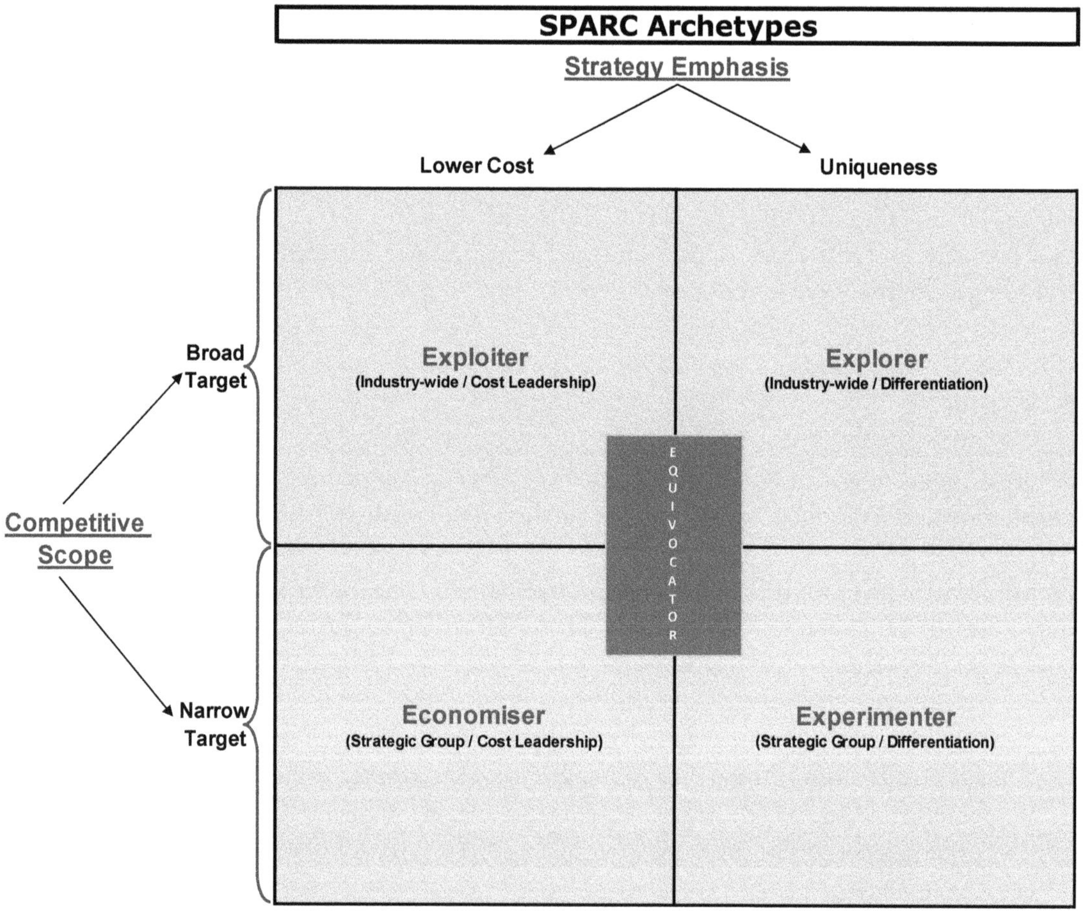

Each of the five archetypes has a certain pattern of characteristics that tend to repeat themselves in firms across domains. These are easy to remember because each starts with the letter E—as in "enterprise."[3] We begin with the key ideas from a classic paper: exploration and exploitation.[4] The ideas that March expressed in his paper reinforce my preference for the Porter matrix over the Delta Model. Here is the opening paragraph from that paper:

3. This connection originated with my friend, colleague, collaborator, and sometime co-conspirator, Russ Hudson, DBA, CPM, founder of StrategeMetrix, LLC. His approach to valuation is also rooted in the strategy discipline.

4. March, "Exploration and Exploitation."

> A central concern of studies of adaptive processes is the relation between the exploration of new possibilities and the exploitation of old certainties. Exploration includes things captured by terms such as search, variation, risk taking, experimentation, play, flexibility, discovery, innovation. Exploitation includes such things as refinement, choice, production, efficiency, selection, implementation, execution. Adaptive systems that engage in exploration to the exclusion of exploitation are likely to find that they suffer the costs of experimentation without gaining many of its benefits. They exhibit too many undeveloped new ideas and too little distinctive competence. Conversely, systems that engage in exploitation to the exclusion of exploration are likely to find themselves trapped in suboptimal stable equilibria. As a result, maintaining an appropriate balance between exploration and exploitation is a primary factor in system survival and prosperity.[5]

And:

> Learning, analysis, imitation, regeneration, and technological change are major components of any effort to improve organizational performance and strengthen competitive advantage. Each involves adaptation and a delicate trade-off between exploration and exploitation. . . . The essence of exploitation is the refinement and extension of existing competences, technologies, and paradigms. Its returns are positive, proximate, and predictable. The essence of exploration is experimentation with new alternatives. Its returns are uncertain, distant, and often negative. . . . [A]daptation [can] lead to a tendency to substitute exploitation of known alternatives for the exploration of unknown ones, to increase the reliability of performance rather more than its mean. . . . An emphasis on exploitation also compromises competitive position where finishing near the top is important. Knowledge-based increases in average performance can be insufficient to overcome the adverse effects produced by reductions in variability.[6]

These excerpts will be instructive as we learn about the characteristics of Exploiters/Economisers vs. Explorers/Experimenters. I hope that readers will remember to see if March's thoughts fit the Equivocator, too.

In the next three sections, I discuss the characteristics and features of each dyad in the context of Strategy, People, Architecture, Routines, and Culture. As I said earlier in this chapter, the only difference between the archetypes constituting each pair is the scope of competition: most SMDCs compete in a strategic group.

Exploiter & Economiser. We chose the Exploiter as our name for Porter's industrywide competitor embracing cost leadership. Its strategic-group sibling is the Economiser. Besides conveying the essential notion of doing more of the same, rather than something different, it also calls attention to the destructive potential of miserliness. Because of their focus on low cost, these two archetypes

5. Ibid., 71.
6. Ibid., 85.

tend to be the market leaders in their domains. They embrace change and innovation—and the variability in performance that attends both—only if lower costs result. That, in turn, enables it to reduce its price and create mischief for its cost-cutting (and self-destructive) emulators and its we're-gonna-do-it-different rivals.

Strategy: Cost leadership. The Exploiter/Economiser has a narrow field of vision. In striving to be the best at what it does, it continually tries to do it faster, better, and cheaper. It believes that low price will insulate it from the ravages of innovation and change. In choosing the sure thing over the maybe thing, it opts for the short term over the long term and for what has worked over what might work better. As March's paper emphasized, there is likely less variation in the performance of Exploiters/Economisers, but at a possible high price, in the longer term: survival.

People: With Exploiters/Economisers, we most often find a scientist or an engineer in the CEO's chair. Given the stereotype of accountants as penny-pinchers, one might believe that they would be high performers as CEOs of Exploiters/Economisers. We have seen that only once. Every other CEO we have seen within these two archetypes was a graduate scientist, engineer, or non-degreed founder who would have graduated in engineering or one of the hard sciences had events, upbringing, or lack of funds not intervened.

Despite the fact that he headed a manufacturer, not an SMDC, my nominee for the textbook CEO of an Exploiter/Economiser is former Intel CEO Andy Grove, holder of a Ph.D. in chemical engineering from Cal/Berkeley. His motto, which was also the title of his best-selling book, was "Only the paranoid survive." Recall the story I told early in Chapter 1 of this *Guide* about his directive to two shift leaders to improve their shifts' productivity at the Albuquerque plant by 15% . . . "per month."

Architecture: The Exploiter/Economiser tends to have a "steep" organization; think "centralized decision-making." At the divisional level, it relies on a functional reporting structure with its attendant "silo mentality." Because of this rigidity, it tends to experience lower turnover, which makes for less diversity, which in itself can create high hurdles in times of external turbulence (think macroenvironment and domain) when new ways of thinking and defining the business might be needed. It emphasizes efficiency—doing things right—sometimes at the expense of effectiveness—doing the right thing.

Information is shared across functions only when it leads to lower cost; employees are seldom cross-trained because the variation introduced by cross-training would increase costs. The goal is low-cost, error-free operations that deliver a simple product or service at a market-leading price. Innovation intrudes only if it pushes the Exploiter/Economiser toward the twin sirens of lower cost and higher quality.

Routines: Exploiters/Economisers want easy-to-replicate routines. If those are intuitive, so much the better. They are by-the-book SMDCs that are obsessive-compulsive about documentation. Their aim is no variation in low value-added routines. In fact, they'll try to eliminate variation in all routines.

Because Routines apply to how decisions are made, Exploiters/Economisers are genetically predisposed to follow what worked before, and that is a good predictor of how they will make decisions. The ringer is when a new approach, a new perspective, or a domain-shaking innovation occurs: Exploiters and Economisers are a new threat, a new opportunity, prone to "going with what brung us," as legendary Texas Longhorn football coach Darrell Royal used to say.

Culture: The culture of Exploiters and Economisers tends toward "quant"—that is, engineering and math. They love to measure. They love certainty. They love efficiency. "You can't manage it if you don't measure it" is their mantra, like a Gregorian chant. Creativity is rewarded only if it reduces costs or enhances quality. The cultural focus emphasizes market share and is willing to absorb lower short-term margins to build it.

The Risks of Exploiters/Economisers: The biggest risk they face is that their focus on efficiency and low cost leaves them vulnerable to being blind-sided by innovation. Exploiters/Economisers also tend to discount the importance of marketing because they think the sole considerations in customers' buying decisions are price and quality.

> ***SMDC context:*** *Although I'm forever pounding my spoon on my high chair about the Experimenter being the strategy of choice for nearly all SMDCs, I would be remiss if I failed to note that no SMDC should think that being a great Experimenter is sufficient. It's not. I expect the margin pressure that now pervades the wholesaling space to increase. That means that SMDCs must focus relentlessly on high productivity employees, getting the work done right the first time, and constantly searching for better ways to execute.*

Explorer & Experimenter. Explorers and Experimenters differ from Exploiters and Economisers about as much as a sand storm differs from a sand flea. These SPARC dyads are almost polar opposites. As noted earlier in this chapter, the Explorer/Experimenter competes on "uniqueness"—recall that Porter called it *perceived uniqueness*, which might sound a bit cynical to some, but, as management guru Tom Peters says, "Perception is all there is." It *is* reality.

Because they thrive on being different and "looking for new," they risk falling short. Their returns tend to have greater volatility, as March's paper leads us to expect—greater risk due to greater uncertainty—but these two SMDC archetypes can also grow faster than the typical Exploiter/Economiser. *Can* grow faster. Not that they *will*, but the potential is there. Where Exploiters and Economisers want tried, true, and low-cost, Explorers and Experimenters embrace untried, maybe-true/we'll-find-out-as-we-build-that-new-plane-while-we-fly-it, and higher price. Where Exploiters and Economisers seek replication and economies of scale, Explorers and Experimenters embrace innovation and economies of scope (more SKUs, for instance).

Explorers/Experimenters have different belief systems about how the world works. Because differentiation is about *unique capabilities*, they seek to make their beliefs a reality. They do so by using Barney's VRINO tool—they aim to create capabilities that are valuable to customers, rare in the domain, inimitable/non-substitutable by rivals except at great disruption to their current operations, and organizationally aligned with their existing incentive systems.

Strategy: Differentiation. Cost matters, but higher margin matters more. That is because Explorers/Experimenters are not market leaders, so increased margins must come from either a higher price point or services that bring customers back—knowledge of complex products is an example. They must continually develop new capabilities *and* survey their customers to ensure that they value these capabilities enough to continue to pay for them. That latter activity is often missing at SMDC differentiators. The key for the Explorer/Experimenter SMDC is to spot unique services embedded in the resources or resource combinations that pervade the company.

People: For Explorers/Experimenters, it's all about marketing. In the SMDC space, it's about logistics, too—which is a key aspect of marketing and one that might not be affirmed the way it needs to be. Top-flight logistics can hold down costs, increase throughput, and raise customer satisfaction and loyalty. CEOs and owners often come from backgrounds in marketing. We also see SMDC CEOs from sales, but not often. This might—*might*—be because people from the sales side often don't make good CEOs for SMDCs any more than the top salesperson at an auto dealership makes a great General Manager of his or her own franchise.

Our exemplar SMDC Explorer CEO is Kevin Murai, who was the #2 guy at market leader Ingram Micro before taking over at the #3 wholesaler of computers, Synnex Corp. This is a sector with paper-thin margins (COGS: 94.5%). Murai's background includes extensive "distribution channel experience." The "core competencies" on the Synnex website emphasize "real-time linkages in the supply chain and after-market product support."

Architecture: With Explorers and Experimenters, most decisions are decentralized. Unlike the steep isosceles-triangle type of organization structure one sees at cost leaders, the structures at differentiators tend to be flat (few layers) with wide spans of control driven by technology and culture. The flat structure allows Explorers/Experimenters to move fast and make quick decisions. Such a structure also discourages silos and the proverbial "it's not my job" attitude.

SMDCs invest most of their assets in receivables and inventory. Therefore, they need high liquidity and strong cash flow. Inventory turns of 12x are common, as are DSO < 45 days. Because wholesalers are under continuous margin pressure in this age of Walmart and the "going-direct" mindset that the Internet can instill, the differentiators in the sector try to avoid long-term debt, though they do need a working-capital line of credit.

Routines: As we noted earlier, one of the keys to minimizing variation in arenas with Internet-induced falling margins is investing in technology. This is especially true in operations, purchasing, invoicing, and collections. An SMDC that still gets its customers' checks delivered via snail mail is an SMDC whose costs are higher than they need to be. Ditto if it mails invoices or, heaven forbid, *statements*. If its website isn't set up for ordering, then it is substituting labor for capital, which means it has it backward.

Culture: Because Explorers/Experimenters are not market leaders, they must de-emphasize price and emphasize something that customers find unique and attractive. In a cut-throat business such as computer-wholesaling, players cannot ignore cost, of course. But, at the same time, an emphasis on product knowledge, trusting business relationships with customers and suppliers, and lightning-fast fulfillment can enable an Experimenter to conserve that most precious of all economic resources, time.

Differentiators seek diversity, not because it's politically correct or legally mandated. They want it because they know that a group-think kind of mindset is fatal. They want "new," so they must hire "diverse." Different worldviews, experiences, and backgrounds can be a key source of innovation in SMDCs. Because successful differentiators tend to have strong and cohesive cultures, "Hire on values" is a mantra we have heard from SMDCs many times.

The Risks of Explorers/Experimenters: The biggest risk they face is that their focus on delivering greater value can cause them to ignore an Exploiter or Economiser whose efficiency widens the price gap. Explorers and Experimenters can also get seduced by the temptation to conserve working capital by reducing the number of SKUs. Telling a retailer whose customer wants to buy a big-ticket item tomorrow that the item is back-ordered can be a real killer for an SMDC.

> ***SMDC context:*** *Complexity increases costs. Therefore, SMDCs should seek to simplify, simplify, simplify. That does* **not** *mean to dumb down. Simplicity is hard to come by in a complex world. "Simple" is not synonymous with "easy," either. Simplicity comes from conscious and ongoing attention to nuances in strategy, customers, and operating efficiencies.*

Equivocator. Last and deservedly least, we have the Equivocator. You will know one when you see it. Most of its decisions are contradictory. Chaos is the norm. It will not commit. It clings doggedly to the impossible idea that it can be all things to all comers. It preaches lower costs one day and branding the next. It ignores the saying I heard in my years growing up in Texas: "There's nothin' in the middle of the road but white lines and dead armadillos."

It has no vision of what it is, wants to be, or might be. It makes it up as it goes along . . . for quite a while, sometimes. Its idea of long-range planning is where to go for lunch tomorrow. It never has enough time to do it right the first time, yet it always can find the time to come back and do it over. And over. And over.

Margin pressure on distributors tends to put Equivocators out of business quickly, so there are few real-life examples of the Equivocator. My favorite is an industrial-supply company client—we'll call it Mid-Atlantic Equivocators, LLC ("MAE")—for whom we did a valuation in the late 1990s. It was a venerable firm then doing about $12 million in annual revenues. Margins were falling due to pricing pressure that came from the Internet and from hard-ball rivals using technology to drive down costs.

MAE had a top-flight IT system that spit out purchase orders based on lead time, safety stock, etc. The problem was that its CEO didn't trust the computer system. So he *manually overrode* almost every automated purchase order. Oh, and did I mention that his company had over 40,000 SKUs in its warehouse? He'd opt for low-cost goods one day and SKUs with differentiating features the next. He wouldn't follow manufacturers' guidelines for pricing because he was sure that he knew his market better than they did. That's not a hanging offense, but he also *changed* prices whenever he felt like it. That stirred up customers, of course, so he and his key people spent a lot of time fighting fires that they could easily have avoided with a disciplined and consistent approach to how they intended for the company to compete. The following is a "SPARC profile" of MAE:

Strategy: MAE had no strategy. It offered beefed-up customer service one day and bare-bones support the next. Differentiation, if it came at all, came on the spur of the moment in terms of which SKUs to promote and which capabilities to develop. MAE's survival was at issue continually.

People: Equivocators are often run by financial professionals. MAE's CEO had been a teacher before going into the family business. I always wondered why because he seemed to think like many accountants I've known. Folks with such career antecedents can be frugal to the point that it boomerangs. Few of the ones I've met seem to understand that there are good ways to save money, and there are expensive ways. A singular focus on minimizing outlays can turn out to be the most self-destructive and expensive choice available.

MAE's CEO had zero use for or knowledge of marketing. He was so focused on cost that he forgot about value. To be sure, the payoffs from marketing are neither immediate nor easy to measure. But he believed that customers bought only on price, despite conclusive evidence to the contrary from a customer satisfaction survey we conducted.

As tight-fisted as MAE's CEO was, he could squander resources in breathtaking ways through all of the flipflops, redos, and mad dashes in opposite directions on successive days. He would never make a thoughtful, disciplined, and well-reasoned commitment—to a clear-eyed and appropriate strategy, first and foremost—and then see it through. The idea of basing strategy on features that were unique to MAE was alien to him.

Architecture: MAE's CEO had no clear vision of Architecture. Like other situations where a little knowledge is dangerous, he changed the organization design often. In the process, he destroyed whatever confidence his employees had in his judgment. Good employees—one in particular who finally threw up his hands and relocated to Roanoke to become the CEO of a substantial company—flew the coop. "Reorganize" was MAE's stock in trade. The CEO's thinking was "linear"—looking at the world through a straw. The idea of multitasking, outsourcing, or thinking ahead is something he never had the time, the money, or the stomach for, yet he always had time to come back and redo and redo and redo. He was like a tippling alcoholic who thrives on the chaos that a booze addiction creates.

Routines: MAE's Routines were conspicuous by their inconsistency. In fact, the CEO documented almost nothing, pleading that he didn't have the time. If an SMDC is behind on its bank recs, as this one was (eight months when I arrived on the scene), you had better fasten your seatbelt. You've only scratched the surface of the chaos.

Since the typical reader of this *Guide* is, like me, a financial professional, I recommend that you spend some time early—before you get the gig, if possible—in the accounting area of the SMDC. When I did that at MAE, I came away stupefied. It was mayhem. And, as I have said before, chaos in accounting is just a reflection of chaos throughout the enterprise. Like other SMDC CEOs and owners we've met, MAE's CEO believed that the accounting department was independent of the operations of the rest of the company. Late and inaccurate financials were the rule, and it was a zoo at inventory time. MAE didn't do cycle-counting because it didn't have time for that, either.

Culture: Measurements at MAE were few. Those it did have were wrong, because politics dominated its culture. There were no core values, no consistent set of beliefs, no predictability. Those from upbringings where chaos was the norm often seem content in the tumultuous daily life inside an Equivocator, and MAE was no exception. MAE had a disproportionate number of alcoholics and food-addicted employees who accepted everything as inevitable, bought into the craziness, stayed, and became part of the problem, even as they watched sane people flee. The sane ones had options. The crazies didn't.

Like other Equivocators, MAE refused to quit. "We'd be letting Grandpa down if we did that," the CEO snapped at me one day. It "bought" orders with low prices, even though it lost money on them. Because it lacked commitment, it assumed everything was temporary. A few years ago, it went through Chapter 7. A few months ago, I drove past the old CEO's home. It was for sale. "By Owner," of course.

The Wrap

Because a given archetype tends to exhibit certain characteristics related to strategy, people, architecture, routines, and culture, each has normative implications. That is, each *should* function in certain predictable ways on each of those five elements. Equivocators are apt to get their backs up if someone like you or me begins to question them about why they do things the way they do.

I've been told, "You just don't understand," "We're too small to have routines—things just aren't that predictable around here," and my favorite: "Our business is different." Sure, it is, but only at the margin. But I've heard that "Our business is different" line so often that we just call it "O.B.I.D." in our shop.

As I have emphasized repeatedly in this *Guide*, the typical SMDC should be an Experimenter. That is, it should implement a strategy of differentiation on a limited-scope basis. Being an Experimenter offers many more ways to be successful than being, say, an Economiser, which has but one: low cost. To the extent that an SMDC is close to its customers, has open and bidirectional lines of internal communication, and monitors how valuable its customers see its unique capabilities, the Experimenter should be successful, even in a perilous sector such as wholesaling. Some SMDCs in small markets are fortunate that their competitors lack the insight to compete on anything except price.

Yet we seldom see Experimenters with commitment—the real commitment of which Pankaj Ghemawat has written.[7] My hunch is that too many SMDCs still don't get it about marketing. In a world of compressing margins, SMDCs have only a couple of choices: reduce costs or differentiate. This is why I like the March paper so much: "exploitation vs. exploration" is just a wonderful way to look at "cost leadership vs. differentiation." The irony is that the owners of these marketing-challenged SMDCs think nothing of buying a Lexus and tossing their Ping golf clubs in the trunk.

Onward and upward: Chapter 12 is about preparing for and conducting the interviews in the on-site visit. This phase of a valuation engagement is a vital, yet underappreciated and underused process in most valuation shops. I'll be pounding my spoon on my high chair about it.

7. Ghemawat, *Commitment.*

Preparing for and Conducting the On-Site Visit

Introduction

Too many valuation professionals treat the on-site visit like a social call. In every engagement I've ever been involved in—not just SMDCs, but *all* of 'em—doing that would have been a mistake. These interviews are *where* we find out *why*. And, as I've said repeatedly in this treatise, if we cannot explain the whys, then, in the middle-market sector of closely helds, we will get the valuation right only by chance. I would sooner take up cordless bungee-jumping than forgo this visit.

Now, we all know that large companies are easier to value than not-large ones.[1] That is by way of saying that the site visit, like the subject of company-level unsystematic risk, has received little ink in the big valuation reference books because those big-book authors don't work in the same markets as you and I. The big guns have priced themselves out of it. You and I are still here, and on-site interviews are the biggest of big deals in our valuation process.

A Key Insight

An organization's ability to grow profitably depends on what Penrose calls "entrepreneurial competence."[2] She defines it as follows:

> [It is] a psychological predisposition on the part of individuals to take a chance in the hope of gain, and, in particular, to commit effort and resources to speculative activity. The decision on the part of a firm to investigate the prospective profitability of expansion is an [entrepreneurial] decision, in the sense that whenever expansion is neither pressing nor particularly obvious, a firm has the choice of continuing in its existing course or of expending effort and committing resources to the investigation of whether there are further opportunities of which it is not yet aware. This is a decision which depends on the "enterprise" [*a.k.a. entrepreneurial competence*] of the firm and not on sober calculations as to whether the investigation is likely to turn up enticing opportunities, for it is, in effect, the decision to make some calculations. This is truly the "first" decision, and it is here that the "spirit of enterprise," or a general entrepreneurial bias in favor of "growth," has perhaps its greatest significance. . . . In any case, the decision to search for opportunities is an enterprising decision requiring entrepreneurial intuition and imagination and must precede the "economic" decision to go ahead with the examination of opportunities for expansion.[3]

---

1. The irony is that they're also willing to pay more.
2. Penrose, *Theory of Growth*: 31-64; bracketed words/italics added.
3. Ibid., 33-34.

I have quoted from Penrose often in this book, and with good reason: her insights are spot-on relevant to our work with SMBs. Although her book first came out over a half-century ago, I cannot recommend it highly enough. *Anyone who is around either high-growth companies or organizations that think they want to grow rapidly will benefit—big time—from reading this book.* It is one of those rare "WOW!" books.

The Primary Purposes of the Visit

There are two of them:

- to get a soup-to-nuts, function-by-function walk-through of the operating side of the business

and

- to conduct interviews with selected employees

Operations Review: This is the full-Monty version of the walk-through you did before you drafted the Engagement Letter for the SMDC.

Interviews: There is a way to conduct these and many ways not to. I have made about every mistake possible in these interviews. As a result, we have a process that took time to create, but is simple and straightforward.

Scheduling the Visit

You should infer from the position of this chapter relative to others in this *Guide* that the visit occurs relatively late in the valuation process. In our shop, where we have a typical cycle of 80-90 days for an engagement, the on-site interviews occur in the Day 60-65 range. They don't happen sooner because we are not ready sooner. We do as much analysis as we can—external risk assessment, constructing a composite, doing the preliminary financial analysis, and taking a first pass at guideline public companies—*before* we ask for time from the client and its employees. If we're not ready, we'll waste everyone's time, including our own.

Preparing the CEO

During the run-up to getting the Engagement Letter signed, we describe the valuation process to the owner or CEO. In fact, we have constructed a short narrative that walks that individual through the valuation process at about a 30,000-foot level. Included in our conversation about the process is the on-site visit. We tell the owner/CEO that we are going to ask questions aimed at uncovering the underlying causes of certain performance metrics whose identity we don't then know. Nor do we know with whom we are going to want to talk. We say that we are also going to solicit attitudes about the company, its work environment, senior management, and how business is conducted. We emphasize that we are *not* looking for negative information, only information that is accurate. We say that we will share what we find, but we will not knowingly betray the identity of any individuals. In other words, what we share is an overall picture of what we learned during those interviews. We have never had an owner or CEO object to this approach. We are very matter-of-fact about it and make it clear that it is a normal part of our process.

We also let the CEO know that how we are received at the SMDC will depend to a large degree on how she or he presents us. We want to get information, of course, but, more than that, we want to help the owner and his or her company become worth more. That applies even in situations where there is no value-map add-on to the basic engagement. Our aim is to deliver more value than we ask the client to pay for. That philosophy has served us well.

E-Mail from the CEO

A key to how we are received is the CEO's e-mail that announces our visit. We draft it for her or his review and comment. Here is an example:

> Hi, everyone—
>
> As you know, we have hired Beckmill Research, LLC, to value our company in the wake of the spurt of rapid growth that we have all experienced. Part of the valuation process involves one-on-one interviews with some of you. No one should draw any conclusions about the significance of being interviewed or not being interviewed or the sequence in which the interviews are conducted. Warren Miller will make those choices. I have agreed to make available on company time whomever he wants to speak to. I want to emphasize that no one has anything to fear from these interviews. Absolutely nothing. It is a normal and important part of the valuation process. You don't need to study or prepare these interviews. Just be yourself, please, and be helpful.
>
> Therefore, I respectfully request that you be open, honest, and candid with him. Whatever you say *will not* be disclosed to me or anyone else. I want Warren to get as accurate a picture of our company as he can because only by having that can we get an accurate estimate of value. Certain aspects of that picture are unlikely to be as pretty as we'd like them to be. That is normal in every company—no organization is perfect. But, we cannot solve problems if we don't know they exist. Warren can help us do that, and he can help us more if you will respond to his questions as honestly and accurately as you can.
>
> Thanks in advance for your help and cooperation.

You might think that that e-mail uses more words than necessary. It does. But the extra words are there to reassure those who might otherwise get jumpy that they have nothing at risk and nothing to fear from those interviews. In this case, more words are better than fewer because people are more likely to jump to erroneous conclusions if the need for their candor and cooperation are not stated gently and then re-emphasized. Of course, even then there will be some cynics who will not be candid under any circumstances. There are others who will try to dish dirt and even political scores with their co-workers. That's all part of what happens, and I roll with it. If I think the interviews are going to be especially difficult, I ask Dorothy or one of our subcontractors to be there with me.

Incentives and Other Programs

As part of your Document Request List, you should ask for a list of incentive programs *and* a copy of the *Employee Manual* or similar document. You should also inquire of the owner or CEO about incentives and other programs that might not be in print. For instance, are there rewards for:

- higher performance on the source(s) of differentiation as a result of customer loyalty/satisfaction surveys?
- either the acquisition of a specific number of new customers, or a threshold percentage of annual sales revenue from new customers?
- drop-shipments of big-ticket items so as not to reduce liquidity?
- through the use of cycle counting, a continual reduction in back-orders and in the time necessary to conduct physical inventories?
- increases in the average revenue per invoice?
- cross-selling?
- dissemination of the monthly financial package within three business days of the next month?
- error-free order-filling?
- reduced lost-time accidents?
- timely replacement of crucial IT equipment?
- prompt electronic delivery of invoices?
- more E-commerce and fewer telephone or mail-in orders?

- online capability for customers to check the status of their orders?
- development of successors in every SMDC function reporting to the owner/CEO?
- economic education for all employees?
- suggestions for ways to increase throughput, raise the efficiency of operations, and improve overall performance?

I could go on, but you get the idea. People tend to enact behavior that is rewarded. That's another way of saying, "Behavior rewarded is behavior repeated." If you've not read Steve Kerr's classic paper on goofy incentives, you're missing something.[4] Goofy behavior rewarded is goofy behavior repeated. Just look at the re-election rates of Congress.

Preparing for the Visit

We invest a slug of time prepping for the "on-site," as we call it. By now, we have done our preliminary financial analysis of the SMDC, and we have completed a near-final version of the external risk assessment. I say "near-final" because I often change my estimates of risk and of value as I write my report. They don't move much, but they do move. That is because, as I write, I see aspects of the analysis in ways that I hadn't seen before. This is also a good argument against using the off-the-shelf report-writing software that floats around the marketplace like an invisible BP oil spill.

We covered what goes on in the first part of the on-site visit in Chapter 10. That is where you get a detailed walk-through. You should ask plenty of questions there, but they shouldn't be hard ones. Save those for the one-on-one interviews later in the day. But that walk-through gives you another opportunity to learn about the SMDC, how it does what it does, and, in some cases, why.

The heavy lifting in this phase will come during those face-to-face interviews. It is to those that you will devote the lion's share of your time in preparing. In our shop, we have two types of questions: those that we ask everyone, and those that we ask only of a certain individual. The latter are function-specific and intended to ferret out underlying causes of the outlier performance metrics that our preliminary analysis uncovered. There are usually about six of these metrics.

You might think that we could then just confine these conversations to three or four people. Not a good idea. That is because other people have insights and observations that the area where a given problem resides might not have. In addition, I don't want to risk frightening a few people by focusing only on them. I typically talk with anywhere from eight to 12 employees, plus the top dog, for 30-90 minutes. The more responsibility the interviewee has, the longer the conversation runs. It's a grueling 12-to-14-hour day.

4. Kerr, "On the Folly of Rewarding A, While Hoping for B."

Basic Questions: We ask two kinds of questions here: those intended to help us learn more about the person to whom we're speaking and those aimed at getting at that individual's perceptions about certain generic aspects of the SMDC. Most people like to talk about themselves and their backgrounds, so that is where we start. In most cases we have résumés, but we go beyond those. We inquire about what the person liked or didn't like about previous jobs, what she or he learned, why they left, and so on. We also learn about their education and why it might have stopped short of a degree. We always ask if someone has served in the military. If they have, we thank them for their service, but we also go on to ask which branch they served in, what they did while they were in, how long they were in, and what they learned from the experience. With few exceptions, we find that those who have served enlisted hitches see the reality of the company more clearly than those who haven't. You won't be surprised to hear me say that Marines usually see the situation as it is.

Below is the basic list of questions that we ask everyone. Sometimes, depending on the situation, we might add a question or two to it, but you'll know when to do that.

1. Why do customers do business with this company and not with its closest competitor?

2. Using three adjectives—hyphenations are O.K.—how would you describe this company?

3. What are the three most important criteria in the assessment of your job performance?

    a.

    b.

    c.

4. What do you need in order to do your job better?

5. What do you see yourself doing job-wise in five years? In 10 years?

6. On a scale of 1 (lowest) to 7 (highest), please pick the whole number that accurately describes your feeling or assessment in response to these questions:

    a. How good do you feel about this company's future?

    b. How well do you like your job here?

    c. How good do you feel about the company's commitment to helping you grow professionally, develop, and be successful?

    d. How fair is the company in its dealings with you?

   e. On its transparency?

   f. On the overall trustworthiness of the people here?

   g. On the criteria used to judge your performance?

7. What do you see as this company's three biggest strengths?

   a.

   b.

   c.

8. What are its biggest weaknesses?

   a.

   b.

   c.

9. The occurrence of what single **external event** would hurt this company the most? (Emphasize that this must be *plausible.*)

10. What **internal event** would do the most damage?

11. If you had a secret that you *had* to share with a co-worker, but you knew that you would be "toast" if it ever got out, whom would you tell?

12. If you could sprinkle a little magic dust and change two things here (not including your pay or job title), what would you change?

    a.

    b.

As these questions imply, I'm trying to get at risk, at culture, at potential sources of differentiation, and at perceptions of distinctive advantage. I am also hoping to identify any influential people whose power isn't obvious on an organization chart. In the event of a follow-on effort to enhance value, knowing these centers of influence will be critical to effecting change and increasing value.

Function-Specific Questions

Most often you will be trying to find out what causes low-performing metrics, not superior ones. People are likely to be defensive and on guard, despite what the CEO's e-mail said. You must try to reduce tension and make casual conversation, no matter how egregious the metric is and no matter how uneasy or uncooperative the employee may be. Here are some practices we have found that have a good track record of eliciting helpful responses in difficult or even contentious conversations:

- Begin by assuring each person of the confidentiality of what she or he says to you. In return, ask them not to disclose your questions, either.

- Think "Columbo." Be understated, and don't be reluctant to use the phrase, "I'm really confused here. Would you help me out, please?" Most folks will respond positively to that.

- Print out your questions in advance and append them to the "generic" set of questions that you ask everyone.

- Your function-specific questions should be in some sort of logical sequence, probably the sequence of tasks surrounding the particular area you're trying to zero in on.

- Speak softly and smile a lot. Make the experience as pleasant as possible for both you and the interviewee.

- Use *lots of adverbs* and "weasel-words." In writing, adverbs are a no-no, but in on-site interviews, they take the edge off what might otherwise look like a missile aimed at someone's paycheck.

- Use qualifiers such as "You know, I probably have this wrong, but it appears to me that blah-blah-blah. Am I getting that right or am I off-base?" Say that even when you're *sure* you have it right. The last thing you want to come off as is a know-it-all. Remember, these folks have forgotten more about how to do their jobs than you and I will ever know.

- Keep it impersonal, even if a response sounds as if it implicates a particular higher-up. For instance, if someone says that she does something a certain way "because So-and-so says to do it that way," ask if that routine is documented that way. Don't say, "Jeez, that doesn't make a bit of sense, does it?" If you say that, it will be around the entire SMDC within about 60 seconds of the end of that particular interview.

- Understate what you know. Part of what you're doing is playing poker. Don't bluff, don't tip your hand, and don't give the slightest hint that you're about to reach for a bunch of invisible blue chips.

- Give the interviewee a chance to ask you questions. Some will. This is just a matter of equity. No matter what they ask, affirm their question. Say it's a good one or an interesting one or one you hadn't thought about.

- Give each interviewee a business card. I do that at the start; at the end, I ask each person to "drop me a line if you have any questions or other thoughts about what we chatted about today." Some have.

Draw a Bead on IT

As I suggested early on in this *Guide*, the deployment of IT is essential to helping protect the SMDC from falling gross margins resulting from Internet competition. You don't have to be a geek to assess IT, but you do have to be willing to go deep into the IT weeds to ferret out a thorough understanding of the client's attitude toward and philosophy about IT. Quite often, it is a basic matter of substituting capital (IT investments) for labor. That doesn't mean that the client needs every new techno-bell and -whistle that comes out, but it does mean that it should be IT-savvy.

Check the IT-related "capital measurements" I provided in Barney's "four types of capital" in the "Resources" section of Chapter 8. An SMDC's IT commitment, or lack of it, starts with the owner or the CEO. If that individual isn't walking the IT talk, no one else will, either. Heaven forbid that she or he be like the owner of one SMDC we saw a few years ago: he had his administrative assistant print out his e-mails, and then he would dictate a response that she keyed in from his work station. In contrast, Jim Henderson, the now-retired CEO of Cummins Engine Co., routinely answered 100+ e-mails a day from his employees around the world.

Even if it has an IT manager with a small staff, the SMDC should still consider outsourcing IT support to a 24/7 managed-services provider. We do that in our little shop, and it is about the biggest bang for the buck that we get. Our IT support company provides Help Desk services as well as monitoring our server and NAS around the clock. They also send a guy out quarterly to check on things and to make sure all of our software is up to date. They even help us with our (not very) smart-phone challenges.

The Implications of Outlier Metrics for Interviews

Whether the metrics in question exceed the composite's or trail them, we choose the ones that really matter. If we go back to Mr. Walton's "Five Rights" admonition—in distribution, the key is to have the *right* amount of the *right* SKU in the *right* place at the *right* time at the *right* price—then the first places to look are inventory turn and purchasing routines. As I said earlier, I have yet to see an SMDC that didn't have too much inventory. If the client is struggling with cash flow, check inventory turnover, billing, and DSO. It's your job to dig and find out what causes those effects, and you do that during the on-site interviews.

The metrics themselves will tell you the functions whose people you need to talk to. When you have chosen the key metrics, you should make it a point to talk to at least two, and preferably three, people in each low-performing function. You want different views, and you want them from the rank-and-file employees who are doing the work as well as those in charge.

Deciding the Sequence of Interviews

I am not aware of any hard and fast rules about the order in which to interview people. You should inquire, first, if there are times during the day where certain functions cannot be at less than full throttle. Ask, too, whether any of the people you've tentatively scheduled to see late in the day leave early to pick up kids or care for aging parents. That might cause you to reshuffle your queue.

If there are no scheduling conflicts, we usually tackle what we think are the easier problems first. We also like to start with a later line function (customer service or operations) and work our way backward. That is because problems tend to accumulate during the operating cycle. If we didn't start at the end, it would take us longer to get to the root causes of some metrics.

As a professional courtesy, we interview the manager of a function *right after* we have spoken with his or her subordinates. We are careful not to divulge what we've already been told. We ask that individual the same set of questions that we asked of her or his troops.

Thoughts on Style

There are also matters of style. In most situations, every person in the company is going to be curious about your questions and what you seem to be driving at. Therefore, show a lot of humility, gratitude, and appreciation for the time people are taking out of their day to talk with you. Other thoughts:

- Dress the same way as the people you'll be talking to. In our neck of the woods, that most often means jeans and a polo shirt. Don't come off as one of "the suits." It's lethal.

- Avoid attaché cases. I carry a zip-up notebook and several pens. That's all.

- Don't drive an ostentatious vehicle. This is no time for a social statement.

- If you're driving a rental car, it shouldn't be red. Besides being the most attractive color for car thieves, red sends a loud message. To some, it might appear flashy; to others, angry. That's not what you want to do if the client is reimbursing you for expenses.

- Do *not* bang responses into a laptop.

- Don't even think about recording these interviews.

- I like to talk to people on their turf, if possible. Therefore, if an interviewee has an office, I'll go there. *However*, in that case I ask them not to take phone calls or let other people intrude while I'm in there. In fact, I carry a "Do Not Disturb" sign that I hang on the knob of a closed door to an office where I'm asking questions. If someone *still* knocks, then boundaries are likely to be a major issue at that SMDC. Expect operational chaos.

- If the person's office door has a window in it, I ask him or her to sit on the same side of the desk with me so that we both have our backs to the door. This avoids distractions. Ditto for glass in a conference room.

- If I'm interviewing a woman in her office, however, I leave the door open. I've never been on the receiving end of any untoward accusations, and I believe that leaving the door open helps reduce that possibility.

- If I expect interviews to be difficult or sensitive, I bring either my bride or a subcontractor with me. I want to avoid "he-said/she-said" fall-out.

- If I talk to a person in a conference room, I sit on the same side of the table with them. It reduces the level of confrontation.

- However, I don't sit too close to them because (a) I want to show respect for "their space," and (b) I don't want them trying to read my notes.

- Sometimes I take my notes during the interview, and sometimes I do it right after it ends, before I talk to the next person. It just depends on my sense of the other person's comfort level.

- I make no phone calls from inside the company facility. I save those for my trip back to the office.

- If the conference room has curtains, we do *not* close them. Openness and a casual tone are important impressions to convey.

- Out of respect for the jobs people do and also for their stamina, I try to make these interviews as short as possible, while still keeping them meaningful and unhurried. That requires meticulous preparation.

- I have had situations where interviews ran into a second day. They are the exception, but it does happen. In the best of circumstances, I expect to spend at least 10 hours talking to people, and sometimes more. It is an intense and draining process for all.

- My conversation with the owner or CEO comes last. In my experience, she or he wants to know how my day went, what my impressions were of the people I talked to, and what I learned. Consistent with the commitment of the CEO's e-mail concerning our visit, I do not disclose anything that would be traceable to a particular individual. If the CEO asks my opinion about a certain individual, I offer it, but *only* with the caveat that an hour with someone gives me only a rudimentary impression, and it might not be an accurate one.

The Wrap

We covered a lot of territory in this chapter. You cannot over-prepare for these interviews. Don't have them too soon, and don't be loosey-goosey in how you conduct them. *Seem* casual, but don't *be* casual. These interviews are vital. They can and should provide you with insights that you would not get any other way. Respect people's positions, don't jeopardize anyone's job, and remember that, but for the luck of the gene pool, you'd be on the receiving end of your questions.

In our next chapter, I explain how to take what you have learned during these interviews and integrate it into a "SPARC Profile." There are no short cuts to constructing these, but they are, in my view, the key to one's credibility in valuing any SMDC.

Chapter 13

Writing the Analysis of the SMDC's Outlier Metrics

Introduction

This is a crucial chapter because it explains how to present your findings in writing to your client company.[1] Because most of a given SMDC's outlier metrics are below those of the median of the composite, the tone of the presentation is a major consideration. It is hard to make critical written comments about the client company without offending someone, but, when the situation calls for candor, we are candid—but respectful. We must not be mean-spirited about it. Nothing we write is personal, which we say up-front. We direct our comments at processes, not people. We also make positive observations—again, not personal—wherever possible. Sometimes, rather than say what the situation is, we say what it isn't. In this chapter, I will give specific examples that I hope you'll find helpful.

Cause-and-Effect Relationships (Redux)

As I said earlier, the crucial aspect of middle-market private-company valuation—and what makes our approach different from the mainstream's—is our commitment to explaining *why*. That is what gave rise to the SPARC Framework, and that, too, is why we put such emphasis on the on-site interviews. As I have noted several times, our aim is to uncover the causes of those outlier metrics. I'm now going to present some hypothetical metrics that one might encounter in valuing SMDCs, along with some plausible underlying causes. Neither the hypotheticals nor the causes are all-inclusive, of course. They are intended to show how you might approach writing about these issues.

Low inventory turnover: In my experience, this is the most common deficiency in SMDCs. I have listed some reasons why turnover might be low. More than one of these might apply to a particular situation . . . or it could be a cause that I've not listed. This is *not* an all-inclusive list:

- Manual overrides of the purchasing algorithms in the software
- Inaccurate built-in purchasing algorithms
- Not doing cycle counting

1. We *never* give an "oral appraisal," and we believe that it is an outrage and a disservice to clients that the AICPA's SSVS-1 allows such nonsense. It encourages recklessness and allows valuation know-nothings to "commit business appraisal." Permitting oral appraisals is the epitome of a member organization pandering to its members. It also invites later litigation *a la* she-said/he-said. Don't do oral appraisals, and don't let your subordinates do them, either.

- Purchasing person(s) with inadequate training about their job
- Agreeing with vendors to deals that are insufficiently profitable—this applies especially to slow-moving inventory when one includes the carrying cost
- Biases of purchasers toward certain vendors or types of goods
- Too many stock-outs resulting in "Expedite Overnight" requests to manufacturers
- Inaccurate physical inventory
- Intentionally inaccurate physical inventory
- Not-clean cut-offs for physical inventory
- Unlabeled warehouse bins
- Inventory that is not barcoded or RFIDed
- An excess of slow-moving or obsolete inventory
- Kickbacks
- Slow payments to vendors, which causes them to suspend credit

High DSO: Take it from an ex-Controller: Slow-paying customers can result from a plethora of causes. Here are some of them:

- Inefficient invoicing routines
- Not using a lockbox
- Not accepting credit cards
- Not enabling customers to pay through the SMDC's website
- Not confirming information on a credit application
- Not checking credit before extending it
- Fictitious customers
- Not submitting invoices electronically

- Not starting collection efforts soon enough (this is a *big one*)
- Incentives that focus on "Net Income" without a capital charge and/or, in the case of pass-through entities, a provision for income taxes
- Not requiring salespeople to convey, repeat, and, where necessary, gently reinforce the SMDC's payment expectations
- Not cutting off sales to slow-paying customers
- Paying commissions based on shipments, not collections
- Not having a trained and effective collector of past-dues (I've never seen a man who could do this as well as a woman—collections can easily be done by a part-time telecommuter who knows what she's doing and can VPN into the SMDC's network)
- No incentives for the Controller to keep DSO below a specific target

Low productivity: As I have said before, this is calculated by dividing annual revenues by full-time equivalent employees. Short of getting into a calculation that is both convoluted and not comparable to what public companies disclose, this simple calculation is the best one. Some reasons that productivity might be low include:

- No external benchmarking using the same revenues ÷ FTEs calculation
- Not having objective measures of at least some of the job performance of *every person* on the payroll
- Not measuring productivity in "staff" jobs[2]
- Lack of documentation in low value-added tasks
- Mismatching jobs with employees' skillsets
- Salespeople working under poorly conceived incentives (i.e., too-great salary component and too-little commission component, of overall compensation)
- A lengthy cash-conversion cycle

2. When I, as a new Controller barely 2½ years out of undergraduate school, instituted productivity measurements in the Accounting Department, my troops thought I was nuts . . . but the CEO loved it. The troops went along and eventually agreed that such measurements were helpful.

- Undisciplined approach/or poor rationale for staffing levels
- Paying employees below market—in normal labor markets, this tends to attract low-performing individuals (TANSTAAFL[3])
- Untrained managers who don't know how to analyze their staffing needs
- Unmotivated employees
- Insufficient capital investment, especially in IT
- Ill-considered incentives
- "Us vs. them" employee vs. management attitude

Low gross margin: How low "low" is depends on how far G.M. is from the composite's median. Except for LIFO, which to date I've seen only rarely in distribution companies, there are few discretionary GAAP choices in how COGS is accounted for. In fact, accounting for COGS is remarkably uncomplicated for SMDCs. That, in turn, implies that the accounting that gives rise to a gross margin figure at the SMDC should be comparable to that of the composite. If the difference exceeds 10%, we worry about either the components of our composite or about the accuracy of our client company's accounting.

That is *not* 10 percentage points, incidentally; it is relative. For instance, if the composite's gross margin was 42%, and the SMDC's was 37%, that difference (.05/.42 = 11.9%) *is* greater than 10%, so it would certainly land on our radar screen and be the subject of in-depth queries during our on-site interviews. We would also review the footnotes to the audited financials in the GPCs' 10-K filings.

In general, the greater the lack of differentiation, the lower the gross margin will be. That has implications for both staffing levels and the capabilities of those who are hired. Low gross margins can arise from the following causes, among others:

- COGS "padding" (result: lower taxes, understated ending inventory)
- Not getting clean cut-offs for physical inventory (ask for a written description of the inventory-taking process)
- Making some SKUs subject to LIFO, and some SKUs not—this can make for complex accounting and inventory costing (we've never seen this, but it *is* a possibility)

3. Acronym for "there ain't no such thing as a free lunch."

- Theft—if the inventory is fungible, be sure to check security and the measures that the SMDC has in place to discourage inventory from "developing legs" (Walmart ties the bonuses of its store managers, in part, to inventory shrinkage—at our suggestion, some clients improved performance by doing the same with their warehouse managers)

Bang-for-the-Buck ratio (gross profit ÷ gross pay $): This ratio is a crucial one. As I wrote back in Chapter 2, the "BftB," as I call it, should be *at least* 2.5; otherwise, the rate of return to invested capital will be too low, and the shareholders will suffer more than the lenders. Potential causes of the BfB ratio being < 2.5 include:

- too many folks on the payroll

- excessive compensation

- failure to deploy technology

More often than not, it's bullet #1, which is caused by #3. If the primary owner of the SMDC is the founder, and it's been in business for more than two decades, expect lots of issues that can be traced back to the refusal to embrace IT to the extent necessary in this Age of the Internet.

Overview of the Section on Outlier Metrics

Because this part of the report is, in my view, its centerpiece, we take care preparing it. That goes in spades if the company is a low performer (i.e., below the 20th percentile of the composite). That means that this section is going to criticize, but, again, we are neither harsh nor personal. And whatever we say in our report will *not* be the first time that the owner or CEO has heard about it.

The SPARC profile has two parts:

- The first looks at the SMDC in terms of the five SPARC components. It presents those as they *are*, not as they should be in terms of consistency and alignment (which our value-maps Excel template helps us gauge).

- The second presents the outlier metrics and their underlying causes in the context of SPARC. The aim here is to explain and to teach, not indict and slam. We want to shine a light, show the way, and try to avoid putting the client's people on defense. In our experience, it's all about tone. Too much "pithy" here can work against a civil tone, so this is the one part of our report where we use the adverbs and wordiness that we otherwise deplore.

Unfortunately—and this might be a tad confusing—these two components are *not* contiguous within the report itself. In fact, there are usually a couple of dozen pages (or more) between them.

That is because the first component above is the linchpin of our initial description of the SMDC. It appears in Chapter 2; Chapter 1 is short boilerplate about valuation approaches and methods. Here is our standard outline of Chapter 2:

SMDC, Inc.

- **Introduction**
- **The SMDC and Its History**
    - Founding and Ownership
    - Key Historical Events
    - Key Personnel (a paragraph about each person)
    - SPARC Profile
        - <u>S</u>trategy
        - <u>P</u>eople
        - <u>A</u>rchitecture
        - <u>R</u>outines
        - <u>C</u>ulture
    - Summing Up
    - Key Customers & Suppliers
    - Key Professional Advisors
    - Litigation
    - Environmental Risk
- **Summary**

Within the "SPARC Profile" section, I present the five SPARC components with a paragraph, sometimes more, about each in the context of the client company. If there are deficiencies in any of them, or a lack of alignment between them, I gently note that (e.g., *The incentives the Company has in place undermine its ability to achieve its goals*), along with a statement similar to, "*Later in this report, we will discuss the implications of these issues in our analysis of the key performance metrics.*" This is to avoid taking readers by surprise later on. And, to repeat, before any of this ever shows up in our "Incomplete Work Product—For Discussion Purposes Only," we have talked to the owner/CEO about it and also suggested some fixes. No surprises.

The second piece (cause-and-effect) is the most important section of our chapter entitled "**Risk Assessment**." Here is our basic layout of that chapter:

Risk Assessment

- **Introduction**
    - Classifying Industries
    - Strategic Groups
    - Strategic Groups Within This Industry
- **Risk**
- **The Macroenvironment**
    - Introduction
        - economy
        - innovation
        - lifestyles & values
        - demographics
        - disasters
        - politics
    - Summary
- **The Domain**
    - Introduction
    - What This Strategic Group Does
    - Domain Framework
        - new entrants
        - competitors
        - suppliers' bargaining power
        - customers' bargaining power
        - substitutes
        - complements
    - Summary
- **The Company**
    - Overview of Our Analysis
        - rationale for measure of economic income chosen
        - measuring size
        - adjustments to financial statements
        - analysis of key ratios and metrics
    - Outlier Performance Metrics and Their Causes
        - metric #1
        - metric #2
        - etc. (usually 4 or 6, but sometimes 8)
- **TOWS (SWOT) Discussion**
    - External Threats and Opportunities
    - Internal Weaknesses and Strengths
    - Assessment of Company's Alignment with External Environment
- **Summary**
- **Appendix: Competitive Analysis**

The Toughest Task in Writing

As an experienced writer who takes the creation of his work product with the utmost seriousness, I have found that the subsection entitled "Outlier Performance Metrics and Their Causes" is the hardest part of the report to write. That is because it usually focuses on negatives. In this subsection, we present each of those outliers *and* explain why each is positive or negative *and* do this by (a) not betraying the trust of anyone we interviewed and (b) not being harsh or personal about any individuals. It is important here, I think, to draw the line between criticizing the person and criticizing the person's performance of his or her job. We go to extra lengths to make that point. It's never personal. Here's an excerpt from a report:

> Much of what follows is negative. Therefore, before getting into my discussion of each key metric and why, in my view, it is the way it is, I emphasize that there is a bright line between the individual, on the one hand, and how he or she does a particular job, on the other. To the extent that I am critical, my intent is to discuss aspects of how the job is done, *not* the individual doing it. In fact, if the Company has not provided, or is unable to provide, an individual with the tools needed to do a job, then, unless I stipulate otherwise, readers should infer that I believe the person is doing the job as well as it can be done, given the organization's failure or inability to provide the proper tools and training. Again, this is not about individuals. It's about process, policy, and performance.

Now, that's not exactly pithy, is it? It's a whole lot of words that say and reinforce the same basic messages: (a) this is unlikely to be fun reading, and (b) it is about how jobs are done, not about the individuals doing them. I cannot overemphasize the importance of drawing this line and drawing it broadly. If I did not do this in our reports, then what I write in this section—despite the fact that it is objective and impersonal—could come off as finger-pointing and personal. I want it to be neither. In this section, I follow the Three Rules of Successful Public Speaking:

- Tell 'Em What You're Gonna Tell 'Em
- Tell 'Em
- Tell 'Em What You Told 'Em

To be sure, what I intend, and how someone reads what I've written, may diverge. When that happens—and it can because many SMDCS have the same lack of boundaries in their business that the families that own them have at home—there is nothing I can do about it. If I am confident that someone is likely to personalize what is not intended to be personal, then I will also include verbiage similar to the following after the sample excerpt above:

> Lest any reader be inclined to take my comments personally, let me observe that doing so reflects an inability, or a choice, to see the person and the job separately. In the family-systems literature, this separation is called a "boundary." To the extent that a company

> has boundary issues, it will have performance issues. It is also apt to have chaos in one or more functions. It is not my intent to recommend possible solutions for issues that are inherently psychological. I am not qualified to do that. Having observed the problem of boundaries in many companies over the years, though, I know it when I see it.

In essence, I am politely drawing a line in the sand. Sometimes the greatest job in the world—mine—is no fun at all. That's the price I pay for the other 98% of the time when it's so much fun that it doesn't feel like work at all. What a country!

The Gunning Fog Index[4]

Most of us with at least one college degree overwrite. Our sentences have too many words, and the words themselves have too many syllables. This combination—number of words and number of syllables in them—gives rise to a writing tool called "The Fog Index." This nifty little algorithm estimates the number of years of education a reader will need in order to be able to understand what she or he is reading. It works. Here are the steps in computing it:

1. Choose a representative excerpt from your report of at least 300 words.
2. In Word, you can Copy (Ctrl+C) and Paste (Ctrl+V) that excerpt into a new Word document, and then hit Alt+F, and see on the right side of the **Properties** section the number of words you have pasted.
3. Subtract the number of proper names from the number in the excerpt.
4. Count the number of sentences. Count compound sentences separated by a semicolon as separate sentences. Also count independent clauses such as "I came, I saw, I conquered" as three sentences.
5. Compute the average number of words per sentence.
6. Then count the number of words that have three or more syllables; omit those that reach three syllables by having an –ly suffix.
7. Divide the number of three-or-more-syllable words by the number in the excerpt (again, exclude proper names from both numerator and denominator).
8. Add the results from steps 5 and 7 above, and multiply the sum by 0.4.
9. The result is the Fog Index of the excerpt.

4. According to Wikipedia (http://en.wikipedia.org/wiki/gunning_fog_index), this algorithm was developed by Robert Gunning, "an American businessman, in 1952."

Just to shape expectations, here is the Fog Index of some publications with which you are familiar:

- 6—the *Bible* and *Huckleberry Finn*
- 9—*Reader's Digest*
- 11—*Wall Street Journal*
- 12—*Atlantic Monthly*

I've read two valuation reports written by different professionals in different firms that weighed in at... fasten your seatbelts... 33. They had no idea what they were saying, and neither did I. Readers who have reviewed such reports have had these root-canals-without-anesthesia. They smart.

Guidelines for the Toughest Task in Writing

What follows applies *only* to the **Outlier Metrics** section of the report. Though I do not intend it as the be-all and end-all, it is a list of ideas that I commend to your consideration. Writing is the hardest work any professional does because the best writing is simple English. And that's not easy.

More words are better than fewer. This applies *only* in this chapter of the report. Compare these two pieces of writing:

> The Company's management is inexperienced, out of its element, and in over its head. That is why profits are falling as revenues skyrocket.

vs.

> In periods of rapid revenue growth, keeping pace with the new demands of such growth requires growing the skills and knowledge of employees. Without that, overstaffing and lagging profitability set in. Sooner or later, people will have to be hired from outside to do the jobs at the level that profitable growth requires. Aside from the discouraging message that sends to employees, hiring senior people from outside carries a ton of risk.
>
> A device that helps avoid bringing in outsiders is the "Personal Development Program" (PDP). The PDP process encourages employees to commit to specific enhancements to their knowledge and skillsets that they themselves select; their supervisors or managers must review those objectives, ensure that the wording is black-and-white so that there will be no doubt whether the employee did or did not reach the goal, and then sign off with the employee on his or her PDP. If a company decides to embrace PDPs, the CEO should take the lead by doing hers (or his) first and then posting it on the intranet, but also in high-traffic locations such as coffee pots, drinking fountains,

> restrooms, and the Break Room. The CEO can then coach her direct reports in the preparation of their PDPs. This process is top-down, *not* bottom-up. It is learning-by-seeing and –by-doing.

Be practical. Speak readers' language, not ours. For instance:

> The Company's low inventory turnover contributes to its burden of debt. If it raised its turnover from the current level of 2.6x to the composite's median of 8x, it would have an additional $675,000 of cash each year. That would go a long way toward paying down the debt that threatens to drown the enterprise.

Be constructive. Suggest solutions to problems. For instance:

> The question then becomes, "How do we increase inventory turn?" The choices that struck us were (a) to invest in software with a good purchasing algorithm and (b) to invest in two employees by helping them develop their skills and knowledge to the point where they will know when to override the computerized algorithm. An effective tool for the latter is PDPs. Among other objectives, these could result in them enrolling in the Certified Professional in Supply Management (www.ism.ws) curriculum of the Institute for Supply Management. The cost of this investment in People would be trivial compared to the potential benefits it would bring.

Pick (only) the metrics that are key to understanding the SMDC's story. Even if the SMDC trails the composite everywhere, it is our job to choose the metrics that are hurting the company the most. The outlier metrics that I highlight in our GPC analysis—an even number (4 or 6, but in a couple of cases, 8)—get discussed here. I don't bog the reader down in metrics that don't matter. We cannot just throw a bunch of ratios into a report and expect readers to figure it out for themselves. That is an unreasonable expectation; yet I see it often.

Wherever possible, quantify the impact of the metric either in terms of its current impact or what it could contribute if it were fixed. There is no substitute for providing this kind of economic education. We had a prospective SMDC client several years ago with atrocious software and horrific purchasing routines. I say "prospective" because the engagement didn't close. That was one of those situations where I quoted the work sky-high because, in all honesty, I saw nothing but problems with the owner's spouse. Among the questions I asked him before we got to the Engagement Letter were about his taking over $1,000,000 in distributions the preceding year when the taxes were only about $400,000. I pointed out that, if he were willing to take some difficult steps, he'd be able to weather the storm of his company's current cash-strapped position. He denied vehemently that he and his wife had pulled anywhere near a million bucks out of the company. I simply handed him the Statement of Cash Flows from his SMDC's reviewed financial statements and said (paraphrasing here), "Well, if that's not the case, then I think you ought to talk with your outside CPA firm and tell them to alert your banker to the fact that they're going to amend the financial statements they have already published."

Sequence your presentation so that the most important metric is first, the second most important next, and so on. The sequence should be dictated by the magnitude of what you're able to quantify as the reward for "fixing the metric." The sequence helps the client company decide which one to attack first, in case it does not have the resources to take on all of them.

Remember that fixing one metric might improve another. In the "Be Practical" admonition a few paragraphs above, I quantified the effect that increasing inventory would have on cash and the ability to pay down on debt. Therefore, there was no need to have a separate discussion of the SMDC's "Excessive Debt Ratio." It speaks for itself, and we highlight it in our GPC analysis.

In most SMDCs that we have appraised, governance is non-existent. This is a big deal. Councils of Advisers should pay their way several times over each year by the economic impact of their advice. Even though public companies are supposedly "scored" in terms of their governance, I doubt that the algorithms used to make those calculations would apply to most SMDCs, especially if their Boards are dormant.

In a small number of cases where we were especially confident about our relationship with the SMDC, we have gone so far as to identify in our report the type of expertise to which we believe the SMDC needs access, but doesn't have. When we present our report to the owner or CEO, we then offer to help them through the process of setting up such a Council. Here are the steps in doing so:

1. Work with the owner to determine the size of the Council. An odd number is essential, and we recommend starting with five. If more are needed, they can be added later.

2. We tell the owner that he or she is allowed one "buddy" on the Council. No more than that.

3. We ask the owner to tell us who his or her "buddy" is. We also ask about the background of the relationship between them and why the boss wants this particular individual. In this discussion process, we also become aware of any particular expertise that individual has, other than the friendship with the lead dog.

4. No one on the Council can be an "insider," a consultant, or any other paid advisor to the SMDC. We want people who will speak their minds without having to think about their "other" relationship.

5. Confirm with the CEO/owner the types of expertise or experience needed. Examples: someone who has successfully integrated acquisitions; someone who has B2B marketing expertise that the SMDC lacks; someone who has either opened a new location for an existing company or overseen someone who has; someone with IT expertise; someone with HR chops; someone who has sold his or her company; and so on.

6. Except for the "buddy," we seek people that the owner/CEO doesn't know well and preferably not at all. The latter allows the Council process to begin with a clean slate unaffected by prior interpersonal histories.

7. However, as a courtesy, we do ask the owner for recommendations for specific individuals who have the areas of expertise sought. That is because we are usually working in a geographical area we're not familiar with, and all of the Council members should be local. Local folks save travel expenses and allow the owner/CEO to get comfortable with the Council process without having to worry about covering the travel expenses of a stranger.

8. I then set out to "round up the suspects" for the (usually three) slots available on the Council. Because my "electronic Rolodex" now exceeds 3,000 individuals, I have yet to meet a situation where I couldn't call at least one person I know to get me started. Often that is a valuation colleague in the SMDC's hometown.

9. I usually call candidates that I don't know at work after work hours and leave a voice-mail telling them who I am and why I'm calling. I also tell them I'll be following up with an e-mail, which I do promptly after leaving the voice-mail. In the e-mail, I do not disclose the client company's name (yet), but I do ask them if the situation I've described in the e-mail is something in which they think they might be interested. The e-mail stipulates that there is a "stipend involved," but doesn't disclose what it is ($1,200–$1,500 per meeting). It also asks the person to reply via return e-mail to indicate their level of interest and also a couple of time slots when I can follow-up with a phone call.

10. I then choose a time and make the call. If all goes well, we schedule a time when I can come to their office for a face-to-face meeting. If it doesn't go well, I move to the second person on my list.

11. Like the questions I prepare for the on-site visit, I ask each Council candidate the same set of basic questions plus an additional set related to her or his expertise. I'm looking for confirmation of the needed expertise, a personality that will not conflict with the owner's, and an ability to communicate clearly, briefly, and without jargon. If someone has SMDC expertise, I'm skeptical, but not close-minded. An "industry mindset" on a Council is not a good thing, especially if it's in the majority. Diversity of knowledge and experience is desirable. And count the owner/CEO and the buddy as two votes toward that mindset.

12. I then schedule one-on-one meetings between the owner/CEO and the person I select as the lead candidate for each type of expertise. In case the lead dog wants to talk to more than one expert in each area, I will add a second person. However, I want to hold the number to two because I don't want the owner/CEO to perceive the process as too time-intensive before she or he ever gets to experience the benefits of having the Council.

13. The owner chooses whom she or he wants and selects the date for the first meeting. We don't recommend meetings before the 20th day of any month because it takes until at least the 10th day of a "meeting month" to get the meeting materials ready and PDFed to the Council. The last Tuesday, Wednesday, or Thursday of the first month tend to work well. The early days of the second month tend not to because Council members often have meetings to attend elsewhere.

14. To the extent possible, we want the meeting to convene on the same relative date each quarter (e.g., "the last Thursday of the first month of the quarter at 1 p.m."). The timing of the meeting is contingent on having the time to put together an agenda and disseminate meeting materials at least 10 days ahead of the scheduled meeting.

15. The owner/CEO then calls each of the interviewees selected. I contact any who were not chosen and let them down gently.

16. I then prepare a "Profile" of the SMDC (including financials), its closest competitors, issues in the domain, and the particular challenges the SMDC itself faces. I draw the first rough draft of much of this profile, of course, from the valuation report I wrote.

Don't overlook succession issues. If there is no succession plan, that is your opportunity to convey to the client, both in writing and in your discussions with the senior people, how important that issue is. I have yet to see a situation where, if the lead person didn't have a successor, anyone else did, either. The entire succession issue also gives you a reason to educate the client about the value of the Council of Advisers I just mentioned. In my experience, the benefit-cost ratio of such a body to most SMDCs is middle-double-digits or higher.

Sustainable Revenue and Risk

In assessing risk at the company level, it is crucial to try to zero in on "sustainable revenue"; it means "revenue from repeat customers." The greater its share of total revenue, the lower its risk. The downside is that less risk from sustainable revenue often carries a slower-growth price tag.

Over the years, dozens of clients have told us that they cannot forecast revenue with any degree of accuracy. As a former controller and CFO, I couldn't disagree more. I take strenuous exception to the traditional small-company approach, which is "last year + X%."

We urge our clients to have their salespeople talk to their customers before SMDC starts Phase 1 of the budget cycle: the sales forecast. Each sales professional should ask each client three questions:

- Do you expect your company's revenues to be up, down, or flat next year?

- If up or down, and you had to name a percentage today, what would it be?

- Is it reasonable, in your view, for our company to maintain about the same "share of wallet" with you that we have this year, or do you think we might be fortunate enough to win a little more space?

From those three simple questions, a decent sales forecast can emerge. No, it's not to the penny. But it *is* bottom-up, which is incredibly valuable, and it does provide an audit trail (to the customers and then to the rep who talked to the customer). Over a few years, the SMDC will learn which of its customers are too optimistic, which are too pessimistic, and which have a clear-eyed view of probable economic reality. It can then tweak its forecast accordingly. Without a good sales forecast, everything else in a budget is speculative frou-frou.

Quantifying the Company Level of Unsystematic Risk

The remaining task is to quantify this most important level of risk. We saw three ways to do so at the macroenvironment and domain levels of the trilevel framework:

- Do it yourself, or
- Use our template, or
- Use a "black box"

We think that using our template adds a level of coherence and accuracy that you are unlikely to get any other way, but then, I make no claim to being objective about our template—I know that it works because we use it all the time. If you doubt the template's utility and accuracy, I recommend (again) that you infer these premiums yourself and then compare your inference with the template result; in other words, triangulate. In the majority of cases, you are going to find, I think, that the risk factor here is in the 2%-8% range.

All we have to do now is to derive the range for the company risk premium. Let's replay some tidbits from earlier in this *Guide*:

Macroenvironment:

$$-3\% \leq P_{MAC} \leq +3\%$$

Domain:

$$-3\% \leq P_{DOM} \leq +9\%$$

Totals

$$-6\% \leq P_{EXT} \leq +12\%$$

We know from our earlier discussions that the lowest possible aggregate risk premium for our three levels of unsystematic risk is –9%. Therefore, the low end of the Company level is, like that of its two external siblings, –3%, too.

As noted in the figures above, the maximum total external risk premium, $\mathbf{P}_{EXT}$, is +12%. We know from the 10 published academic papers summarized in Chapter 3 that internal sources of variation in rate of return are, on average, 3.0x as great as external ones. Therefore, the top end of the company range is a simple matter of multiplying 12% by 3.0 and rounding, or **36%**.

Here, again, is the table with the highs and lows of the unsystematic-risk premiums that account for the range of estimates of the cost of equity capital in virtually all of the engagements that most of us will have:

The Range of Empirically Derived Equity Discount Rates – 2011

	Low	Both	High
▪ Risk-free rate		4%	
▪ ERP		5%	
▪ P_{size}		4%	
▪ P_{mac}	– 3%		3%
▪ P_{dom}	– 3%		9%
▪ P_{com}	– 3%		36%
Totals	4%		61%

In early-stage venture-capital situations, it could go higher for a variety of situation-specific reasons. For instance, the uncertainty that attends technological gadgets and gizmos could ratchet up the rate. So could a "key-person" premium in a situation where the success of the venture depended on one person.

The Wrap

I began this chapter with a short discussion of the five most likely symptoms of difficulty in increasing the value of an SMDC. I listed some possible causes of those symptoms. Here are the five:

- Low inventory turnover
- High DSO
- Low productivity
- Low gross margin
- Low bang for the buck

We have often seen a high debt ratio as a symptom, but that can be fixed in almost all cases by fixing the other outliers. Diagnosing these tripwires is not difficult. Fixing them can be.

We then discussed the SPARC profile in an early chapter of our typical report and of the format of the "outlier metrics" section in the longest chapter in the book, **Risk Assessment**. I emphasized the importance of following a policy of "no surprises" by saying that the report should not be the first time that the top person has heard of the issues that your "outlier metrics" subsection discusses. Much of the valuation process is about orchestrating expectations, and this is no exception.

In my view, the most important part of this chapter was about what I call "the toughest task in writing": the wording of the **Outlier Metrics** subsection. It is all about tone. Be honest, but not hurtful. Criticize how the job is done or call attention to deficient routines or identify the tools to do the job not being available, but *do not criticize any person as a person*. I gave some examples of how to write difficult paragraphs and, in one case, of how not to write it.

After presenting the step-by-step sequence we use to help an SMDC create a Council of Advisers, I also pointed out the importance of the succession issue in most SMDCs. If succession is a problem, it gives you a chance to sell the idea of a Council of Advisers, where you, of course, might become the outside facilitator to help the owner/CEO figure out what knowledge or expertise that the company needs (or will need in its near future), identify candidates with the requisite expertise or experience, screen them, and seat them. You can also help the SMDC's top people write their PDPs, if the owner decides that she wants to go in that direction. In our experience, PDPs are essential in high-growth situations: they increase productivity, reduce personnel turnover, and improve performance.

We wound up this chapter by deriving the risk premium range for the company. We also computed the maximum upper range for the company's cost of equity capital. We now move to Chapter 14, the penultimate chapter in this *Guide*, where we will discuss writing the rest of the Report.

Writing the "Incomplete Work Document—for Discussion Purposes Only" Document

Introduction

Writing is the hardest work we do. We saw that in the last chapter when we discussed the delicate wording that attends the "Outlier Performance Metrics" subsection of the report. Even without that part, writing is still a monumental task, even for those who love writing as much as I do. I'm reminded of how Red Smith, the legendary sports writer for the *New York Times*, described it: "There's nothing to writing. All you do is sit down at a typewriter and open a vein." For the over-educated, which includes your Humble Servant and everyone reading this book, writing seems doubly hard. I think it comes from our failure to see writing as a conversation. Instead, we think we have to compete with Eudora Welty or John Steinbeck or *The Wall Street Journal* and be a wordsmith of some kind.

It's not like that.

Tell a story. If you're a good joke-teller or story-teller, you should be a fine writer. Just listen to yourself speaking, and then write it down. But if you don't read much—especially good books—writing is apt to be a grind. I love story-telling, and that's how I approach report-writing. But when I write a technical paper or something like this *Guide*, I do my best to carry on a conversation in everyday English with a friend—you, the reader. To be sure, it is going to be more of a monologue than a give-and-take exchange. But I am still going to "listen" for your questions and I'm going to "watch" your facial expressions for any sign of puzzlement. And I am going to do my best to respond to those "questions" and "confused looks" as I write. I do the same thing in report-writing. I want to devote this chapter to helping you write better. I have some tips and tricks that I think you'll find helpful.

Where to Read Good Writing

I mention "good writing" because good writers are also readers. Funny how that works. Don't read business books if you are looking for fine writing. They are a literary wasteland.

The best writing is found in books. One should read the classics, though most folks these days haven't. However, they will be a big help if one does. Valuation reports are non-fiction. Therefore, I recommend biography and history. Biography is personal, and history is narrative. I find that combination to be compelling when it comes to writing about businesses and their owners. I'm no critic, but I know good writing when I read it. These days, of course, such writing is the exception, not the rule.

Here is a sampling of writers that I recommend without hesitation or qualification:

- A. Scott Berg—*Maxwell Perkins: Editor of Genius*
- Ron Chernow—*The Warburgs: The Twentieth-Century Odyssey of a Remarkable Jewish Family*; *Washington: A Life*
- Alistaire Cook—*Six Men*
- Richard Ellmann—*Oscar Wilde*
- Noemie Emery—*Washington: A Biography* (out of print, but worth looking for)
- Doris Kearns Goodwin—*Team of Rivals: The Political Genius of Abraham Lincoln*
- Don Higginbotham—*The War of American Independence*
- Woody Holton—*Abigail Adams*
- Daniel Walker Howe—*What Hath God Wrought: The Transformation of America, 1815-1848*
- Paul Johnson—*A History of the American People*; *George Washington: The Founding Father*
- Robert W. Merry—*A Country of Vast Designs: James K. Polk, the Mexican War, and the Conquest of the American Continent*
- William Manchester's biographies of Churchill and MacArthur
- David McCullough—*John Adams*; *1776*
- anything by H.L. Mencken
- Thomas Sowell—*Migrations and Cultures*
- Ira Stoll—*Samuel Adams*
- C. James Taylor (Ed.)—*My Dearest Friend: The Letters of John and Abigail Adams*
- anything by E.B. White
- Kathleen C. Winters—*Anne Morrow Lindbergh: First Lady of the Air*
- Gordon S. Wood—*The Radicalism of the American Revolution*

Anyone who doubts that reading economics can be a treat hasn't tried *Socialism* by Ludwig von Mises or *Economics in One Lesson* by Henry Hazlitt. For sheer clarity, those two guys are hard to beat. So is Warren Buffett's annual letter to his Berkshire Hathaway shareholders. But stay away from Mises' protégé, Hayek, unless you have a high tolerance for turgidity. He's tough going.

Examples of Good Valuation Reports

As I said, all but a few business books stink. So do most court cases. The exception, as many readers know, is the *Delaware Open MRI* case; you can download it here: www.bvresources.com/wholesaledownloads. Reports by top-tier securities analysts are also worthy nominees. We don't value technology companies, but Goldman Sachs's Rick Sherlund is a pleasure to read. Notwithstanding Jim Cramer's manic style on CNBC, he is a fine writer. If you've not read *One Up on Wall Street* by Peter Lynch, it, too, is worth your time.

Report Templates vs. Report Formats

There is a difference. A "template" is a special kind of file in Word. It can make report-writing less difficult, if not downright easy. If you have the technical skills to create a template, or are willing to pay someone to create one for you, I recommend it. You'll get your money back in a flash because of the increased productivity. That goes in spades if your reports have complex formatting; ours do, so we paid a "Word consultant" in Alabama to make our basic template.

Report formats, on the other hand, are common. I assume you have yours; I have mine. I confess I find it curious that the organization of most reports I read is dreadful. The sequence makes no sense. Organizing a report that "flows" isn't rocket science. In our shop, except for an initial chapter that is largely boilerplate, the order of the report mirrors the order of our valuation process. Why anyone would do it any other way is beyond me. Then again, maybe the chaos I read reflects the chaos of the writer's valuation engagements. I dunno. Below is a format that I find congenial for a traditional valuation report (i.e., *not* valuation for financial reporting or for litigation support):

[Personal & Confidential]
[This page left blank intentionally]
[Title Page]
[This page left blank intentionally]
Letter of Transmittal
Contingent & Limiting Conditions
Appraiser's Certification
Appraisal Summary (Table)
Table of Contents
1. Overview of the Business Valuation Process

Purpose and Approaches
- Purpose
- Approaches
  - asset-based approach
  - market approach
  - income approach
- Valuation is prospective, not retrospective

2. SMDC, Inc.
- **Introduction**
- **Founding and Ownership**
  - Key Historical Events
  - Key Personnel (a paragraph about each person)
  - SPARC Profile
    - <u>S</u>trategy
    - <u>P</u>eople
    - <u>A</u>rchitecture
    - <u>R</u>outines
    - <u>C</u>ulture
    - Summing Up
  - Key Customers & Suppliers
  - Key Professional Advisors
  - Litigation
  - Environmental Risk
- **Summary**

3. Risk Assessment
- **Introduction**
  - Classifying Industries
  - Strategic Groups
  - Strategic Groups Within This Industry
- **Risk**
- **The Macroenvironment**
  - Introduction
    - economy
    - innovation
    - lifestyles & values
    - demographics
    - disasters
    - politics
  - Summary

- **The Domain**

- Introduction
- What This Strategic Group Does
- Domain Framework
    - new entrants
    - competitors
    - suppliers' bargaining power
    - customers' bargaining power
    - substitutes
    - complements
- Summary

The Company

- Overview of Our Analysis
    - rationale for measure of economic income chosen
    - measuring size
    - adjustments to financial statements
    - ratio analysis
- Aberrant Performance Metrics and Their Causes
    - metric #1
    - metric #2
    - etc.

TOWS Discussion

- External Threats and Opportunities
- Internal Weaknesses and Strengths
- Alignment

Summary

Appendix: Competitive Analysis

4. Valuation

Revenue Ruling 59-60

Estimates of Value

- Asset-Based Approach
    - net asset method
    - asset accumulation method
- Market Approach
    - internal stock transactions
    - guideline public company method
    - merged-and-acquired-company method
- Income Approach
    - discounted cash flow

Premiums and Discounts

- The Pass-Through Entity (PTE) Premium
- Discount for lack of control
    - ownership

control premiums
shareholder agreement
state corporation laws
a fifth factor
Conclusion—DLOC
Discount for lack of marketability
Mandelbaum v. Commissioner
empirical studies
court decisions
marketability at SMDC, Inc.
Conclusion—DLOM

5. Synthesis of Value Estimates
Reconciliation of Estimates of Value
Opinion of Value

6. Appraiser's Qualifications

Should You Prepare an Executive Summary?

In "traditional valuations"—those not related to litigation or valuation for financial reporting [VfFR]—I do not. Not yet anyway. The letter of transmittal includes the results of the valuation. The table of contents in our reports has enough detail that, if a reader is looking for a particular topic, chances are that he or she can turn to it from our TOC.

Litigation support is different. The weighty dockets of most judges oblige me to include an executive summary for reports that are subject to discovery by the other side. Ours typically runs no more than one page (two, max) and includes page-number citations adjacent to each bulleted item in the summary. Be pithy: the trier of fact's time is limited.

Report-Writing Software

No way. No how, no way. It will *never* happen in this shop. In my view, such software is a torpedo aimed straight at the analyst's head. Software insults the client, mocks a judge, and doesn't do nearly as good a job as you and I can. It is *not* that I want to spend the time to be paid for writing a report. Given my choice, I'd rather not, even though I type 85 wpm. But I also know that every company is different, and each has its own story. My job is to be the story-teller, and I can't do that if software is going to boilerplate most of it. In my view, this is *not* a productivity issue. It is an ethical issue. I'm not being sanctimonious or preachy; I just can't imagine sticking my finger into a reader's eye by using such junk.

Boilerplate

Something less than 10% of our report is boilerplate. Most of it is in Chapter 1 and the introductions to the other chapters. Again, each client is unique. Heavy use of boilerplate detracts from that uniqueness every bit as much as report-writing software does.

Once Upon a Time . . .

I've never begun Chapter 2 with that phrase, but I have thought about it. It is tempting. Even though I don't use that opener, I keep it in mind as I tell the client company's story. I don't get cutesy, fawning, or flowery. I just tell the story in simple English. I also use the "Fog Index" (see Chapter 12) to put a damper on my tendency to overwrite—too-long sentences with too-long words. That the flow of our report reflects the flow of our work makes the story-telling easier. It just comes out naturally.

What if My Opinion of Value Changes as I'm Writing?

The better question is, What if it *doesn't*? I cannot recall writing a report where my opinion of value didn't move a little. The first time it happened, it rattled me. Then my wife reminded me that I do my thinking as I type. In that process, I see the company in different shades and hues, and that leads to modest adjustments in the opinion of value. If you're not at least *tempted* to change your opinion as you write your report, I'd worry about your work. Let your thinking flow through your keyboard, and don't be afraid to make a change.

Report Aesthetics

How the report looks is important. Most clients are paying more for your report and ours than they thought they'd have to pay. That creates expectations on their part, and it is our job (and yours) to meet what we have created.

Our printer is a Xerox 8550DP model that generates the report using solid ink, not toner. Solid ink is sharper and more vivid. In fact, if I hold a page at a certain angle, I can see the light reflecting off the header (I use a maroon fill with bolded white letters in the header). We also print our reports "duplex" on 24-lb. paper whose "brightness" is 100. The heavier paper and the high brightness combine with the printer technology to make a great visual impression.

We paste excerpts from Excel into the body of our report. To do otherwise, I think, is to diss readers. Asking them to flip back and forth between what we say on p. 22 to an Exhibit buried 30 pages later asks too much. I don't do it.

For that same reason, I don't use "end notes." Those are also killers of readers' time. I just finished McCraw's excellent biography of economist Joseph Schumpeter, one of the finest economists of the 20th century; had he not died about 15 years before the Nobel Prize in Economics was created, I'm confident he would have won one. For me, the voluminous end notes in the McGraw biography disrupted my reading and distracted me. The text of the book was about 505 pages; the end notes consumed almost 200 more. Worse, they were at the end of the book, not the end of each chapter. And some notes went on for more than a page and in notably smaller font than the one used in the text. I have e-mailed Prof. McCraw and asked why he did it that way, but no reply yet. The end notes undermined a Herculean effort by a fine biographer. We use footnotes because we don't want to punish those who do us the honor of reading what we write.

Tips on Writing

What follows is idiosyncratic and incomplete. I aspire to these goals, but I sometimes fall short, often by choice.

Words and Phrases to Avoid:

- *methodology*—the most pretentious word of all; why not *method*?
- *a lot*—only if you're writing about real estate
- *as to whether*—*whether*
- *as yet*—*yet* will do in most cases
- *basically*—the Siamese twin of *hopefully*
- *currently*—*now*
- *different than*—*different* **from**
- *due to the fact that*—*because*
- *firstly, secondly, thirdly*—first, second, third . . . *nextly*?
- *foreseeable future*—an oxymoron
- *hopefully*—surely this dangling nonentity needs no elaboration
- *interestingly*—to whom? Why?

- *irregardless—regardless*
- *more unique / most unique—unique* is already a superlative
- most words ending in *–ize*—e.g., *customize, finalize, incentivize, prioritize*
- most words ending in *–oriented*—these are *tortuous* to the point of being *torturous* (see below)
- *personally*—superfluous when used with *I*
- *possess—have*
- *presently*—this means *soon*, **not** *now*
- *pretty*—only if you're describing scenery or a person
- *stated—said*
- *stuff*—argggggggggg
- *things*—why not *stuff*?
- *utilize—use*
- *very*—a garbage word that adds nothing to any conversation

Words <u>Not</u> *to Be Used Interchangeably*:

- *aggravate* vs. *irritate*
- *among* vs. *between*
- *continuous* vs. *continual*
- *disinterested* vs. *uninterested*
- *farther* vs. *further*
- *fewer* vs. *less*
- *fortuitous* vs. *fortunate*

- *its* vs. *it's*
- *lend* vs. *loan*
- *shall* vs. *will*
- *that* vs. *which*
- *tortuous* vs. *torturous*
- *transpire* vs. *happen*
- *type* vs. *kind of*
- *verbal* vs. *oral*

Writing Practices to Avoid:

- adverbs
- beginning a sentence with numerals, unless it is a specific year
- dangling participles ("Hanging on the clothesline, I saw the clothes")
- the passive voice
- run-on sentences
- more than two (2) numbers embedded in one paragraph—few can assimilate these the way you and I can—use charts and graphs
- one-sentence paragraphs
- more than two pages without a heading or subheading—the reader wants to make progress reading—would you rather read a one-chapter 500-page book or a 50-chapter 500-page book?

Good Writing Practices:

- use "transition" words and phrases to connect paragraphs—a non-inclusive list of examples:
  - However
  - As a result
  - Nonetheless
  - In addition
  - In contrast
  - Despite
  - Likewise
  - Indeed
  - In fact
  - Furthermore
  - Thus
  - For example
  - For instance
  - Yet
  - Conversely
  - Nevertheless
  - Moreover
  - Besides
  - Consequently
  - Therefore
  - Otherwise

- the active voice

- action verbs

- sentences of varying lengths

- headings and subheadings

- fonts *without* serifs (we favor Verdana and Calibri)

- 12-point (or larger) fonts, except in footnotes and long quotations

- text boxes for lengthy quotations and sidebars

- footnotes

- an occasional fragment (e.g., "More later in this chapter.") unless your reader is a judge or a former English teacher
- teasers (e.g., "I'll have more on that later in this chapter.")
- colors (mild—dark blue, dark green) in headings and subheadings
- graphs
- charts
- pictures
- a .JPG of your signature in blue ink
- Adobe's "secure" signature feature (if you use Acrobat)
- detailed tables of contents
- pasted excerpts from financial statements and analysis in your text
- highlighting in excerpts
- symbols in excerpts (ellipses, rectangles, arrows, and so on)
- bigger and different-colored fonts for emphasis in spreadsheet excerpts
- colored fill in spreadsheets and tables
- "reverses" (dark fill, bolded white words or numbers)

The Wrap

This chapter contained fewer words than all the others except Chapter 4. However, word volume bows to word value. I believe what I have said here is worth heeding. As readers can infer, I am passionate about my love of the craft of business valuation and of the craft of writing. And both *are* crafts. As I said back in Chapter 1, we get good at craft by doing craft. The more you write *and* read, the better your writing will become. But you must be serious about it, and you must work at it.

My message in this chapter was simple: good writing is an essential tool in the kit of the valuation professional. Readers also have a right to stay awake reading a valuation report. They have paid for it. We should never ask them to read something that sounds as if it was written by a garbage salesman with a keyboard full of samples. Between using a sensible format, avoiding report-writing software, genuflecting to report aesthetics, and embracing the tips I have provided, I hope you have found this chapter worthwhile. I also hope you will take your writing task as seriously as I take mine. If you do, we will work together to elevate the craft of business valuation.

Preceding the index of this *Guide*, I have included a bibliography. It has a section with a short list of recommended books on writing. I commend them to your attention.

Our 15th and final chapter is about a subject near and dear to my heart: value maps. I do so in the SMDC context. Done right, business valuation presents opportunities to assist clients in separate engagements after you write and deliver the report. I think you will find the last chapter useful, stimulating, and, dare I say, valuable.

Chapter 15

Value Maps for SMDCs

Introduction

For this writer, this *Guide* would be incomplete without a chapter on value maps. They are the heart of our valuation practice; over half of our 2009 and 2010 revenues came from work related to them. I touched on value maps early in Chapter 2, but I want to return to my favorite subject now.

What Is a Value Map, and Why Should I (or My Client) Care?

A value map results from a comprehensive, in-depth analysis of the operations and capabilities of a client company, in this case, an SMDC. The value map is an enriched and separate deliverable with two primary purposes:

- to identify an SMDC's value enhancers and value destroyers, and
- to provide a practical plan of action that gives the SMDC and its people a path—a ***value map***—that shows the way to increasing the value of the company

A typical value-mapping engagement takes 75-90 days from start to deliverables. Its benefit-cost ratio is usually at least 20 times. The deliverable is a "value map" that is custom-tailored to the resources of the SMDC *and* to the capabilities of its people. It is *not* a one-size-fits-all cookie-cutter document. It is rigorous and demanding. It incorporates a comprehensive analysis of value creation, of the durability of distinctive business advantage, and of risk. Because of its laser-like focus on cause-and-effect relationships, it also surfaces issues and processes that can be dealt with to enhance the value of shareholders' equity. The report provides practical, step-by-step, how-to guidance in the context of the capabilities and skills *of existing employees.*

Because every business is different, every value map is different. Therefore, those looking to "leverage" personnel in the professional-services-firm context are likely to be disappointed unless they can build a full-time practice devoted solely to value maps. The value-maps practice can be an extension of an existing *valuation* or *consulting* practice; existing practices should have that leverage already. That makes the value map an addition to the services portfolio and one with high value-added, to boot.

A client SMDC might well need a value map for one or more of the reasons below—this is *not* an all-inclusive list:

- the SMDC's risk is much higher than it needs to be
- the company might be sold in the next few years
- value destroyers are costing the owner(s) a lot of money
- customers are not as satisfied with the SMDC as they need to be
- the SMDC is starting/considering a value-based management program
- the SMDC is expecting growth to ramp up
- the SMDC is in danger of losing one or more major customers
- an uneasy lender might require more collateral or require its loan(s) to be paid off or moved to another institution
- the SMDC is overstaffed
- the SMDC is at risk of losing one or more valuable employees because of their frustration with lack of promotion, lack of pay increases, or, for reasons beyond their control, the inability to earn bonuses

In short, the client SMDC might need and benefit from a value map and not even know it. That is where you, the analyst, come in. Because of either the valuation you are doing or an existing relationship you have with the SMDC, you could be looking at an opportunity to help the SMDC enhance its value and, at the same time, allow you to do interesting and value-enhancing work. Value maps are truly win-win situations for your clients and for you.

More on the Value Map

Since 1993, our extensive research, writing for publication, and experience in over 400 engagements and transactions have resulted in the development of the trilevel framework of unsystematic risk discussed earlier in this *Guide*. Along with that framework, we developed the five elements of SPARC: <u>S</u>trategy, <u>P</u>eople, <u>A</u>rchitecture, <u>R</u>outines, <u>C</u>ulture. SPARC's components are the universe of potential causes of performance that is either well above or well below that of a risk-adjusted public-company industry composite. Risk matters because reducing it increases value.

A key aspect of the value-mapping process is establishing cause-and-effect relationships between aberrant performance metrics and the underlying factors (embedded in SPARC) that give rise to each. If a valuation precedes the value-mapping engagement, then the valuation process should uncover these relationships. At that point, the value-map deliverable becomes a straightforward matter of:

- assessing durability of sources of distinctive advantage (using VRINO and a statistics-driven customer survey)
- in the context of the SMDC's current SPARC profile, determining the best way to hedge, neutralize, outsource, or otherwise minimize value destroyers and other risk-raisers
- creating practical, doable implementation steps for existing employees
- aligning the value map with the goals of the owner(s)
- writing the document

If the value map is not preceded by a valuation, then one should be included in the value-map engagement. The length of the valuation report, however, should be minimal.

As I wrote earlier in this *Guide*, traditional tools from finance and accounting will *not* suffice. That is why we use non-traditional ones, starting with strategic management. Then, and only then, can value drivers be enhanced and value destroyers be neutralized, hedged, or outsourced. The trilevel framework is shown again on the following page.

As we work our way from the perimeter to SPARC, we meet all the factors that drive or destroy value. We identify ways to reduce risk, increase free cash flow, and raise the expected growth rate in cash flow. When we reach the epicenter, **SPARC**, we conduct a disciplined and comprehensive examination of the panoply of the factors, processes, and attributes that affect value from within the company itself.

The five SPARC elements are circumscribed by11 functions, which are themselves surrounded with the firm's resources. Those running the business are responsible for identifying services that can be obtained from the resources and then configuring those services into routines and bundling one or more routines into value-creating capabilities. Those capabilities should maximize opportunities, minimize threats, buttress strengths, and neutralize weaknesses. This sounds easier than it is. That few companies' managements can and do accomplish it is a major reason that only about one in 20 enterprises makes it to the third generation of ownership.

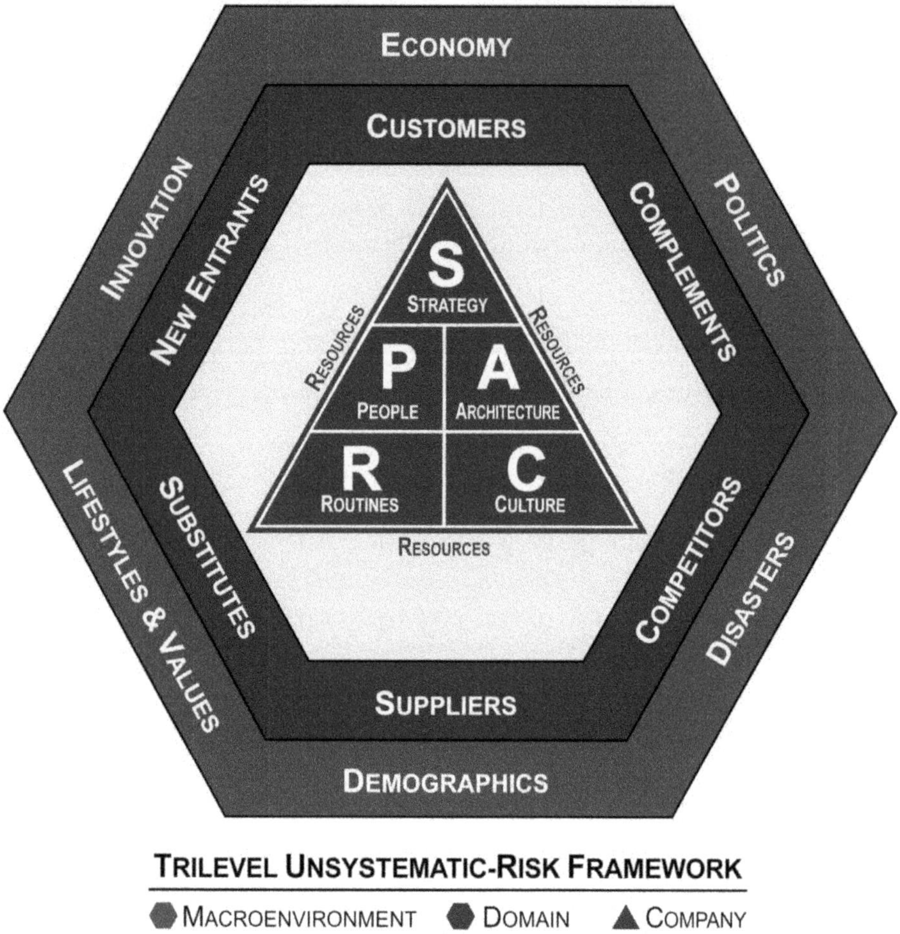

What Can a Value Map Do for an SMDC?

The value map offers new insights to SMDC owners about what creates and destroys value in their business. It is a blueprint for reducing risk, increasing margins, and growing free cash flow. A value map is a reasonable, practical, doable, and sequenced action plan. You can work with owners not only to increase the value of their businesses, but also to help them see the strategic impact of their decisions. They will have a powerful tool with which to preserve and enhance their life's work. In most cases, that is the most valuable asset they own: their company.

What Can Value Maps Do for Your Practice?

Obviously the value map gives you another service to sell. Unlike, say, money management or pension consulting or IT advising, the value map is a logical extension of your existing valuation practice. It should not require major investments in software or hardware. The only people who should be hired are those needed to accommodate growth in the valuation/value-map practice. There is no big regulatory overhang, no licenses to get, no tests to take (except the one that the market for services gives you every day), and no major outlays for intangible ideas with unknowable horizons for reaping benefits. Creating value maps for clients helps you leverage the company- and domain-specific knowledge that your calculations or valuation engagement provided to you.

Value maps should do something else for your practice: they give you a relatively larger-fee service to sell to clients that will pay for value. Value maps are not about compliance: they are about increasing shareholder value. However one configures one's engagement—and some CPAs will want to check their state's statutes about contingency fee arrangements—the value map should be wealth-enhancing for both clients and service-providers. As I said a few pages ago, it's win-win.

The Book

There is no need to belabor this one. *Value Maps* is an extended treatment of this subject. I commend it to your consideration.

Bringing It Together

The fact that the value proposition for value maps is not compliance-driven and does not culminate in a beefy report that clients will read once (if that) makes it unusual. Combining calculations with a mini-value-map, which I wrote about in Chapter 2, is a world-beater. When you and I deliver value, clients can't get their checkbooks out fast enough.

Make no mistake about it: marketing matters. It matters in business valuation and it matters in building a successful value-maps practice. Like business valuation, value maps are a one-off service. Unlike BV, value-map engagements tend to have an extended shelf life. That goes in spades if you are helping an owner prepare an SMDC for sale.

Still and all, the owners and executives of prospective client companies must be educated about the value maps. Work with your chamber of commerce or prominent law firms with M&A practices and exit-planning specialists to offer freebie education to captive audiences. This can be done easily over lunch . . . and the lawyers can get CLE credit for it.

Let's talk more about marketing of value-map services. There are ways to do that and ways not to. I have arranged the following subtopics in order of their importance in our shop. It might be different in yours. Either way, though, the mantra in marketing is replication, replication, replication.

Branding/Logo/Tag Line: This is a key aspect of marketing and one to which, in my view, most valuation professionals pay too little attention. We developed our logo and tag line in 2005. We chose the deep maroon color to match that of my beloved high school, Culver Military Academy in Indiana. Next to my wife, Culver is the best thing that ever happened to me. That maroon has a particular mix of RGB (Red, Green, Blue). You will also notice a spooky resemblance to our trilevel framework:

BECKMILL RESEARCH

Valuation + Strategy → Value Enhancement

At the same time we made that choice, we also made two others that have come in handy. We chose a shade of green and a shade of blue to use in certain places in our spreadsheets and reports. When we formed Beckmill Capital, LLC, in 2008, Birch Studio, Inc. made our maroon logo into a green one. I came up with a decent tag line, and here is the result:

BECKMILL CAPITAL

Capital Ideas for the Middle Market

During the summer of 2010, at the urging of a client CPA firm in Alabama, we decided to offer home-grown CPE. That is, instead of teaching for someone else—which I have done with NACVA, ASA, and AICPA—Dorothy and I went through the process of providing the necessary information to the National Association of State Boards of Accountancy in Nashville; NASBA is the arbiter of CPE program sponsors in the United States. At the urging of a meeting planner we know who quickly said, "Brand, Warren, brand," Beckmill Education, LLC, was a no-brainer. So was the tag line. Look:

BECKMILL EDUCATION

Value-Added Business Education

I liked "Eclectic Business Education for Professionals," but clients and colleagues whistled me off it. I'm not crazy about the existing tag line, but either I'll get comfortable with it, or we'll change it. And I hope we don't come up with a fourth business idea because I'm fresh out of good colors.

Herewith a little tale: The one-woman ad house that had come up with our original logo, tag line, and ingenious brochure design called me during the summer of 2005 and said that our logo and tag line were, and I quote, "long in the tooth, Warren—it's time to get something new, something jazzy." In a nanosecond, I went from right-brain strategy guy to ****-retentive, left-brain dullard, put my head down, and dug in my heels. I *liked* that brochure. I *liked* our logo. I *liked* our tag line.

Then I made a mistake. I said to our then-ad woman (we later parted amicably because she couldn't stand my eagle eye and insistence on precision in her work), "Barb, if it ain't broke, I'm not gonna fix it."

Her quick response: "Terrific, you genius. Don't change the oil in your Lexus. Or Dorothy's. Ever."

I caved.

She was tough enough to take me on when she disagreed with me. I like that because we do it with our own clients. I gave her a budget and, after many prints, reviewing graphics with a magnifying glass, and file transfers back and forth, we didn't have much. I then suggested making the trilevel framework the center of the logo. (I had drawn it only a month before on a cocktail napkin over supper with Jim Travis, ASA, at a meeting in New York. He liked it.) Barb was all over my trilevel-framework idea. She also made two watermarks—one for everyday use and one with **DO NOT COPY** on the perimeter of the inside triangle of our logos; that second watermark is on every page of our reports. Replication, replication, replication.

Business Cards: Too many of my colleagues take these too casually. Barb and I then collaborated to hatch a tag line that embedded our strategy-based perspective on valuation. She then came up with a "vertical" business card. That is, one reads the card in "portrait" mode. She flipped the tag line along a vertical edge, perpendicular to everything else printed on the card. She then used the back of the card for bullet points about each service we offer. And if she said, "White space is your friend, Warren, white space is your friend" once, she said it a hundred times. Like most in this line of work, I suspect, I wanted to cram words into every last millimeter of the card. It looked like a centipede on steroids.

Website: A good website is important. A quarterly newsletter is a real plus. You will be ahead of the game if you can buy one, rather than write it yourself. Try to find one that allows you to pick the articles from a group or, if you choose, provide occasional content yourself.

Writing: If you can write—and I hope that, if your writing skills could stand some polishing, my tips in Chapter 14 will enhance yours—writing for publication can be a great marketing vehicle. The impact of such a weapon goes up if it is aimed at a specialized target: a specific domain or industry, for instance. Legal journals and industry-specific trade publications come to mind. Start with state trade associations, not the national biggies. Get the kinks and hiccups out of your stand-up routine on the smallest scale possible. Once it's polished and ready for prime time, that state association will line you up with other states and the national group, and you'll be off to the races.

Target a domain that has a significant presence in your area *and* that is growing. Or at least not contracting (in the current economy). Talk to any group that will have you. Get a booth at their convention and a slot on their program. Don't be a shameless huckster, though. Teach. Educate. Enlighten.

Webinars: We will add webinars to our Beckmill Education portfolio by the end of 2011. I have been privileged to conduct webinars sponsored by the publisher of this *Guide* (www.bvresources.com), Valuation Products and Services (www.valuationproducts.com), and NACVA (www.nacva.com). If you can do some of those, go for it. It's a good way to get your name out.

Public Speaking: I recommend speaking to industry groups. Speak as often as you can. You'll probably never get completely over the butterflies—I've been doing it for 45 years, and I still get them. Public speaking hones platform skills. Those in lit support will find that it's invaluable, especially if they join a local chapter of Toastmasters International (www.toastmasters.org). TI is a fabulous education-and-leadership organization. Its structured curriculum will improve your performance giving prepared speeches. But TI does something more valuable than that: it teaches members to think on their feet. Put that in your expert-witness hat. It's a great skill to have.

Ad Agencies: A small shop that is big on big ad agencies will make its checkbook smaller. But a small outfit that is willing to invest the time to learn about you and about your practice can be a walloping bang for the buck. Our current "ad-visor" (as it were) is Birch Studio Graphics Inc. (www.birchstudio.com), Charlottesville, Va., about 70 miles from us. Birch hosts our website, takes care of our business cards, and works with us to develop web content.

Sponsorships: In recent years, Beckmill Research, LLC, has been a cosponsor of an annual May gathering called the Atlanta Competitive Advantage Conference; the acronym, ACAC, is pronounced "ack-ack." It is a conference of strategy academics and consulting yokels like me. It is small enough to be personal and big enough to be interesting. It is my favorite conference every year. As a pointy-headed "practitioner" (their word, not mine—shudder), I am slowly gaining traction and respectability among these high-end scholars. It's a kick.

Articles for Potential Clients (and Lawyers): When we find one, whether it's about their business, their hobbies, or their kids, we grab our trusty "Business Reply Card." It is on thick white linen stock that shoehorns right into a #10 envelope. It also has our logo, tag line, contact information, and, in the upper right corner, the logo of the CFA Institute. I write a short note on that card, clip the article to it, and slide them into an envelope with our logo and return address on it. We then bang an address into our labeling software, and then our little Brother P-Touch QL-500 spits out a pretty mailing label.

An Atlanta CPA, David Ringstrom, is arguably the pre-eminent Excel expert (www.acctgadvisors.com) in the U.S. and maybe the world. He led me to a nifty piece of software called SnagIt (www.snagit.com). It is screenshot software like no other, and, for a one-time payment of $49.95, you can slap it on your workstation and your laptop. It is way cool. Sometimes I take a screenshot with it, copy the .JPG into a Word document, print it on the beautiful Xerox 8550DP, staple the Business Reply Card to it, scribble a note, and stuff the envelope. I'd never do it without the software. It's the best 50 bucks I've spent in at least a decade.

Social Media: Use 'em, especially LinkedIn. Chris Mercer is a LinkedIn guru. He gave a boffo presentation on the subject at the June 2010 NACVA conference.

YouTube: Use it so long as you don't come off as an embalmer or a deer in the headlights. I'm fortunate to have a three-part interview on there with NACVA's Brien Jones from the 2010 NACVA conference. My grandson thinks it really cool for his Grandpa to be up on YouTube.

Blogs: The bloom is off the blog rose. They were white-hot for a while. A professional whom I admire a ton, Jack Ciesielski, CFA, CPA, owns The Analyst's Accounting Observer (www.accountingobserver.com). Jack has forgotten more about GAAP and IFRS than most people will ever know. He is the *OED* of financial reporting. He wrote a fabulous blog for several years and then quit. It turned out that blog freebies didn't bring him high-dollar clients. As much as I believe in marketing, I'm not keen on blogs.

If you're not a blogger, but decide to become one, you'd be wise to learn how to use some HTML commands. That will help you **bold**, *italicize*, embed links, and the like. I'm told that the key to making business connections in blogging is to get links to your blog from the "Blogroll" of other bloggers, and, in return, put links to their blog on yours. Be sure to post to someone else's blog, too, and then link that post to your blog—the other blogger will thank you for helping to broaden her audience.

The Wrap

This chapter was about value maps and the need for marketing in all its many incarnations. Some of the marketing tools I talked about might not be your cup of tea. That's fine—it's a great country, you know. But I'm as serious as a heart attack when I urge you to market your services. Value maps are a natural extension of business valuation. They require a small investment—this book and the time to read and get acquainted with its Excel template. As business investments go, this one should pay a walloping return. If you run into trouble, email me at SPARC@beckmill.com.

In fact, please e-mail me anytime (SPARC@beckmill.com) with questions, comments, and constructive criticisms. We are all in this thing together. There is more than enough business out there, even in a hyper-weak economy, for all of us make nice livings. We can and must be colleagues, not throat-cutting competitors. In so doing, we will do our part to raise the practice of the craft of business valuation and value maps in the United States and around the world. As professional legacies ago, I don't think it gets any better than that, does it?

Bibliography

Augier, Mie, & James G. March. *Models of a Man: Essays in Memory of Herbert A. Simon.* Cambridge, Mass.: MIT Press, 2004.

Barney, Jay B. *Gaining and Sustaining Competitive Advantage* (4th Ed.). Upper Saddle River, N.J.: Pearson/Prentice-Hall, 2010.

Becker, Markus C., & Nathalie LaZaric. *Organizational Routines: Advancing Empirical Research.* Northampton, Mass.: Edward Elgar Publishing, 2009.

Burd, Steven A. How Safeway is cutting healthcare costs. *Wall Street Journal,* June 12, 2009: A15.

Caves, Richard E., & Michael E. Porter. 1977. From entry barriers to mobility barriers. *Quarterly Journal of Economics* 91 (1977): 241-262.

Deming, W. Edwards. *Out of the Crisis.* Cambridge, Mass.: MIT Press, 1982.

Ellison, Sarah. *War at the Wall Street Journal: Inside the Struggle to Control an American Business Empire.* Boston: Houghton Mifflin Harcourt, 2010.

Fridson, Martin S., & Fernando Alvarez. *Financial Statement Analysis: A Practitioner's Guide* (4th Ed.). Hoboken, N.J.: John Wiley & Sons Inc, 2011.

Ghemawat, Pankaj. *Commitment: The Dynamic of Strategy.* New York: The Free Press, 1991.

Goldratt, Eliyahu. *The Goal: A Process of Ongoing Improvement* (2nd Revised Ed.). Great Barrington, Mass.: North River Press, 1992.

Hax, Arnoldo C., & Dean L. Wilde II. *The Delta Project: Discovering New Sources of Profitability in a Networked Economy.* New York: Palgrave Macmillan, 2001.

Israel, Ted. A generous helping of company-specific risk may be included in your size premium. *Business Valuation Update,* vol. 17 (2011), no. 6: 7-13.

Kets de Vries, Manfred F.R., & Danny Miller. *The Neurotic Organization: Diagnosing and Changing Counterproductive Styles of Management.* San Francisco: Jossey-Bass, 1984.

Kerr, Steve. On the folly of rewarding A, while hoping for B. *Academy of Management Journal* 18 (1975): 769-783.

Langlois, Richard N. *The Dynamics of Industrial Capitalism: Schumpeter, Chandler, and the New Economy (The 2004 Graz Schumpeter Lectures).* New York: Routledge, 2007.

Langlois, Richard N., & Paul L. Robertson. Business organization as a coordination problem: Toward a dynamic theory of the boundaries of the firm. *Business and Economic History* 22 (1993): 31-41.

Lintner, John. The valuation of risky assets and the selection of risky investments in stock portfolios and capital budgets. *Review of Economics and Statistics* 47 (1965): 13-37.

Magnasson, Lars, & Jan Ottosson. *Evolutionary Economics and Path Dependence.* Cheltenham, U.K.: Edward Elgar Publishing, 1997.

March, James G. Exploration and exploitation in organizational learning. *Organization Science* 2 (1991): 71-87.

Mattson, Michael E., Don Shannon, & Don Drysdale. 2001. Adjusting guideline multiples for size. *Valuation Strategies* 5 (2001), no. 1: 24-29.

McGahan, Anita M. *How Industries Evolve: Principles for Achieving and Sustaining Superior Performance.* Boston: Harvard Business School Press, 2004.

McKenzie, Richard B., & Dwight R. Lee. *Managing Through Incentives: How to Develop a More Collaborative, Productive, and Profitable Organization.* New York: Oxford University Press, 1998.

Miles, Robert H., & Charles C. Snow. *Fit, Failure, and the Hall of Fame.* New York: The Free Press, 1994.

Milgrom, Paul, & John Roberts. *Economics, Organization, and Management.* Upper Saddle River, N.J.: Prentice-Hall Inc., 1992.

Miller, Warren D. *Value Maps: Valuation Tools That Unlock Business Wealth.* Hoboken, N.J.: John Wiley & Sons Inc., 2010.

Mintzberg, Henry. Patterns in strategy formation. *Management Science* 9 (1978): 934-948.

———. *Structure in Fives: Designing Effective Organizations.* Englewood Cliffs, New Jersey, 1992.

Morczek, Magdalena (Ed.). *2011 Valuation Yearbook: Market Results for Stocks, Bonds, Bills, and Inflation, 1926-2010.* Chicago: Morningstar, Inc., 2011.

Nelson, Richard R., & Sidney G. Winter. *An Evolutionary Theory of Economic Change*. Boston: Belknap Press, 1982.

Penrose, Edith T. *The Theory of the Growth of the Firm* (3rd Ed.). New York: Oxford University Press, 1995.

Porter. Michael E. *Competitive Strategy: How to Analyze Industries and Competitors*. New York: The Free Press, 1980.

———. *Competitive Advantage: Creating and Sustaining Superior Performance*. New York: The Free Press, 1985.

Rumelt, Richard P. *Strategy, Structure, and Economic Performance*. Boston, Mass.: Harvard Business School Press, 1974.

Schumpeter, Joseph A. *Capitalism, Socialism, and Democracy* (3rd Ed.). New York: Harper Perennial, 1962.

Scherer, Frederic M., & David Ross. 1990. *Industrial Market Structure and Economic Performance* (3rd Ed.). Boston: Houghton Mifflin Company, 1990.

Sharpe, William F. Capital asset prices: A theory of market equilibrium under conditions of risk. *Journal of Finance* 19 (1964): 425-442.

Simon, Herbert A. *Models of Man: Social and Rational*. New York: John Wiley & Sons, Inc., 1961.

Teece, David J. Economies of scope and the scope of the enterprise. *Journal of Economic Behavior and Organization* 1 (1980): 223-247.

Uttal, Bro. The corporate culture vultures. *Fortune* 108 (1983), no. 8: 66-72.

Williamson, Oliver E. *Markets and Hierarchies: Analysis and Antitrust Implications—A Study of the Economics of Internal Organization*. New York: The Free Press, 1975.

———. *The Economic Institutions of Capitalism*. New York: The Free Press, 1985.

———. *The Mechanisms of Governance*. New York: Oxford University Press, 1996.

Winter, Sidney G. The satisficing principle in capability learning. *Strategic Management Journal* 21: 981-996.

Index

N.B.: A ***bolded italicized*** page number refers to a graphic or exhibit on that page.

W

www.ingramcontent.com/pod-product-compliance
Ingram Content Group UK Ltd.
Pitfield, Milton Keynes, MK11 3LW, UK
UKHW050945290926
15470UKWH00005B/1644

9 781935 081722